I0815743

A BLOODY BUSINESS

A BLOODY BUSINESS

Convoy PQ 17

JOHN HENSHAW

Published in the United States of America and Great Britain in 2025 by
CASEMATE PUBLISHERS
1950 Lawrence Road, Havertown, PA 19083, USA
and
47 Church Street, Barnsley, S70 2AS, UK

Hardback Edition: ISBN 978-1-63624-607-9
Digital Edition: ISBN 978-1-63624-608-6

A CIP record for this book is available from the British Library

Printed and bound in the United Kingdom by CPI Group (UK) Ltd, Croydon, CR0 4YY

Typeset in India by Lapiz Digital Services, Chennai.

For a complete list of Casemate titles, please contact:

CASEMATE PUBLISHERS (US)
Telephone (610) 853-9131
Fax (610) 853-9146
Email: casemate@casematepublishers.com
www.casematepublishers.com

CASEMATE PUBLISHERS (UK)
Telephone (0)1226 734350
Email: casemate@casemateuk.com
www.casemateuk.com

Front cover image: This photograph shows the last moments of one of PQ 17's merchantmen still flying its barrage balloon. (Public Domain)

The Publisher's authorised representative in the EU for product safety is Authorised Rep Compliance Ltd.,
Ground Floor, 71 Lower Baggot Street, Dublin D02 P593, Ireland.
http://www.arccompliance.com

Dedication

Dedicated to the memory of all those who served in Convoy PQ 17, on whatever ship, in whatever manner.

Contents

Author's Notes and Acknowledgements

Unlike other renderings of this story where authors often take for granted technical details of which most readers simply have no knowledge, my narrative, drawings, maps and photographs give readers a more balanced grasp of the naval events and the ships and aircraft involved for this brief period of time.

As with my previous books, I have created scale drawings of the principal warship classes, merchant ships and aircraft involved, with appropriate specifications. While some of these CAD (Computer Aided Drawing) illustrations have been based on existing drawings – ones of varying quality, scales and detail – a number of them have been based solely on the interpretation of photographs, particularly those which show a profile view. The purpose of these drawings is not to provide a definitive drawing of any one ship, nor is this book about any particular ship or aircraft. Rather, it covers the variety of ships – both warships and merchant ships – and aircraft that took part in either attacking or defending Convoy PQ 17. Readers should regard my drawings as a means of understanding the basic designs of the ships and aircraft, and providing the ability to make comparisons between types, rather than thinking of any one of them as being a micro-detailed representation. Although I exclusively use the metric system in my drawings, I have quoted dimensions, tonnages and the like in the imperial system as that was in use at the time.

Readers should note that when I refer to a warship by name, it is assumed that it is one of His Majesty's Ships (HMS) unless otherwise stated, and the warship is therefore mentioned without an HMS prefix. Once ships of the United States Navy have been first mentioned and prefixed by USS, thereafter they are similarly referred to without the prefix. Similarly, warships of the Kriegsmarine are first mentioned with the KMS prefix and thereafter the prefix becomes redundant. To distinguish merchant ships from naval ships, I have used SS for steamship unless a motor vessel, in which case the prefix is MV. Likewise, once first mentioned any prefix is deleted.

All times quoted are in what was called Zone B, in use in this period; that is, Greenwich Mean Time (GMT) plus two hours. However, I cannot vouch that all the times quoted are absolutely accurate, as I have taken at face value those quoted in the various sources.

I acknowledge the dedication and time devoted by my son to sourcing photographs and improving them where possible and preparing the maps. My heart-felt thanks, Andrew.

Casemate's Group Publisher and Vice-President, Ruth Sheppard, not only had faith in publishing this work but was a tower of support before the publishing process began and then throughout.

Of the six books I have had published, this was by far the most streamlined and pain-free. My eternal gratitude, Ruth. I also acknowledge the patience and understanding of Casemate's editor, Lizzy Hammond, in working through the details that escaped my attention in the manuscript and its several iterations.

John Henshaw, Cape Schanck, Victoria, Australia

Preface

The title of this book comes from a conversation between Commander Jack Broome (captain of the destroyer *Keppel* and commander of the Russian-bound Convoy PQ 17's Close Escort) and Commodore J. C. K. Dowding on SS *River Afton* (commodore of PQ 17's 33 merchant ships), shouted via megaphones across the gap between their two ships shortly after the disastrous order for the convoy to scatter had been given by the Admiralty in London at 2136 hours on 4 July 1942.

Sorry to leave you like this. Goodbye, and good luck. It looks like a bloody business.

And so it was, indeed, a bloody business.

This book tells the story of what happened to this ill-fated delivery of vital war *matériel* from the Western Allies to the Soviet Union in July 1942 on a day-by-day, hour-by-hour, position-by-position basis.

* * * * *

The year 1941 was the major turning point of World War II, one that was easier to see in retrospect than at the time.

At the beginning of June 1941, few optimists would have forecast that a beleaguered Britain would see victory or, perhaps more-so, be joined by new military allies in World War II. Yet, on 22 June 1941, Nazi Germany launched Operation *Barbarossa*, its surprise attack on the Soviet Union, which in six months reached the very gates of Moscow. Then, in the closing days of 1941, on 7 December, Japan launched an even more astonishing surprise attack on the US Navy's Pacific Fleet, off-watch in its home base of Pearl Harbor, Hawaii. Co-incidentally, this was on the same day (8 December, GMT) that Adolf Hitler signed Directive 39, ordering the Wehrmacht onto the defensive and effectively abandoning the Moscow offensive just when it had reached its territorial zenith, Khimki, 22 kilometres north-west of Moscow's centre.[1]

Without these two surprise attacks – and possibly without either one of them – the end result of World War II would have been vastly different. If *Barbarossa* had not been undertaken, Germany would not have been involved in a two-front war and all its might could have been directed against Britain. Similarly, if there had been no attack on Pearl Harbor, American involvement in World War II would not have eventuated. However, it is impossible to predict how long the impasse regarding the American requirement for Japan to make considerable concessions in return for lifting sanctions could have lasted.[2] Something had to give eventually.

When the Red Army under General Georgy Zhukov began its winter offensive on 5 December 1941 and pushed the Wehrmacht back from Moscow, the Oberkommando der Wehrmacht

(OKW – the High Command of the German armed forces) began to realize that Germany had bitten off more than it could chew and that Hitler's comment that 'we have only to kick in the door and the whole rotten structure will come crashing down' was a typical falsehood.

Japan's unheralded strike on Pearl Harbor failed to deliver the knockout blow similar to that envisaged in its Mahan-inspired Decisive Battle Doctrine (*Kantai Kessen*).[3] The attack sank or damaged obsolescent battleships but failed to destroy the vital aircraft carriers and their aircraft, which were away on manoeuvres. The important fuel reserves at Pearl Harbor (being that this was before the Red Hill underground storage facility was completed) were left intact because of Admiral Nagumo's reluctance to launch a third wave. Instead of bringing the United States to some sort of favourable *détente* – a very unlikely outcome – Japan had bitten the tail of a sleeping tiger.

Both Axis powers grossly underestimated the ability of their opponents to fight back in scale, speed and dedication. In doing so, these attacks – despite the advantage of surprise and the absence of a declaration of war – failed to achieve their ultimate goals and irrevocably changed history; for the better.

The following year saw momentous events that gave impetus to the basic direction in which World War II was heading even more positively in the Allies' favour:

- the German retreat from the gates of Moscow
- the Russian winter offensive
- the battle of the Coral Sea
- the battle of Midway
- the Guadalcanal campaign
- the second battle of Alamein and the retreat of the Afrika Korps
- Operation *Torch* and the Allied invasion of French North Africa
- the failure of Germany's *Fall Blau* (Case Blue – the drive for the Caucasus oil fields)
- the prelude to the fall of Stalingrad in February 1943

However, these successes were marred by many reversals of fortune – on land, in the air and at sea. While not singularly as significant, their effects had a negative impact at the time, often requiring a rethink of strategy and tactics.

One of the Allied reversals of 1942 involved the almost complete destruction of a convoy supplying vital war *matériel* from Britain and the United States to Soviet Russia: PQ 17. Of the 33 merchant ships that finally made up the convoy (after three early retirements), 20 were American-flagged (60.6 per cent). Of the 22 ships lost – that's two-thirds of the convoy – 15 (68.1 per cent) were American.

What made this sad event worse was that it didn't need to have happened. But for the decision of one man, Chief of the Naval Staff and First Sea Lord of the Admiralty Sir Dudley Pound, the massacre could have been avoided. Pound micro-managed the operation from London instead of leaving the men on the spot to make the necessary decisions. Under the mistaken belief that the German battleship *Tirpitz* and attending warships had put to sea and would intercept PQ 17, instead of a more prudent course of action to reverse the course of the convoy until the situation clarified itself, he contradicted his staff advice and issued the fateful order, 'Convoy is to scatter.'

The Soviets were being supplied by the West because if the invasion of Russia succeeded, all of the Nazi force might be brought to bear on Britain and its Commonwealth (or Empire, as some still thought of it despite the change of status as a result of the Imperial Conference and Balfour Declaration of 1926). Despite this spectre, in many respects the decision to send supplies to Russia via the Arctic route was more political than it was strategic. There is an old saying, which some attribute to Sanskrit literature, specifically in the *Arthashastra* around the 4th century BC, that 'the enemy of my enemy is my friend.' And so it was that Operation *Barbarossa* brought two most unlikely bedfellows together, in the form of democratic, capitalist and royalist Britain alongside the communist, totalitarian and dictatorial Soviet Union.

The same day that news came through that Germany had begun an invasion of the USSR, Winston Churchill said,

> No one has been a more consistent opponent of Communism than I have for the last twenty-five years. I will unsay no word that I have spoken about it. But all this fades away before the spectacle which is now unfolding … Any man or state who fights on against Nazidom will have our aid. Any man or state who marches with Hitler is our foe … It follows, therefore, that we shall give whatever help we can to Russia and the Russian people. We shall appeal to all our friends and allies in every part of the world to take the same course and pursue it, as we shall, faithfully and steadfastly to the end.[4]

Hard-pressed as Britain was after almost two years of warfare, Prime Minister Churchill, ever the pragmatist, gave President of the Soviet Union Joseph Stalin a quite extraordinary commitment: to deliver, by sea, 1,200 tanks a month from July 1942 to January 1943, followed by 2,000 tanks and another 3,300 aircraft more than had already been promised in the initial commitment of 440 fighters. Despite the fact that these tanks (Matildas and Valentines to begin with) were obsolescent, even obsolete, and certainly inferior to the Soviet T-34s and German Panzer Mk IIIs and Mk IVs, and that the aircraft (Hawker Hurricanes to begin with) were also no longer front-line fighter aircraft, they still represented a significant proportion of Britain's industrial production capacity which could have been applied towards its more direct and immediate needs. However, by diverting production and providing *matériel* aid to the Soviets, it was recognized that this was basically in Britain's overall best interests. Ultimately, about 25 per cent of the tonnage of Allied supplies of all sorts was delivered to the Soviets via Arctic convoys, some 70 per cent was via the Persian Gulf and the remainder from the US West Coast to Vladivostok, Nikolayevsk-on-Amur and Petropavlovsk-Kamchatski. The ships that were loaded on the US West Coast took about 18–20 days to make the crossing, and to this must be added the time that it took to transport goods to the US ports and later westwards by rail across the Soviet Union. After 7 December 1941, only Soviet ships could be used on this route, observing a neutral status, although some ships were apparently sunk by the Japanese.

The Persian Gulf route took significantly longer; some 75 days via the Cape of Good Hope.

Thus, the Arctic convoy route was the shortest, but it was also the most dangerous.

Return convoys from Russia brought such diversified cargoes as timber (particularly mine pit props), ore (magnesite, chrome and iron), wax, potash (potassium chloride), apatite, tobacco, arsenic, pine pitch, horsehair, mandrake root and – controversially – caviar. Passengers were often carried too, including Polish soldiers who had escaped to Russia from Germany's invasion.

Matilda tanks being loaded in Britain bound for the Soviet Union. (Public Domain)

The first aid convoy to Russia – Operation *Dervish* – departed from Liverpool on 12 August 1941 via Scapa Flow (16–17 August) and Hvalfjörður (Hvalfiordur, or Whale Fjord) in Iceland (20–21 August), arriving at Arkhangelsk on 31 August, just 70 days after Germany's invasion began. It comprised six merchant ships and an accompanying oiler with a close escort of one cruiser, three destroyers and a mixed bag of seven anti-submarine trawlers and minesweepers. As if a ratio of almost two escorts to each merchant ship was not deemed sufficient protection, units of the Home Fleet acted as a Distant Cover Force (a fleet aircraft carrier, two heavy cruisers and three destroyers). In addition, indirect support was offered by Operation *Gauntlet* and Operation *Strength*. The former was an Allied combined operation (25 August–3 September) involving Canadian, British and Free Norwegian troops landing on the Norwegian Island of Spitsbergen to destroy the mining and port infrastructure and deny German access to a weather-reporting station. Operation *Strength* (30 August–14 September) involved the delivery of 24 Hawker Hurricane IIBs to Vaenga on the Kola Peninsula. The RAF's 151 Wing (two squadrons) had been established at the end of 1941 at Vaenga through 15 Hurricanes being delivered in crated form and reassembled. The old aircraft carrier, *Argus*, delivered the Hurricanes in September from a position south of Spitzbergen, where they were flown off in clear weather.

Convoys to and from Russia were a perilous undertaking. While trans-Atlantic convoys had to run the gauntlet, mainly, of German submarines, the Russia route was subject to extremes: almost continual daylight in summer and almost continual darkness in winter, the latter made worse by below-freezing temperatures, ice and frequent storms. Ice in the water was one danger,

Arctic Sea conditions. (Public Domain)

Typical icing conditions. If allowed to build up, a ship's stability could be adversely affected. (*The Globe & Mail*, Canadian War Museum)

made worse by frequent fogs. Ice which formed from sea spray was another threat. It could form instantly from breaking green water and build up on a ship's superstructure, guard rails, masts and rigging, deck cargo and guns, all adding to a ship's topweight; if not removed by steam and/or chipping, it could threaten to capsize the vessel.

To make matter worse, navigation in these waters was affected by being so close to the Earth's magnetic pole.[5] This resulted in magnetic compass needles wanting to dip alarmingly and gyro-compasses to tilt upwards, all contrary to accurate navigation. Mists, fog and storms all reduced visibility and opportunities for astronomical sightings to be taken, sometimes for days on end. This resulted in Dead Reckoning (DR) having to be used to estimate – rather than calculate – a ship's position. DR involved using estimates of course made good (having allowed for leeway), speed over the ground and distance achieved. It was far from precise, as we shall see later.

Leamington was one of 50 Town-class destroyers transferred to the RN from the USN in the 'Destroyers-for-Bases' agreement in September 1940. It formed part of PQ 17's close escort. Beneath the accumulated ice there is a 4-inch gun and a three-level bridge, a DF aerial and a Type 271 radar. (Public Domain)

The routes to and from northern Russia were determined by the presence of the ice barrier and the necessity to stand off from the German-occupied Norwegian coast as far as possible in order to reduce the chances of being spotted by Norway-based Luftwaffe reconnaissance flights. In addition to Nazi submarines patrolling the most logical routes, this theatre also had the threat of follow-up Luftwaffe dive-bombers, level bombers and torpedo bombers, plus the Kriegsmarine's warships. The latter ranged from fast coastal forces to destroyers, cruisers, pocket-battleships and their modern battleship, *Tirpitz* – hence the need for a large escort and covering forces.

The summer route was a 14-day voyage: west of Iceland, west of Jan Mayen Island and north of Bear Island towards Novaya Zemlya (New Land), hugging the ice barrier to the north. The 10-day winter route was forced south by the build-up of ice – sometimes within 80 miles of North Cape – and proceeded east of the Faroes, south of Bear Island, then hugged the north coast (Kola Peninsula) of Russia, where it could receive promised Russian protection – sea and air – which often failed to materialize.

A total of 41 convoys and 13 independent sailings to Russia involved 865 merchant ships, of which 728 arrived, a 15.84 per cent loss rate (refer to the table in Chapter 1 as this data varies between sources). This average, while considerably higher than that which pertained to the trans-Atlantic convoys (approximately 4 per cent), pales into insignificance with PQ 17's 66 per cent.

While there have been several books written on the subject, albeit none recently, including the very controversial David Irving account, *The Destruction of Convoy PQ 17*, this book is the only account of Convoy PQ 17 which illuminates the narrative with scale drawings of the principal warships and aircraft involved. It begins by putting PQ 17 into its true context of all the Allied supply convoys sent beyond the Arctic Circle to support the Soviet Union in its fight against Hitler's invading armies.

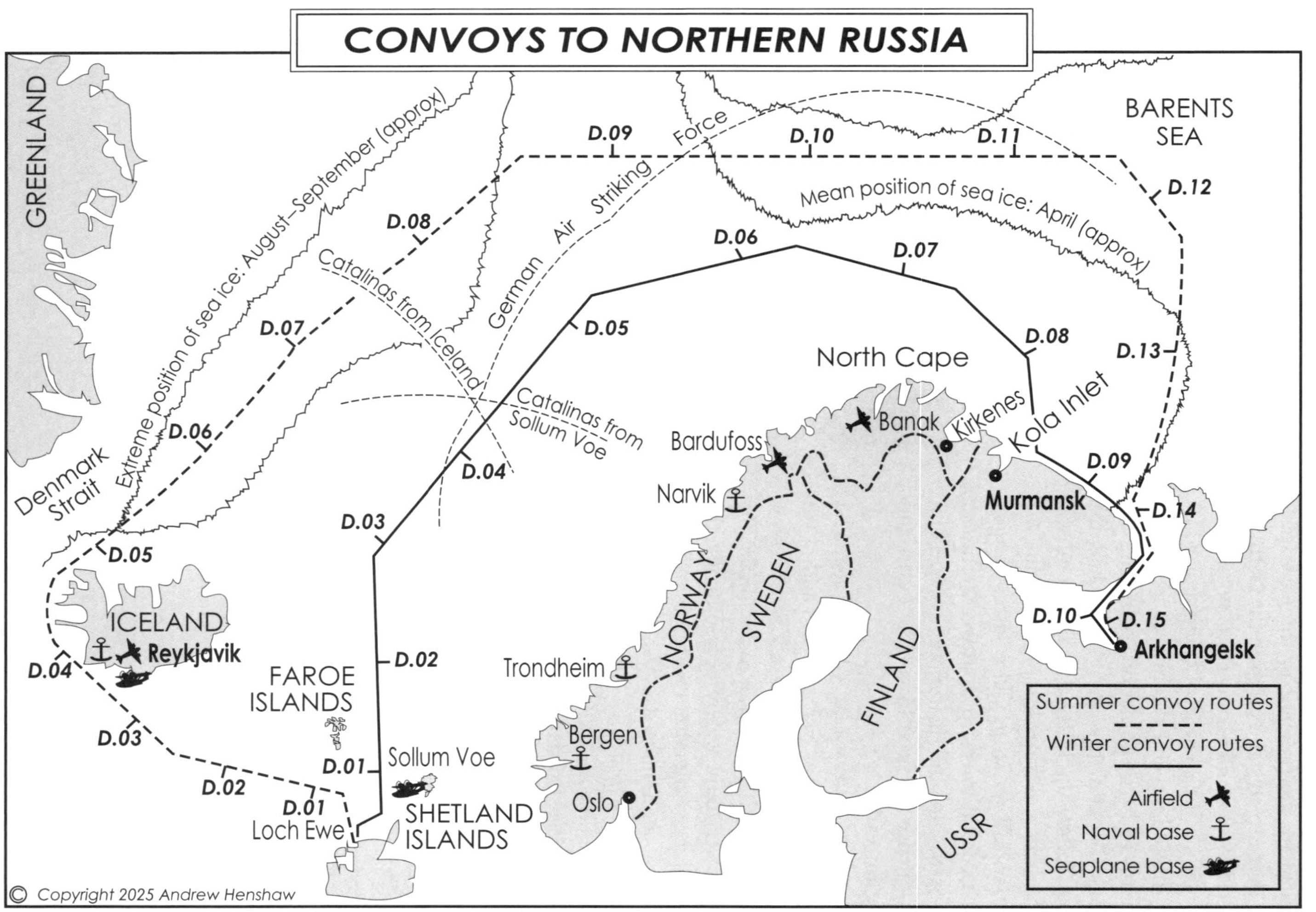

This map shows the longer (15-day) summer route from Scotland to Arkhangelsk, west of Iceland and Jan Mayen Island and north of Bear Island, and the shorter (10-day) winter route avoiding, if possible, the edge of the ice. All dates are for the year 1942.

PART I

The Enemy of My Enemy

CHAPTER 1

Background

There would have been no need for convoys to supply the Red Army had Adolf Hitler not decided that his Third Reich needed *Lebensraum* – living room in German, but code for a new German Empire – seizing neighbouring resource-rich lands and subduing what the Nazi regime referred to as *Untermenschen* (literally under-men, more usually sub-humans) who did not fit the Aryan racial template; basically, the Slav peoples and Jews. Operation *Barbarossa* was to be the means to this end, at least insofar as the Soviet Union was concerned. World domination was the ultimate goal; a One Thousand-Year Reich.[1]

It is logical, therefore, if somewhat hard to comprehend considering the disparity of doctrines, that upon the commencement of German hostilities against the Soviet Union on 22 June 1941, the British must have breathed a collective sigh of relief and changed from a viewpoint of the Soviets as potential enemies to being somewhat unprincipled allies. After all, the two countries had not seen eye-to-eye since the October Revolution of 1917, which toppled the three-century-old Romanov dynasty. This animosity was inflamed by Russia's withdrawal from World War I on 3 March 1918 (the Treaty of Brest-Litovsk), which freed up some one million German servicemen, leaving Britain and its allies to fight on alone on the Western Front against a much larger force than previously.

When Germany invaded Poland from the west on 1 September 1939, it was France and Britain that declared war on Germany for doing so, albeit two days later. However, both countries conveniently chose not to declare war on Soviet Russia when it similarly invaded Poland, from the east, on 17 September. These two invasions resulted in the annexation of what had been the Second Polish Republic by the two powers on 6 October 1939. The Polish–British Common Defence Pact, more particularly termed the Agreement of Mutual Assistance between the United Kingdom and Poland, was a brief document of only eight articles, pledging Britain to give Poland 'all the support and assistance in its power' if Poland was 'engaged in hostilities with a European Power in consequence of aggression by the latter'. It was executed, hurriedly it would seem, as late as 25 August 1939, only two days after the Molotov–Ribbentrop Pact. Irrespective of the agreement, neither Britain nor France ever fired a shot or dropped a bomb in Poland's direct defence, despite the French promise of May 1939 to launch a major offensive within two weeks of any German attack and the July 1939 promise that Britain would support this action with a strategic bombing campaign against targets within Germany.

By not fulfilling these obligations – one must understand that bombing would have been difficult to accomplish anyway, given the distance involved and the capabilities of current aircraft – Britain and France gave a certain tacit legitimacy to German and Soviet aggression.

The German–Soviet Non-Aggression Pact (more often known as the Molotov–Ribbentrop Pact after the names of the Soviet and German foreign ministers who negotiated the deal) was executed on 23 August 1939. Communism and fascism were philosophically diametrically opposed to one another, and the pact dismayed the Western democracies, particularly Britain and France, which had been exploring a collective-security agreement after the outcome of the 1938 Munich Conference. What was perhaps not well-known at the time was the degree of military co-operation that had taken place between the two regimes' countries from as early as 1922 and which reached its peak in the mid-1930s. The Versailles Treaty had placed severe restrictions on Germany's armed forces – as to size and equipment – and by allowing the Germans to have secret bases in Soviet territory, where new equipment (forbidden by the treaty) could be tested, the Soviets had the benefit of technology transfer and training. While the construction and testing of submarines never took place in Soviet territory, as late as April 1940 the incomplete Hipper-class heavy cruiser *Lützow* was sold to the Soviets. It was still incomplete when Germany attacked on 22 June 1941.

For Germany, the pact removed the spectre of fighting on two fronts at the same time. For Russia, in an undeclared war on its eastern borders with Japan since 1932, it bought time to build up its defences and gain territories to provide defence-in-depth.

Molotov signs the German–Soviet Non-Aggression Pact on 23 August 1939, with Ribbentrop and Stalin looking on. (Public Domain)

There was a symbiosis in this Faustian bargain. Germany was rich in technology and poor in many vital resources, whereas the Soviet Union was rich in resources and poor in the technology to develop them.

However, there was far more than a you-scratch-my-back-and-I'll-scratch-yours element to this unlikely German–Soviet arrangement. A secret protocol of the pact divided Eastern Europe into German and Soviet spheres of influence – for the time being at least. While the pact had a 10-year duration with a five-year extension, it lasted less than two years. In that time, goods flowed between both countries via a generous German–Soviet Commercial Agreement of February 1940: raw materials to Germany, such as over 900,000 tons of oil, 1,600,000 tons of grain and 140,000 tons of manganese ore and rubber, in exchange for manufactured goods such as locomotives, machine tools, generators and diesel engines.

When Germany began Operation *Barbarossa* and the German–Soviet Non-Aggression Pact was broken, the Nazi regime was fighting a two-front war. Indeed, it was not so much a two-front conflict at the time as one very big conflict and one – by comparison – sideline.

Having recently won battles for Yugoslavia, Greece and Crete, Hitler chose to divide his forces in what was almost a stalemate situation with Britain, where the only real confrontation was in the Atlantic and in the North African desert and adjoining Mediterranean Sea. From Britain's point of view, still standing alone, any watering-down of aggression, anything that took the pressure off, was welcome. However, the very concept of providing *matériel* aid to the Soviets in order for them to fight the Nazis was another matter. While it was expedient to do so at the time, it was far from practical, considering that Britain's own lines of communication – particularly the west-to-east trans-Atlantic supply route – were constantly under threat. Furthermore, it was losing merchant ships faster than they could be replaced, and the Royal Navy (RN) was trying to fight a three-ocean war with only a two-ocean fleet. Short of practically everything needed to wage (and win) war, could Britain afford to give *matériel* aid to a regime with diametrically opposite political doctrine, aims and objectives?

It was a question of pragmatism, particularly as the opening months of *Barbarossa* saw German victory after victory, causing seemingly unsustainable Red Army losses and the very real possibility of a Nazi victory. The only land campaign Britain was fighting against the Axis forces was in the North African desert, where a mere 14 divisions were involved, many of which were from the Commonwealth. To put this into perspective, *Barbarossa* involved some 150 German divisions along a front of almost 3,000 kilometres. Despite the relatively small British forces actively battling the Axis forces, and the American build-up which only got underway in early 1942, there was no prospect of the Western Allies opening a second front in 1942, despite Stalin's urging for it to take pressure off the Red Army. To suit Stalin, that second front would have to involve some form of amphibious assault, somewhere on the European coastline from Norway to France. Amphibious assaults are risky, major undertakings and require considerable preparations – none of which were in the current experience of Britain or the United States, or at least not on the scale that would be required.

One could well argue that there was already a second front in existence: the daylight and night-time strategic bombing campaign by the United States Army Air Force (USAAF) and the Royal Air Force (RAF) designed to cripple Germany's infrastructure. Stalin had little appreciation of Britain's position, particularly the war at sea and the desert war. In many respects,

Stalin was asking for aid – both *matériel* and the opening of some offensive to take the load off the Soviets – in excess of what Churchill was offering. Further, the Arcadia Conference (First Washington Conference), which ran from 22 December 1941 to 14 January 1942, established the 'Germany First' principle, with the Pacific conflict relegated to an uncomfortable back seat. In view of the fact that this conference started only 15 days after the Japanese attack on Pearl Harbor, it is significant that the United States did not press for a 'Japan First' strategy, adopting instead a war plan previously established with Britain between 29 January and 27 March 1941 (the ABC-1 Plan). The emphasis on defeating Germany rather than Japan favoured the Soviet Union, further helped by the invasion of Sicily and Italy in mid-1943 just as Germany's Kursk offensive was taking place in south-western Russia.

Admiral of the Fleet of the Soviet Union and People's Commissar of the Navy N. G. Kuznetsov said in his memoirs:

> The British government claimed that it [a second front] was impossible, that it was not in their power, to land a descent directly in France. On September 13, 1941, Stalin proposed that Britain should land 25–30 divisions in Arkhangelsk or bring them through Iran to the USSR's southern regions. However, Churchill was unwilling to aid the USSR with troops. He offered to replace our units in Iran or to send British troops to the Caucasus to protect Soviet oil fields. This unseemly proposal revealed the real reasons why Britain was constantly delaying the opening of a second front not only in 1941–1942, but also in 1943 … Though the situation demanded the opening of a second front in 1942 and though agreement had actually been reached on the matter, the Allies refrained from executing this operation. This is an indisputable fact. We foundedly [*sic*] believed that Great Britain with its powerful Navy could exert pressure on Nazi Germany in the north … It could have executed an operation in Varangerfjorden [Norway] to put the Germans in a difficult position … I must say that the Navy of the 'ruler of the seas' rendered rather limited aid to its fighting ally.[2]

But could Britain afford *not* to support a somewhat dubious ally? As the British historian A. J. P. Taylor remarked: 'Nearly every Western observer was convinced that Soviet Russia was useless as an ally: her ruler a savage and unscrupulous dictator, her armies in chaos, her political system likely to collapse at the first strain.'[3] Soviet Russia would not be an ally so much as simply Germany's co-enemy. However, in the simplest and most basic of terms, every German life lost, every German plane shot down, every German tank destroyed by the Red Army was just that much less available – at some future date – to threaten Britain and its allies in their aim to liberate Western Europe.

On 7 July 1941, Churchill wrote to Stalin to open negotiations. Churchill was concerned that due to the way the Nazi invasion seemed to be rolling back the Red Army and gaining territory so quickly, Stalin might make a separate peace. The usually perspicacious Churchill got that wrong. Like Hitler, he underestimated the capacity of Russia to fight back.

On 12 July – only 20 days after Operation *Barbarossa* commenced – an Anglo-Soviet Agreement was executed between Britain and the Soviet Union. This was a military alliance which pledged both powers to assist each other and not make a separate peace with Germany. The way in which assistance was to be rendered, one to the other, was not spelt out.

On the same day, the Admiralty issued an order that a new striking force for Arctic waters was to be established, which was fine in theory but difficult in practice. The battle-cruiser *Hood* had been lost fighting the *Bismarck*, and the battleship *Prince of Wales* was earmarked for transporting Churchill to and from Placentia Bay for the Atlantic Charter meeting. Other Home Fleet units were also unavailable. The battleships *Nelson* and *Rodney* were on detached duties and under repair in America, respectively. Heavy cruisers *Dorsetshire* and *Norfolk* were under repair, while *London* was at Freetown in western Africa. Light cruisers *Kenya* (under repair) and *Birmingham* (due in Durban, South Africa) were out of the picture too.[4]

On 31 July, the Director of the Lend-Lease programme, American statesman Harry Hopkins, broached the subject of providing aid to the Soviet Union with Stalin.

On 12 August, Churchill and US President Franklin D. Roosevelt cabled Stalin to assure him that the Western Allies were co-operating to provide Stalin's most urgent military supplies. Still at peace, the United States Navy was to be responsible for escorting American-originated supplies from East Coast ports to Iceland. In October, the destroyer USS *Kearney* was damaged by a torpedo and the destroyer USS *Reuben James* was sunk. Aid to Russia was costing more than America expected.

On 14 August, Prime Minister Churchill and President Roosevelt issued the Atlantic Charter statement after conferring in Placentia Bay, Canada. Of the eight principal clauses, none referred to providing aid to the Soviet Union. However, their discussions resulted in a proposal to meet with the Russians to further discuss aid. A rather strange combination of personalities – the American W. Averell Harriman and the Canadian Lord Beaverbrook – flew to Moscow in late

President Franklin Roosevelt and Prime Minister Winston Churchill on the quarterdeck of the newly completed battleship *Prince of Wales* prior to the announcement of the Atlantic Charter. (Public Domain)

September 1941 to meet with the Soviet Foreign Commissar, Vyacheslav Molotov, to discuss a long-range aid programme. The meeting became known as The First Moscow Conference. The First Protocol, signed on 1 October, promised 400 aircraft, 500 tanks and 10,000 trucks a month, in addition to other supplies such as aluminium, lead, tin, nickel and rubber. Churchill also asked of Roosevelt that American output be increased from 1,200 tanks per month to 2,000 per month, and aircraft to 3,600 per month, by the end of 1942 or beginning of 1943 – seemingly impossible numbers.

Beaverbrook was ambivalent as to whether the Soviet Union could be kept in the war, even with the Western aid. Nonetheless, in October, Churchill gave Stalin the assurance of a convoy every 10 days. It was totally unrealistic. The British Chiefs of Staff had stated that any more frequent than one every 40 days was impractical due to the lack of the necessary escort resources. Churchill was made well aware of the difficulties and risks to an overstretched RN, but chose, typically, to ignore them. The bigger picture, to him at least, was the importance of keeping Russia in the war, no matter the cost. Ultimately, the inability to meet the 10-day schedule was seen by Stalin as having broken a promise, with the Western Allies not committed to the task of supporting the Soviets.

To ensure secure overland supply lines, an Anglo-Soviet invasion of Persia (Iran) was formulated – Operation *Countenance*. It would also secure oil fields and pre-empt a possible Axis advance from the west via Turkey and from the south-west through Egypt should the Western Desert campaign fail.

On 6 October, as well as Churchill cabling Stalin advising of his intention to despatch convoys at 10-day intervals from Iceland, he reiterated that American output be increased to 1,200 tanks and 3,600 aircraft.

In order to obtain an appreciation of how difficult it was to gather the necessary merchant ships and their defending escorts, some data as to shipping losses is necessary. By the time the first convoy (Operation *Dervish*) was assembled, almost 4,000 merchant ships and some 13 million tons of commercial shipping had been lost, mainly in the Atlantic.[5] New emergency construction, coming primarily from orders placed with American shipyards and secondarily from Canadian shipyards, was augmented by hard-pressed British shipyards, all streamlining their output in the form of standardized designs. A 10,000-ton tramp-steamer design from the Sunderland shipyard of Joseph L. Thompson & Sons Ltd (SS *Empire Liberty*) formed the basis of an order of 60 ships from Henry J. Kaiser; 30 in Richmond, California, and 30 in Portland, Maine, and known as the Ocean class. These ships, in turn, formed the base design for what became a run of 2,710 Liberty ships. The hull and machinery remained unchanged, with the Liberty ships using welding instead of riveting, and oil-fired boilers instead of coal, and with the superstructure redesigned by Gibbs & Cox. Readers can find more detail in the book *Liberty's Provenance*.[6] Liberty ships formed the largest single ship class in PQ 17 and in many of the Russian convoys. They are easily distinguished by being named after people and using their full legal names (such as *Woodbridge N. Ferris*), plus the almost constant tonnage data (7,191 GRT). Also, around 177 Liberty ships were made available to Britain under Lend-Lease and all but one bore 'Sam' prefixes in their names, another distinguishing feature.

The 353 Canadian-built versions of the Ocean class had either a 'Fort' or 'Park' prefix, another useful identifier (see drawings in Chapter 6).

The most authoritative work on World War II convoys is Arnold Hague's *The Allied Convoy System 1939–1945: Its Organization and Operation.* Unfortunately, Hague devotes less than five of almost 200 pages of his book to northern Russian convoys, and then only in Appendix 4.

There were 42 convoys plus one unescorted operation to northern Russia between August 1941 and May 1945. According to Hague, of the 848 ships which sailed, 65 were lost (7.67 per cent). Of the 36 convoys back from Russia, Hague states that of the 735 ships, 40 were sunk (5.44 per cent).[7] These figures have been quoted as gospel without inspection by many authors.

The website devoted to furthering Hague's work, www.convoyweb.org.uk, would appear to have updated Hague's research (dating from 2000), as there are many discrepancies between what that site reports and Hague's book. On their data (and much greater detail), the number of ships on the outbound convoys was 864, and the figure lost was 60 (7.23 per cent). Comparing the data for the convoys returning from Russia, their data reflects 771, of which 30 were lost (3.89 per cent).

Unfortunately, Hague's data is not presented consistently in his book as to the number of ships which were scheduled to set out, those which retired or failed to depart and those which were lost, to arrive at a net-arrived-vessels total. If we look at PQ 14, for instance, Hague states that this was an eight-vessel convoy, but there were actually 25 in the convoy; 16 returned to harbour due to being damaged by ice. Also, one was sunk and this is not mentioned. Further, his totals include Royal Fleet Auxiliary (RFA) oilers, in effect Merchant Navy oilers (whose sole purpose was to service the escorts to and from Russia) and dedicated rescue ships. These vessels should not be included as being ships that delivered aid to Russia. I suspect that the total of these oilers was probably greater than I ascertained. Some unidentified tankers may have been used to transport fuel to Russia. I have, therefore, recast all of Hague's data, making known adjustments accordingly.

My totals are, as tabled below, therefore: 728 merchant ships to Russia, 693 merchant ships back from Russia. The number of ships lost was 61 (8.38 per cent) to Russia and 31 (4.43 per cent) from Russia. Five ships were lost while in harbour, at Murmansk and Arkhangelsk. My summary is as follows:

Summary of Outbound and Homebound Convoys, 1941–45

		Hague	Convoyweb	Deductions*	Returned	Lost	Net Arrived
OUTBOUND: 42 convoys	1941	66	67	3	2	1	**61**
	1942	264	284	13	21	55	**195**
	1943	115	116	6	6	0	**104**
	1944	296	294	11	5	2	**276**
	1945	107	104	9	0	3	**92**
		848	**865**	**42**	**34**	**61**	**728**

(Continued)

(Continued)

		Hague	Convoyweb	Deductions*	Returned	Lost	Net Arrived
HOMEBOUND: 36 convoys	1941	49	49	1	4	0	**44**
	1942	218	221	7	6	20	**188**
	1943	94	94	4	3	5	**82**
	1944	262	259	8	2	4	**245**
	1945	142	142	6	0	2	**134**
		765	**765**	**26**	**15**	**31**	**693**

* Deductions are non-aid-carrying merchant ships such as RFA oilers, merchant ship oilers, rescue vessels, etc.

Before we look at PQ 17's travails, we need to briefly review the 18 convoys to Russia and the 13 return convoys that preceded it.

CHAPTER 2

Arctic Convoys Begin

Before any convoys could be despatched, arrangements had to be put in place for handling their arrivals, the unloading of the merchant ships, the refuelling and rearming of the escorts and the provision of local air cover. To make matters worse, in order to threaten Murmansk, German aircraft only had a short flight, 100 kilometres (60 miles) from Petsamo (Pechenga), and Soviet anti-aircraft defences at Murmansk were poor. Petsamo had a history of changing hands: originally part of Russia, then part of Finland when Finland became independent in December 1917, then lost to Russia in the Russo-Finnish War of 1939–41, then taken by the Germans during the advance on Moscow in late 1941.

Murmansk had very poor port facilities with limited effective wharfage. Arkhangelsk was marginally better, but the port was ice-bound to various degrees for five to six months of the year, depending on the severity of winter. At Murmansk, the wharves had fallen into disrepair, having been hurriedly built by the British in 1915 to provide aid to the Tsar. Despite the urgency frequently expressed by Stalin to provide aid, the Russians did little to improve let alone remove the bottleneck of the inadequate unloading facilities or the poor defences. Also, there was no crane capable of unloading tanks: the Matilda (12 tons), Valentine (16 tons) and later the Sherman (33 tons). A specialized heavy-lift ship eventually had to be positioned at Murmansk, and possibly one later at Arkhangelsk, though records are vague in this respect.

More in hope than expectation, some sort of facilities for crews – both naval and merchant – needed to be established for the turn-around period before setting sail for Britain and America. As it stood, there were no adequate facilities provided by the Soviets. But Soviet promises and Soviet delivery of those promises were two vastly different things. In a hostile environment, weather-wise, politically and socially, this was always a major problem and will be discussed in Chapter 4.

The organization of Arctic convoys was substantially the same as the pattern established for trans-Atlantic convoys, although defences varied considerably.

Before each convoy departed there were collective briefings of all the ship captains to establish, or reinforce, procedures. Each ship was allocated a position within the convoy and given a two-digit identification number; the first number indicating which column of ships it was in and the second indicating its location within that column. Thus, 53 was column five, third from the front. A convoy commodore, most often a very senior and retired Royal Navy officer, was usually in a ship in the middle column at the front. He had a staff, mainly of signallers. Communications between the commodore, the escort and the ships of the convoy were via signal flags, semaphore and signal lamps. Until short-range Talk Between Ships (TBS), which operated in the Ultra

High Frequency (UHF) and Very High Frequency (VHF) bands for line-of-sight communication over distances of less than 25 miles, became available later in the war, radio communication was avoided for fear of being detected by the enemy. Depending on the size of the convoy, a vice commodore and sometimes a rear commodore were appointed in the event the commodore's ship was disabled or sunk.

Merchant ships were often provided with a Royal Navy party. This consisted of an officer – usually a lieutenant – to liaise with the ship's master, plus a number of ratings, mainly signallers, proficient in visual signalling (flags and signal lamps) as W/T and R/T tended not to be used for security purposes. For some reason, personnel expert in visual signalling do not seem to have been used for PQ 17, where visibility was expected to be poor, but were certainly employed on ships attempting to reach Malta in Operation *Pedestal* in August.

Each ship within the convoy was armed. For British ships, or those outfitted in Britain, this generally consisted of a low-angle 4-inch naval gun, previously part of the main armament of a long-ago scrapped destroyer or from the secondary armament of decommissioned cruisers. They were not intended for anti-aircraft use – which would have been much more useful – but to engage surfaced submarines, an unlikely event when in convoy. Anti-aircraft weaponry was varied, depending on what was available – most often a QF 12-pounder 12 cwt of ancient vintage but which was an effective and simple weapon to operate. American ships were, most usually, fitted with similar 4-inch guns from scrapped destroyers and the 3-inch Mk 20-22 dual-purpose guns which were, in many respects, the more modern American equivalent of the 12-pounder. Later in the war, some ships received newer dual-purpose guns; 4-inch in British ships and 5-inch in American ships. When it came to short-range weapons, the most common was the 20 mm Oerlikon cannon in single mounts. The 40 mm Bofors was a harder-hitting weapon but required a bigger and more co-ordinated crew to be effective, and the guns were in short supply anyway. The 20 mm Oerlikons were located where they could offer the best possible firing arcs free of the forest of masts, samson posts, derricks and rigging. It appears that these Oerlikons may have come in mass-produced, prefabricated towers with circular tubs that would facilitate quick fitting-out. Whether the Oerlikons were the Mk I type with separate elevating wheel or the pedestal-type Mk IIA, which relied on two or three rings of surrounding steps for the gunner to achieve elevation, is not recorded. The former required more co-ordination between gunner and whoever manned the elevating wheel, whereas the latter saved a crewman but required some deft footwork by the gunner to negotiate the steps while tracking an aircraft. The former had the complication of mechanics for elevation; the latter had the complication of building up the steps, which also required taller surrounds for protection.

A mixture of rapid-firing weapons ranged from 0.5-inch heavy machine guns (most usually water-cooled ex-USN weapons) through to rifle-calibre machine guns such as World War I Lewis, Vickers, Hotchkiss and Marlin types. Machine guns were fitted to bridge wings, where they could be easily if not necessarily usefully manned. Undoubtedly, shooting back with something was better that just standing by and hoping for the best!

Though they tended to be more of a hazard to the ships fitted with them, the desperate Parachute and Cable (PAC) device was frequently fitted, but fortunately not often used. This consisted of a Schermuly rocket that fired a cable some 600 feet into the air, which then descended by parachute to trap a low-flying aircraft. An even more useless weapon was the Holman Projector, a steam-fired mortar-like weapon which launched hand grenades or, most usually, potatoes and other vegetables at friendly, or rival, ships.

The guns on British ships were manned by members of the Royal Artillery Maritime Regiment (RAMR, originally the Maritime Anti-Aircraft Regiment, Royal Artillery), the Royal Navy and Royal Marines (RM), the British Army and the Merchant Marine under an Admiralty Trade Division programme, generally referred to as Defensively Equipped Merchant Ships (DEMS). This title, somewhat confusingly, applied to ships equipped with self-defence armament of a wide variety of types, the personnel who manned the weapons and the on-shore establishment that organized the programme. Personnel were often retired servicemen or hostilities-only ratings, and were usually under the command of an RN petty officer or an RM sergeant.

American merchant ships with their own self-defence armament used the United States Navy Armed Guard (USNAG), starting in January 1942. These detachments had a similar organization to DEMS but were usually a bit more generously staffed and often under the command of a junior officer. Armed Guard detachments could sometimes be found on non-American ships. Because there were often more weapons than the DEMS and USNAG parties could fully man, it was the duty, indeed the necessity, of DEMS and USNAG parties to train their ship's merchant seamen to assist them. Merchant seamen earned an extra nine pence per day if they had official two-day training as a gunnery rating. It was not necessary that they were able to be a gunlayer, trainer, loader, sight setter, breech worker or rammer number as required by the large guns (4-inch to 6-inch calibre), but they had to act as ammunition handlers, keeping the guns supplied. They were able to man the smaller-calibre guns such as the single 20 mm Oerlikons or rifle-calibre machine guns. Richard Woodman, in both *Malta Convoys 1940–1943* and *Arctic Convoys*, makes the point, many times, that gun crews in American ships were trigger-happy and that fire discipline was poor. There were numerous friendly fire incidents when ships in a convoy were hit and damage inflicted (lifeboats holed and the like), along with Fleet Air Arm aircraft shot down when escort carriers were introduced, despite the fact that there were never any single-engine German aircraft involved in attacks on convoys.

At sea, spells of duty were called 'watches' and usually consisted of alternating four hours on and four hours off – sometimes eight hours off between watches if there were sufficient personnel. All personnel 'stood-to' during 'action stations'.

Unlike Atlantic convoys, what is referred to as the Close Escort used some armed trawlers and whalers, the reason being that they were more suited to the wild Arctic weather and the slow speed of the convoy. An average speed of 8 knots was within their usual 10-knot capabilities. It would appear from where they tended to be positioned, at the outside corners of the convoy, that their lack of speed and weak armament made them more suited to detection and deterrence of U-boats and to rescuing survivors.

An opening gambit in the action to support the Soviets involved Operation *EF* on 30 July 1941, with the cruiser-minelayer *Adventure* delivering mines and other war *matériel* to Arkhangelsk on 1 August. The Russians showed little interest in the mines, but they were eventually laid between 10 and 15 September off Rybachiy Peninsula (Fisher or Fishermen's Peninsula), the northernmost part of Russia.

Operation *EF* was ineffectual at best, an unmitigated disaster at worst. For the loss of 12 of the Fleet Air Arm's Fairey Albacore biplane torpedo bombers and four Fairey Fulmar two-seat fighters launched from aircraft carriers *Victorious* and *Furious*, one small ship was sunk and another set on fire in Kirkenes harbour in Norway, and minor damage was caused to the port at Petsamo in Finland, Germany's ally. The midnight sun conditions and cloudless skies meant that the element of surprise was lost and German fighter aircraft caused havoc, only two being lost.

While various sources dispute the numbers of aircraft shot down generally, Operation *EF* was not an auspicious start to the campaign to supply Soviet Russia: two fleet carriers, two cruisers and six escorting destroyers travelled around 2,000 miles and were put at risk for a very limited objective and with almost nothing positive to show for it.

Operation *Dervish* was the first convoy, which sailed before a decision was taken on 13 September 1941 to give each convoy a serial number in accordance with established practice. Thereafter, the next 19 convoys had a 'PQ' prefix, believed to have been adopted from the initials of Commander Peter Quellyn Roberts RN, an operations officer in the Admiralty from August 1940 to April 1943. At the end of 1942, 'JW' was used as the prefix but despite extensive research I have been unable to establish why the change was made and what the basis was for the initials chosen. The six merchant ships and an RFA oiler of Operation *Dervish* departed Liverpool on 12 August and arrived at Arkhangelsk via Scotland's Scapa Flow and Iceland's Hvalfiordur on 31 August. There do not appear to have been any weapons or munitions transported, the cargoes reported as being wool, rubber and tin.

The convoy had a Close Escort consisting of a light cruiser, three destroyers, an auxiliary anti-aircraft ship and a mixture of nine trawlers and minesweepers. The composition of this force varied during the convoy and was supported by a Distant Cover Force consisting, variously, of a fleet aircraft carrier, two heavy cruisers and three fleet destroyers. Despite travelling in almost uninterrupted daylight,[1] the convoy arrived safely. This format of Close Escort backed up by an Ocean Escort and a Distant Cover Force (sometimes referred to as a Heavy Cover Force) may not have been a constant tactic and seems to have been mainly used as a precaution for convoys sailing in daylight-type conditions or where intelligence suggested that Kriegsmarine assets threatened – principally the pocket-battleships/heavy cruisers *Admiral Scheer* and *Lützow* (ex-*Deutschland*), or the battleship *Tirpitz.*

Convoys PQ 1 to PQ 6, departing at dates between 29 September and 8 December, proceeded similarly without loss, a total of 48 merchant ships arriving safely. Return convoys were prefixed QP, and in the same period QP 1 to QP 4 also brought back 48 merchant ships, again without loss.

PQ 1 delivered 20 tanks (Matildas and/or Valentines) and 193 fighters (almost certainly disassembled Hawker Hurricanes).

In mid-November, a shortage of fuel oil and the prospect of another *Bismarck* incident caused Hitler to veto a recommendation that *Tirpitz* venture forth and attack convoys. However, the pocket-battleship *Admiral Scheer* was moved north and the T-class torpedo boats (small destroyers) were replaced by larger destroyers, despite them being plagued with defective high-pressure boilers. The very nature of the Norwegian coast, indented by fjords, offered innumerable jumping-off points for *Admiral Scheer* and/or *Tirpitz* to sally forth and attack. *Admiral Scheer* had been used effectively to attack convoy HX 84 from Halifax to Liverpool in the North Atlantic on 5 November 1940, sinking five merchant ships and the escorting armed merchant cruiser *Jervis Bay*, also damaging another merchant ship, while yet another was later sunk by German aircraft. The efficacy of this methodology was thus well established. When would it be next used?

By the time of PQ 5, from 27 November to 13 December, it was necessary for Russian icebreakers to force the passage into the White Sea. PQ 6 was too late to reach Arkhangelsk and was forced to dock at Murmansk.

Convoy PQ 7A – strangely a two-ship convoy – witnessed the first loss. Although the convoy departed on 26 December, the loss took place on 2 January 1942 after *Waziristan* became stranded in ice and was attacked by aircraft and then by *U-134*. Ironically, *Waziristan* was the first merchant ship to load military supplies in the United States for Russia.

Convoy PQ 7B of nine merchant ships arrived safely.

The four return convoys, QP 1 to QP 4, delivered 44 ships of 48 for reassignment. Two turned back in each of QP 3 and QP 4.

The Germans were slow to react to the Russian convoys. They controlled the whole of the vast Norwegian coast and the 1,750 nautical mile route from Kirkenes (in the north) to Oslo (in the south), allowing the free transportation of important materials, including Swedish iron ore from the Norwegian port of Narvik. The control of Norway also reduced the possibility of a repeat of the World War I blockade via the Northern Barrage minefield. Somewhat irrationally, Hitler feared a possible repeat of the 1940 Anglo-French invasion of northern Norway, especially after the Anglo-American occupation of Iceland in June 1941. The importance of convoys to northern Russia was not recognized by the OKW until September. Prior to that, there was a belief that the supplies were purely to support Soviet activity on the Murmansk front, with the possibility of a move against the nickel mines in nearby Petsamo. It was not until 10 October 1941 that Hitler issued *Führerweisung #37* for the Kriegsmarine to act against shipping to Murmansk and the 5th Air Fleet to return to Norway. However, because of bad weather conditions little was known about the convoys. On 14 December, Hitler took the measures a step further. He built up defence measures and deployed more assets, such as moving from Brest the battleships *Scharnhorst* and *Gneisenau* and the heavy cruiser *Prinz Eugen* (the 'Channel Dash', 11–13 February 1942) plus additional S-boats (E-boats to the Allies). By 22 January 1942, the Führer believed there was an immediate danger that the Allies could mount a landing between Trondheim and Kirkenes, thereby shortening the supply route to the Soviets and gaining some control of the northern Baltic. What Hitler failed to appreciate was the inability of the Allies, in manpower and amphibious vessels, to mount such an operation.

The true purpose and *modus operandi* of the Russian convoys did not become apparent to Germany's Naval Warfare Directorate until mid-January 1942. Until then, there was a belief that the convoys only originated in Scottish ports, with the Germans unaware of the significance of the convoys from Nova Scotia to the rendezvous in Iceland. A month later, the Naval Warfare Directorate was of the opinion that the convoy route from Iceland went near to the southern tip of Bear Island then southward to latitude 70° north, where the routes separated to Murmansk and Arkhangelsk – weather permitting.

The year 1941 saw a total of 62 arrivals and one loss in the convoys. Fifty merchant ships had delivered 800 fighter aircraft, 750 tanks and 1,400 military vehicles, plus ammunition and raw materials.[2] The never-satisfied and paranoid Stalin complained that deliveries were inefficient, claiming they were poorly packed and loaded, with parts missing and broken, particularly the fragile aircraft. Stalin's contrary attitude may have been attributable to the Western Allies' failure to recognize the Soviet annexation of Latvia, Estonia and Lithuania. It is difficult to reconcile his claims as to the waterside workers' supposed mal-intent when one considers the very pro-communist attitude of such workers in both Britain and the United States largely responsible for the packing and loading of these supplies.

In July 1940, the British government had imposed the Conditions of Employment and National Arbitration Order, known as Order 1305. This banned all strikes and lockouts, and imposed binding arbitration. Then, on 22 June 1941, Hitler attacked the Soviet Union. This changed everything. The workers of Britain supported the USSR as their ally in a war against Hitler and the Nazis. The conduct of the war changed.

However, while 1942 would see a considerable rise in the number of ships departing for Russia, it would also witness an increase in losses as the Germans devoted more resources to their destruction.

Convoys to Northern Russia

Designation	Departure Port	Departure Date	Arrival Port	Arrival Date	Merchant Vessels*
Dervish	Liverpool	12/08/1941	Arkhangelsk	31/08/1941	7
PQ 1	Hvalfjord	29/08/1941	Arkhangelsk	11/10/1941	11
PQ 2	Liverpool	13/10/1941	Arkhangelsk	30/10/1941	6
PQ 3	Hvalfjord	09/11/1941	Arkhangelsk	22/11/1941	8
PQ 4	Hvalfjord	17/11/1941	Arkhangelsk	28/11/1941	8
PQ 5	Hvalfjord	27/11/1941	Arkhangelsk	13/12/1941	7
PQ 6	Hvalfjord	08/12/1941	Murmansk	20/12/1941	8
PQ 7A	Hvalfjord	26/12/1941	Murmansk	10/01/1942	2
PQ 7B	Hvalfjord	31/12/1941	Murmansk	11/01/1942	9
PQ 8	Hvalfjord	08/01/1942	Arkhangelsk	17/01/1942	8
PQ 9	Reykjavik	01/02/1942	Murmansk	10/02/1942	10
PQ 10	Loch Ewe	26/01/1942	Reykjavik	31/01/1942	Part PQ 9
PQ 11	Kirkwall	14/02/1942	Murmansk	22/02/1942	13
PQ 12	Reykjavik	01/03/1942	Murmansk	12/03/2025	17
PQ 13	Loch Ewe	10/03/1942	Murmansk	31/03/1942	19
PQ 14	Oban	26/03/1942	Murmansk	19/04/1942	8
PQ 15	Oban	10/04/1942	Murmansk	05/05/1942	26
PQ 16	Reykjavik	21/05/1942	Murmansk	30/05/1942	36
PQ 17	Reykjavik	27/06/1942	Disprsed	04/07/1942	39
PQ 18	Loch Ewe	02/09/1942	Arkhangelsk	21/09/1942	44

(Continued)

(Continued)

Designation	Departure Port	Departure Date	Arrival Port	Arrival Date	Merchant Vessels*
JW 51A	Loch Ewe	15/12/1942	Kola Inlet	25/12/1942	16
JW 51B	Loch Ewe	22/12/1942	Kola Inlet	04/01/1943	15
JW 52	Loch Ewe	17/01/1943	Kola Inlet	27/01/1943	14
JW 53	Loch Ewe	15/02/1943	Kola Inlet	27/02/1943	29
JW 54A	Loch Ewe	15/11/1943	Kola Inlet	24/11/1943	19
JW 54B	Loch Ewe	22/11/1943	Arkhangelsk	03/12/1943	15
JW 55A	Loch Ewe	12/12/1943	Arkhangelsk	22/12/1943	19
JW 55B	Loch Ewe	20/12/1943	Arkhangelsk	30/12/1943	19
JW 56A	Loch Ewe	12/01/1944	Kola Inlet	28/01/1944	20
JW 56B	Loch Ewe	22/01/1944	Kola Inlet	01/02/1944	17
JW 57	Loch Ewe	22/02/1944	Kola Inlet	28/02/1944	43
JW 58	Loch Ewe	27/03/1944	Kola Inlet	04/04/1944	50
JW 59	Loch Ewe	15/08/1944	Kola Inlet	25/08/1944	34
JW 60	Loch Ewe	15/09/1944	Kola Inlet	23/09/1944	31
JW 61	Loch Ewe	20/10/1944	Kola Inlet	28/10/1944	30
JW 61A	Loch Ewe	31/10/1944	Murmansk	06/11/1944	2
JW 62	Loch Ewe	29/11/1944	Kola Inlet	07/12/1944	31
JW 63	Loch Ewe	30/12/1944	Kola Inlet	08/01/1945	38
JW 64	Clyde	03/02/1945	Kola Inlet	15/02/1945	28
JW 65	Clyde	11/03/1945	Kola Inlet	21/03/1945	26
JW 66	Clyde	16/04/1945	Kola Inlet	25/04/1945	27
JW 67	Clyde	12/05/1945	Kola Inlet	20/05/1945	26

Note:
* Convoy numbers may include naval oilers, rescue ships, etc., (Arnold Hague, *The Allied Convoy System 1939–1945: Its Organisation, Defence and Operation*, pp. 188–89).

Convoys from Northern Russia

Designation	Departure Port	Departure Date	Arrival Port	Arrival Date	Merchant Vessels*
QP 1	Arkhangelsk	28/09/1941	Scapa Flow	10/10/1941	14
QP 2	Arkhangelsk	03/11/1941	Kirkwall	17/11/1941	12
QP 3	Arkhangelsk	27/11/1941	Dispersed	03/12/1941	10
QP 4	Arkhangelsk	29/12/1941	Dispersed	09/01/1942	13
QP 5	Murmansk	13/01/1942	Dispersed	19/01/1942	4
QP 6	Murmansk	24/01/1942	Dispersed	28/01/1942	6
QP 7	Murmansk	12/02/1942	Dispersed	15/02/1942	8

(Continued)

(Continued)

Designation	Departure Port	Departure Date	Arrival Port	Arrival Date	Merchant Vessels*
QP 8	Murmansk	01/03/1942	Reykjavik	11/03/1942	15
QP 9	Kola Inlet	21/03/1942	Reykjavik	03/04/1942	18
QP 10	Kola Inlet	10/04/1942	Reykjavik	21/04/1942	15
QP 11	Murmansk	28/04/1942	Reykjavik	07/05/1942	13
QP 12	Kola Inlet	21/05/1942	Reykjavik	29/05/1942	14
QP 13	Arkhangelsk	26/06/1942	Reykjavik	07/07/1942	35
QP 14	Arkhangelsk	13/09/1942	Loch Ewe	26/09/1942	20
QP 15	Kola Inlet	17/11/1942	Loch Ewe	30/11/1942	31
RA 51	Kola Inlet	30/12/1942	Loch Ewe	11/01/1943	14
RA 52	Kola Inlet	29/01/1943	Loch Ewe	09/02/1943	10
RA 53	Kola Inlet	01/03/1943	Loch Ewe	14/03/1943	30
RA 54A	Kola Inlet	01/11/1943	Loch Ewe	14/11/1943	13
RA 54B	Arkhangelsk	26/11/1943	Loch Ewe	09/12/1943	10
RA 55A	Kola Inlet	22/12/1943	Loch Ewe	01/01/1944	23
RA 55B	Kola Inlet	31/12/1943	Loch Ewe	08/01/1944	8
RA 56	Kola Inlet	03/02/1944	Loch Ewe	11/02/1944	39
RA 57	Kola Inlet	02/03/1944	Loch Ewe	10/03/1944	33
RA 58	Kola Inlet	07/04/1944	Loch Ewe	14/04/1944	38
RA 59A	Kola Inlet	28/04/1944	Loch Ewe	06/05/1944	43
RA 59A	Kola Inlet	28/08/1944	Loch Ewe	05/09/1944	9
RA 60	Kola Inlet	28/09/1944	Loch Ewe	15/10/1944	32
RA 61	Kola Inlet	02/11/1944	Loch Ewe	09/11/1944	37
RA 61A	Kola Inlet	11/11/1944	Loch Ewe	17/11/1944	2
RA 62	Kola Inlet	10/12/1944	Loch Ewe	19/12/1944	29
RA 63	Kola Inlet	11/01/1945	Loch Ewe	21/01/1945	31
RA 64	Kola Inlet	17/02/1945	Loch Ewe	28/02/1945	33
RA 65	Kola Inlet	23/03/1945	Loch Ewe	01/04/1945	26
RA 66	Kola Inlet	29/04/1945	Clyde	08/05/1945	27
RA 67	Kola Inlet	23/05/1945	Clyde	30/05/1945	25

Note:
* Convoy numbers may include naval oilers, rescue ships, etc., (Arnold Hague, *The Allied Convoy System 1939–1945: Its Organisation, Defence and Operation*, pp. 188–89).

CHAPTER 3

Aid Now Comes at a Price

On 12 January 1942, Hitler approved moving *Tirpitz* from the River Jähde at Wilhelmshaven to Trondheim in Norway. While the battleship arrived undetected on 16 January, the absence of *Tirpitz* from Wilhelmshaven was noted by RAF reconnaissance on 17 January, delaying the departure of PQ 9 from Iceland. On 23 January, *Tirpitz* was finally located in the steep-sided Aas Fjord (also known as Aasen Fjord, Asenfjord, Asenfjorden, Åsenfjord or Åsenfjorden), north-east of Trondheim. A bombing raid by the RAF on 24 January caused no damage.

On 19 February, *Tirpitz* up-anchored. The next day, *Admiral Scheer*, heavy cruiser *Prince Eugen* and three escorting destroyers were spotted by aircraft heading north. The aircraft carrier *Victorious*, heavy cruiser *Berwick* and four destroyers were sent to seek and destroy the enemy force, but failed to find it. Instead, the submarine *Trident* managed to get one torpedo strike on *Prince Eugen* on 23 February when off Trondheim. *Admiral Scheer* and the damaged *Prince Eugen* made it into Aas Fjord that night.

The malign threat that *Tirpitz* posed was to dominate Admiralty thinking, strategy and tactics for several years. In many ways, the possibility of *Tirpitz* breaking loose into the North Atlantic was greater than the reality. *Bismarck* had tried it in May 1941 and was lost. Hitler was never maritime-oriented, and other than the U boats, the Kriegsmarine was largely ineffectual in World War II, its ships being laid up towards the end due to lack of fuel and its personnel used as troops. After the *Bismarck* breakout in May 1941, a cruiser patrol had been instigated in the Denmark Strait, known as Patrol White, together with a similar patrol, augmented by Coastal Command aircraft, in the Iceland–Faroes gap called Black Patrol. But the efficacy of any such patrol depended on the right ship or aircraft being at the right place at the right time. Given the area to be covered and the prevailing weather conditions, it was a big ask.

The commander of the 10th Cruiser Squadron, Rear Admiral Burrough (soon to be famous for his leadership in Operation *Pedestal*),[1] covering the Bear Island–Kola Inlet area, had been frequently disappointed by Russian failure to supply anti-submarine patrols and provide air-cover to convoys, despite aircraft having been delivered partly for that purpose.

In 1942 there were 13 outbound and 12 return convoys, plus a separate Operation *FB* which involved 13 merchant ships making independent voyages. While there had been only one ship loss in 1941, the year 1942 saw a large increase in the numbers of ships which arrived safely – 199 – but also a disproportionate increase in the number of ships lost, 54.

The much-feared, but in the end comparatively toothless, KMS *Tirpitz.* (Public Domain)

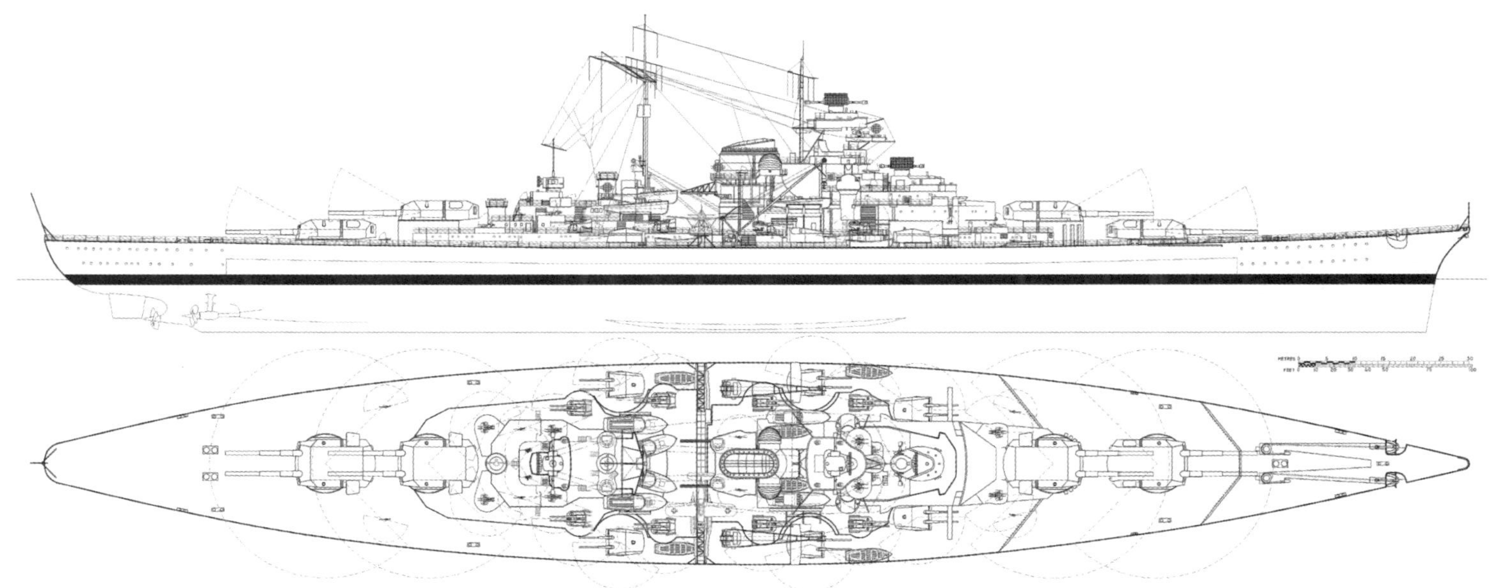

Notes on the drawing: *My drawing of the villain of the piece,* Tirpitz, *is based on its sister-ship,* Bismarck, *which was sunk in an action on 26–27 May 1941. It was not possible to establish precisely what equipment by way of armament and radar may have been fitted to* Tirpitz *at the time of Unternehmen Rösselsprung against PQ 17. While a handsome and powerful-looking battleship, note that effective firing arcs were somewhat limited by the position of the secondary and anti-aircraft guns plus the various ship's boats, the aircraft carried and two cranes to service aircraft and boats. Also note the unusual arrangement for aerials at the head of the mainmast.*

Duke of York. The King George V class was the last multi-ship battleship class built for the Royal Navy and suffered from having to make too many compromises, mainly to meet Washington Treaty obligations. (Public Domain)

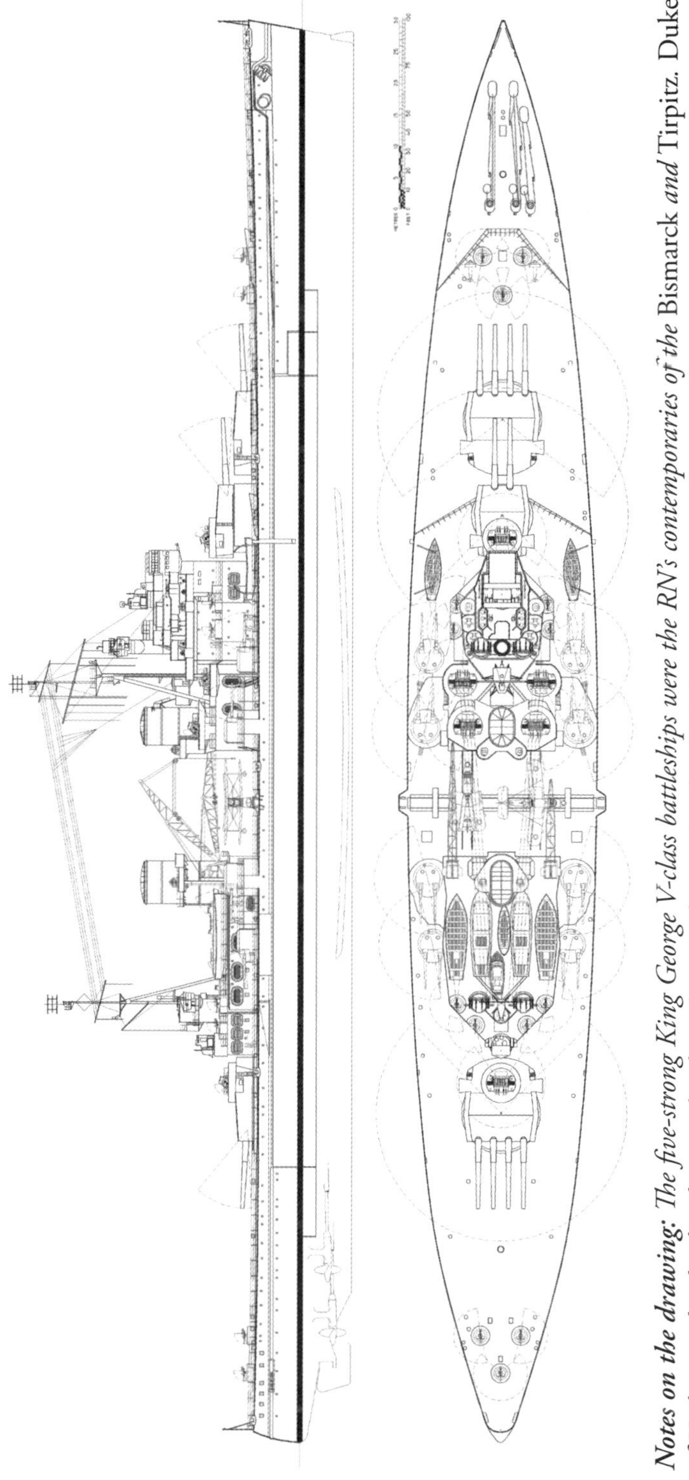

Notes on the drawing: *The five-strong King George V-class battleships were the RN's contemporaries of the* Bismarck *and* Tirpitz. Duke of York *was the third to be completed on 4 November 1941, shortly before sister-ship* Prince of Wales *was sunk by Japanese aircraft on 10 December 1941, proving conclusively that battleships operating without significant air cover and adequate anti-aircraft weaponry and control were more a liability than an asset. The class was not generally considered a success. For example, the 14-inch main armament was considered under-gunned, they had structural problems affecting the main guns, had low freeboard forward – making the ships 'wet' – and range suffered due to poor efficiency and inadequate bunkerage.*

The Focke Wulf Fw 200 Condor in flight – a view rarely seen by convoys that they shadowed beyond the range of anti-aircraft guns. Condors took their toll on unescorted merchant ships or stragglers from convoys. (Public Domain)

Convoys PQ 8 to PQ 11 passed without loss, with 31 ships arriving at Murmansk; one was torpedoed and towed to port. The Tribal-class destroyer, *Matabele*, was torpedoed by *U-454* while escorting the convoy.

Convoys QP 5 to QP 7 passed 18 ships back for reassignment without loss.

On 26 February, Admiral Tovey, Commander in Chief Home Fleet, suggested that westbound and eastbound convoys should depart on the same days in order that they would both be in the most dangerous seas at the same time and their defence could be synchronized. PQ 12 and QP 8 were the first to adopt this tactic.

On 5 March, a Focke-Wulf Fw 200 Condor long-range patrol bomber (termed 'The Scourge of the Atlantic' by the Allies, the name generally attributed to Winston Churchill), spotted the 18-ship PQ 12 70 miles southwest of Jan Mayen Island. Fortunately, the submarine *Seawolf* reported a sighting on 6 March of a large unidentified warship off Trondheim heading north. This information did not reach Admiral Tovey until the early hours of 7 March, not long before the outbound and homebound convoys were due to pass each other. Tovey, in the battleship *King George V*, faced multiple dilemmas. Was this *Tirpitz* trying to break out, like *Bismarck*? Was *Tirpitz* heading to threaten one or both convoys? Was *Tirpitz* going to meet up with *Admiral Scheer*? Were they going to make separate forays? His one fleet aircraft carrier, *Victorious*, was his best asset. Its obsolescent Fairey Albacore torpedo bombers could search for, and hopefully find and attack, *Tirpitz*, heading north and east into the area where it was anticipated the mighty battleship would seek. However, the first air-search scheduled for the early morning of 8 March was cancelled due to snow and fog patches. Worsening weather put paid to any air reconnaissance.

Tirpitz and three or four destroyers (depending on sources) had in fact ventured to sea in Operation *Sportpalast* (sometime referred to as Operation *Nordmeer*) in search of prey, leaving Trondheim at 1100 hours, preceded by patrolling seaplanes. The same weather that prevented *Victorious* launching aircraft also prevented *Tirpitz* from launching its Arado Ar 196 reconnaissance floatplanes. Both forces were thus temporarily blind, although the Germans had four U-boats deployed across the likely paths of the convoys.

What neither force knew was that at one time they were within 60–70 miles of each other, although one of *Tirpitz*'s destroyer screen, *Z-25*, came to within 12 miles of QP 8 as it battered its way south into a heavy head sea. One of QP 8's vessels, the Russian *Ijora*, had become

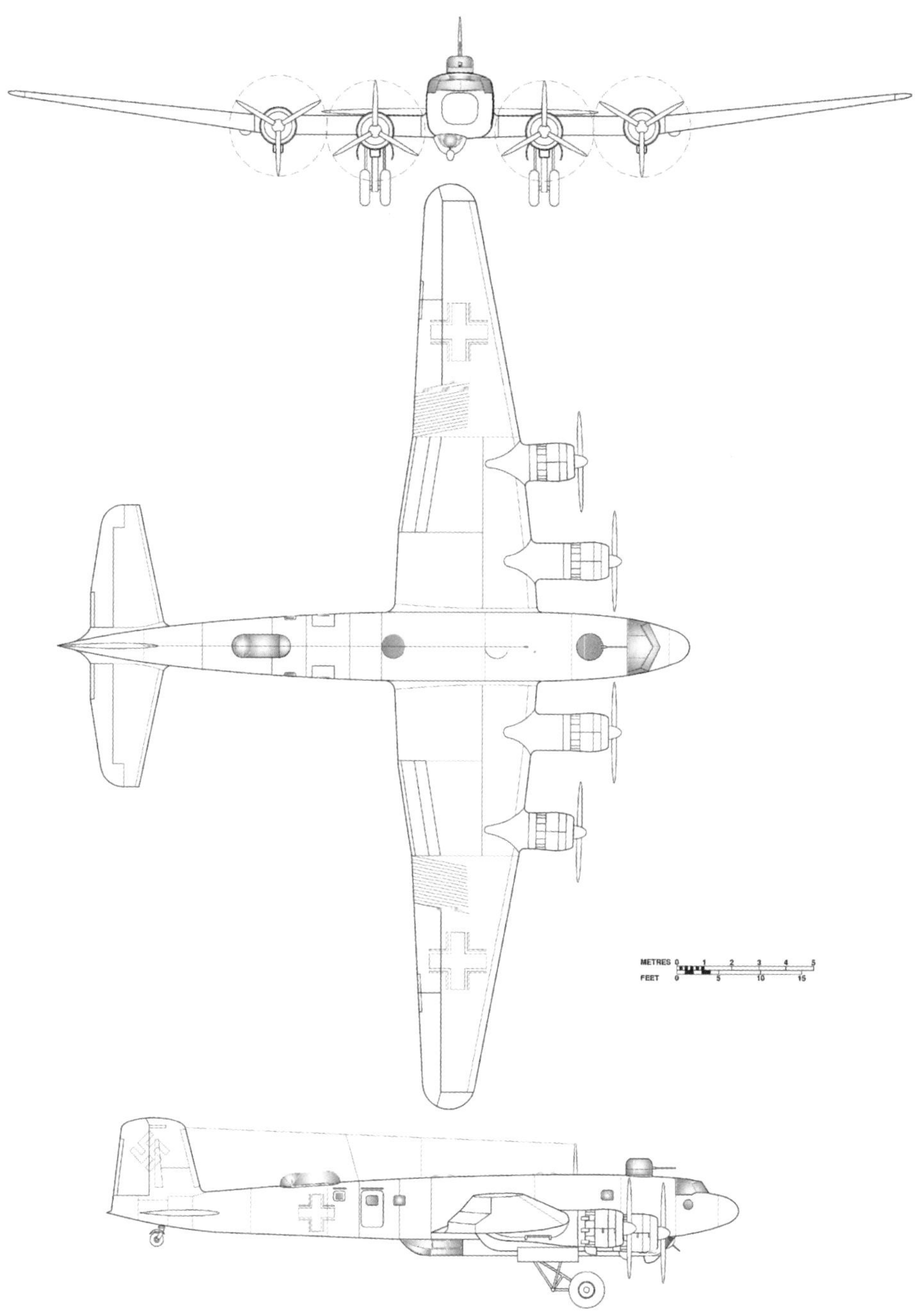

__Notes on the drawing:__ The Focke Wulf Fw 200 Condor was a successful conversion of a long-range passenger aircraft to a maritime patrol bomber. Often referred to as 'The Scourge of the Atlantic', its endurance allowed it to cover large areas and, having found a convoy, send continuous reports as to position, speed and course in order to home submarines and/or aircraft to the location. The Condor had a significant weakness: the fuselage wing join was susceptible to damage from attacking aircraft.

separated. A distress call from it stating that it was being attacked by a warship resulted in PQ 12 changing course to east-north-east despite doubt as to the accuracy of *Ijora*'s reported position. The attacking warship turned out to be the German Type 1934A-class destroyer *Friedrich Iln*, and *Ijora* was duly sunk.

Since the German destroyers were short of fuel, they headed for Tromsø and *Tirpitz* pressed on, searching alone. Six of the RN's destroyers were also forced to detach and head for Siedisfiord to refuel. At about the same time, the decryption of ULTRA intelligence[2] resulted in PQ 12 heading north of Bear Island and then, at noon, changing direction to the south-east, keeping the ice barrier well to port. The convoy sighted Bear Island 40 miles north-east at 1700 hours, and at 1800 hours was some 110 miles from *Tirpitz* and moving in the opposite direction. *Tirpitz* turned south, heading for Vestfjord. PQ 12, protected by sea-smoke, worked its way around the edge of the ice and most reached Murmansk unmolested on 12 March, four arriving separately having become detached from the main body at different times. Again, Stalin complained about the condition of British cargoes as compared with American ones due to different, or indifferent, stevedoring practices. The British practice was to stow the heaviest cargo as low as possible, making ships too stiff, causing rolling to be short and rapid, putting an extra strain on lashings.

Although there had been no ship-to-ship confrontation yet in any convoy, there had already been one casualty. Unfortunately, one of the Norwegian escorting whalers, the *Shera*, capsized on 9 March due to ice build-up, with only three survivors.

The cat-and-mouse game with *Tirpitz* continued. Further ULTRA intelligence informed the Admiralty that the battleship was heading south. Accordingly, at 0240 hours on 9 March, the Home Fleet altered course, heading for the Lofoten Islands with the expectation that *Victorious* would launch reconnaissance aircraft at first light. At 0800 hours, an Albacore made a sighting of two ships heading south, 80 miles east of the Home Fleet. These were *Tirpitz* and an accompanying destroyer, which had refuelled and rejoined it.

At 0820 hours, the trailing Albacores sighted their targets and gradually manoeuvred into an attacking position, given their slow speed and the 30 knots of the warships. The first sub-flight of Albacores launched their torpedoes at too long a range and too fine an angle to be effective – a common fault with torpedo bombers of all navies. The second, third and fourth sub-flights attacked from the starboard quarter, but also missed due to the evasive manoeuvres of *Tirpitz*. Two were shot down. *Tirpitz* escaped.

Having more or less disclosed its likely position when attacking *Tirpitz*, the Home Fleet – now withdrawing to Scapa Flow – was bombed by three Junkers Ju 88s at 1545 hours on 9 March, without success. Despite assigning seven destroyers and four submarines to intercept the *Tirpitz*, it arrived back at Aas Fjord and was discovered there on 18 March by air reconnaissance.

True to its unlucky number, Convoy PQ 13 was less fortunate than any of its predecessors. It was also the harbinger of worse to come.

As was standard practice, both PQ 13 and its return counterpart, QP 9, were scheduled to leave their respective ports on the same day. However, perceived submarine activity in the Kola Peninsula approaches delayed QP 9's 18 vessels. On 23 March, two days after leaving, QP 9 ran into a heavy gale with snowstorms, and the next day the Halcyon-class minesweeper *Sharpshooter* spotted *U-655* on the surface. The U-boat was too close to man its guns and fire, so

The Illustrious-class fleet aircraft carrier *Victorious* in Icelandic waters, 4 October 1941. (Public Domain)

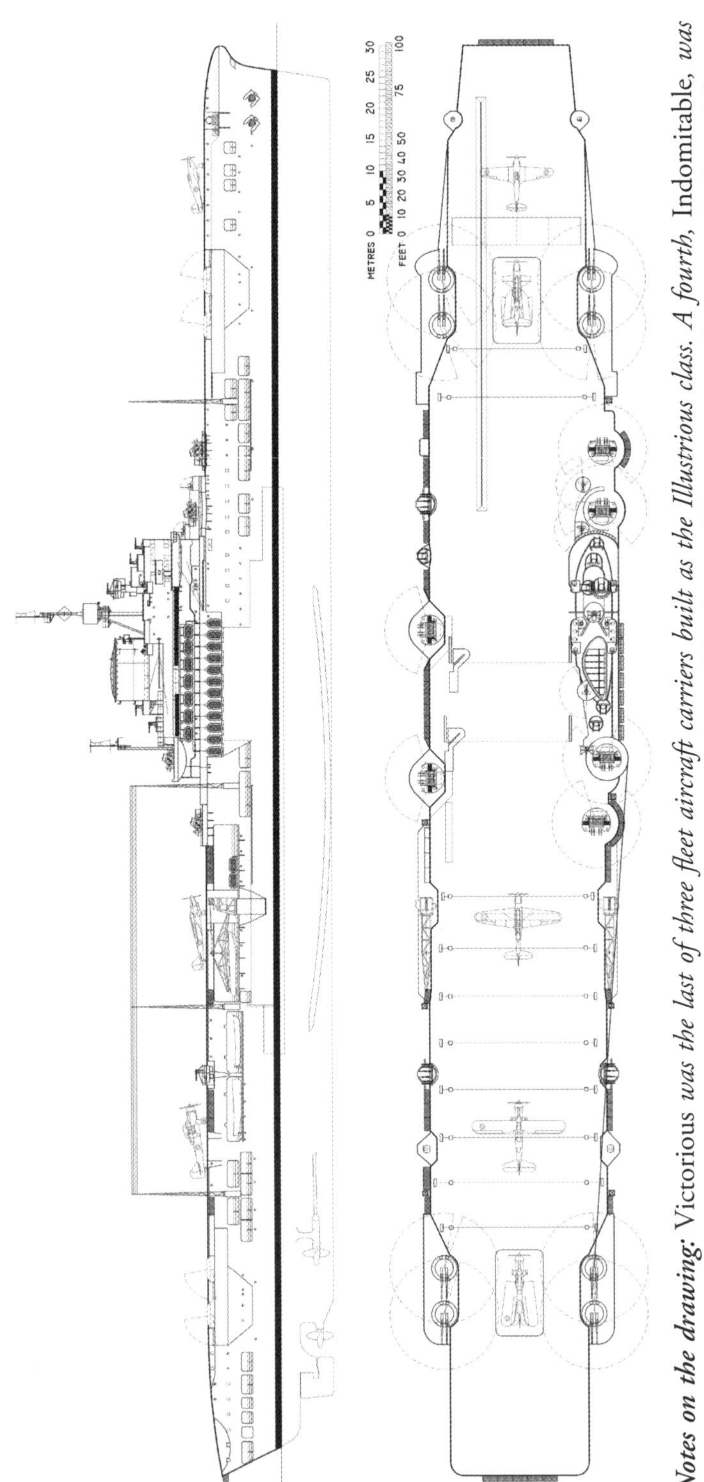

Notes on the drawing: Victorious *was the last of three fleet aircraft carriers built as the* Illustrious *class. A fourth,* Indomitable, *was basically similar but with a higher freeboard to accommodate a partial second-level aircraft hangar to remedy, in part, the basic deficiency of the class in that their armoured flight deck and hangar sides reduced their aircraft complement. The rationale for such armour was that they were expected to operate within the range of land-based aircraft and would rely on their anti-aircraft weaponry for defence. Considering the inferior performance of their current fighter aircraft, this was probably an evil necessity.*

Sharpshooter increased speed and rammed the submarine, sinking it. The damaged *Sharpshooter* retired to Iceland.

PQ 13 was pushed north-east by the same storm, a knot faster than expected, before it turned into a headwind. Two days of this scattered the convoy, and the Distant Force's *Victorious* and the Tribal-class destroyer *Tartar* suffered sufficient damage to require them to head for Scapa Flow.

By 28 March, the weather had improved to the point where ships had gathered in several mini-convoys, albeit spread over a vast area. A patrolling Luftwaffe Blohm & Voss BV 138 flying boat spotted the Crown Colony-class light cruiser, *Trinidad*, which had left Kola on 22 March with 10 tons of bullion aboard and was using its radar to round up scattered ships into some form of order. Predictably, the sighting drew bombing and dive-bombing attacks. *Trinidad* survived, as did SS *Raceland*. But SS *Harpalion* was damaged and, later, SS *Empire Ranger* was sunk, survivors being picked up by one of three German destroyers that had been deployed from Kirkenes to take advantage of the expected scattering of the convoy. SS *Bateau* fell foul of *Z-26*, which sank it after the crew had abandoned ship. But there was to be more drama with these destroyers.

A group of five merchant ships and an escorting whaler, *Silja*, had strayed into ice after losing contact with one of their number after an air attack. *Silja*, running low on fuel, had to be taken in tow. Just before 0900 hours on 29 March, *Trinidad* and *Z-26* exchanged fire. *Trinidad* was hit twice but scored damage midships to the destroyer, which came off worse with three hits. After both ships manoeuvred in mist and snow, they came upon each other, *Z-26* emitting dense black smoke. *Trinidad* closed to 1½ miles, opened fire and prepared to launch torpedoes. The second of two torpedoes malfunctioned after launching and headed straight back to *Trinidad*, striking the ship below the bridge at 0924 hours and bringing it to a stop, listing to port. Fortunately, F-class destroyer *Fury* lived up to its name and chased after *Z-26*, but in a friendly fire incident ran into near sister-ship *Eclipse* and two Russian destroyers, one of which opened fire on *Fury*, which returned fire. *Eclipse* then located *Z-26* and a stern-chase ensued. Despite being hit twice, *Eclipse* managed to bring *Z-26* to a halt by 1022 hours and was about to administer a *coup de grâce* when *Z-24* and *Z-25* appeared. Outnumbered, *Eclipse* had to retire, and although aided by snow squalls it suffered several hits. Licking its wounds and making itself seaworthy, *Eclipse* then sighted a U-boat close by which fired torpedoes – unsuccessfully – before diving.

Meanwhile, *Trinidad* was limping at a bare 6 knots, later increasing progress to 12 knots, heading for Kola Inlet. It finally arrived at 0930 hours on 30 March, having had problems with a northerly gale and salt water in the boiler feed which almost reduced the ship to a halt. *Trinidad* and its escorts were now safe, but PQ 13 was still at sea – somewhere.

Of the group that had strayed into ice, *U-435* torpedoed one, SS *Effingham* (on 30 March), and the ship that had taken *Silja* in tow, *Induna*, was torpedoed by *U-376*.

In all, some 30,000 tons of war *matériel* and five ships were lost: two to bombing, one to a destroyer and two to U-boats. *Trinidad* was badly damaged and did not leave until 13 May 1942, together with the damaged *Forester* and *Foresight* (see later). Steel plate for repairs had to be brought to Russia by the light cruiser *Edinburgh*. Russian non-co-operation in its repairs saw the crew having to pilfer disused railway lines to be used for bracing. After leaving for America for permanent repairs, the Soviets again failed to deliver air cover; only three British-supplied Hurricanes turned up, while none of the promised Petlyakov Pe-3 long-range heavy fighters appeared, making a

Two Junkers Ju 87 Stukas doing what they did best – dive-bombing. (Public Domain)

A Junkers Ju 88 on a snow-covered airfield – probably the A-17 version – with twin torpedoes. (Public Domain)

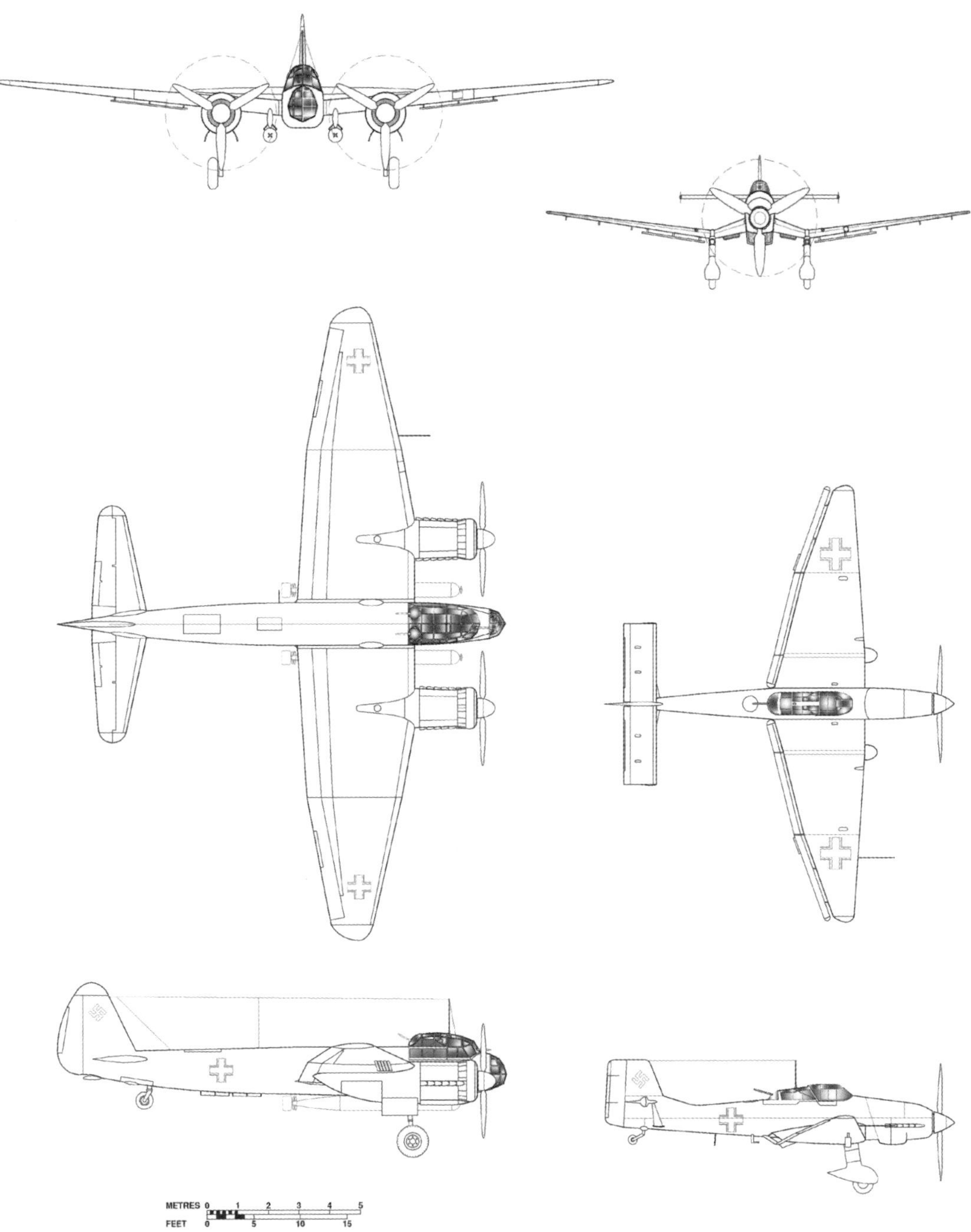

Notes on the drawing: *The famous, or infamous depending on your point of view, Junkers Ju 87 Stuka dive-bomber was less of an influence on the Russian convoys than the more versatile Junkers Ju 88, particularly when equipped with torpedoes, something the Ju 87 could not manage. Different variations of the Ju 88 were used as a level bomber, dive-bomber, heavy fighter, night fighter and for long-range reconnaissance.*

This photograph of *Fury* shows that it retained its full main armament but only has Type 291 radar at the masthead. The aft bank of torpedoes has been replaced by a QF 12 pounder 12 cwt for improved anti-aircraft defence. (Public Domain)

mockery of the efforts and costs endured to make aid available.

On this subject, it is worth quoting the Soviet view as expressed in the memoirs of Admiral Nikolai Kuznetsov, the Soviet Chief of Naval Staff:

> In autumn 1941, a boundary was established between the operational zone of the British Navy and that of the Northern Fleet to assure the safe passage of convoys. In the beginning it was 18 degrees and then 20 degrees east. The British Naval Mission in the USSR had offices in Polyamoye and Arkhangelsk. All the practical questions bearing on convoys were decided by the Northern Fleet command together with the Senior British Naval Officer on the spot. Both in Polyarnoye and Arkhangelsk the British Mission had radio stations for communication with the Admiralty, the British naval base in Iceland, ships and convoys at sea. Before a convoy sailed from Britain the mission informed the command of the Northern Fleet of its composition, the date and time of departure, the route and other essential details. *The Soviet command, for its part, would inform the mission about the measures to be taken to protect and receive the convoy. Attaching special importance to Allied supplies GHQ, Supreme Command, displayed constant interest in reliable protection of the convoys. But things did not always go off without a hitch.*[3]

The history of the Russian convoys is replete with failures of the Soviets to comply with what had been agreed by way of Soviet contribution towards the safe arrival of the convoys, or the safe departures for that matter. That 'things did not always go off without a hitch' is a gross understatement.

Trinidad was attacked by Ju 88s the next day, suffering further damage in the previously hit area and causing fires to break out. The ship was abandoned and scuttled by three torpedoes the next day. The whaler *Sulla* was never seen again, feared to have capsized due to ice build-up. *Edinburgh*, with *Trinidad*'s gold bullion on board, was torpedoed by *U-456* on 30 April. Convoy PQ 13 was, truly, 'unlucky for some'.

PQ 14, a convoy of 25 ships, suffered bad fortune of an altogether different type. During the night of 10/11 April, when south-west of Jan Mayen Island, the convoy encountered unusually heavy ice and dense fog, a very dangerous combination that prevented the ships from extricating themselves. Sixteen merchant ships and two escorts were so damaged they had to return to Iceland on 13 April. One of these was the heavy-lift ship, SS *Empire Bard*, necessary to unload tanks and heavy equipment. Eight ships continued on, with one holed forward and with a damaged propeller. A group of six met up with the homeward-bound QP 10 and fell in with them. On 15 August, the group of eight were spotted by a Blohm & Voss BV 38 flying boat, and this was relieved by a Focke Wulf Fw 200 Condor which directed Ju 88 bombers to the convoy. However, the high-level attacks were not successful. After several unsuccessful submarine attacks, SS *Empire Howard* was hit by two of three torpedoes fired from *U-403*, north-west of North Cape, on 16 April. The second torpedo exploded ammunition in the after holds, splitting the ship in two. It sank in less than a minute.

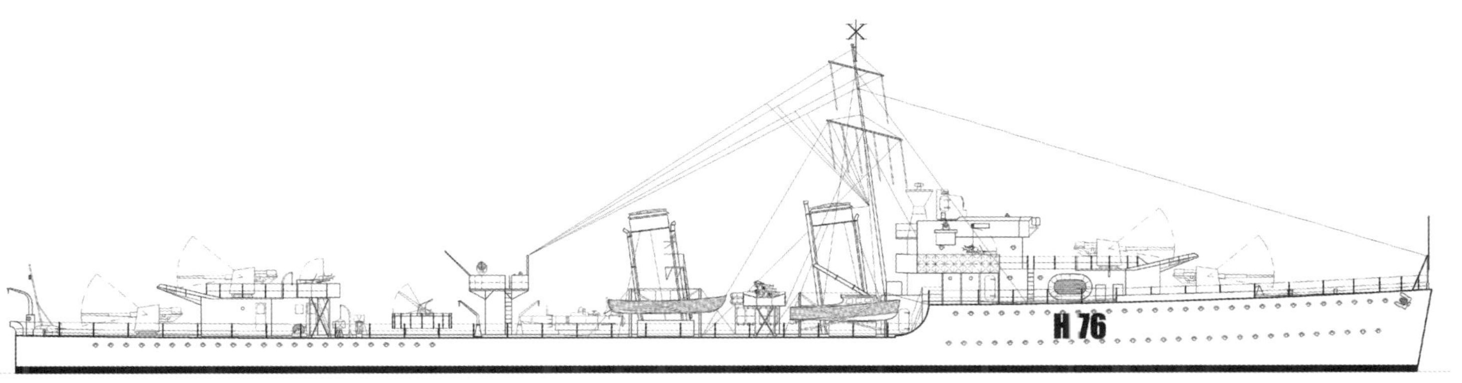

Notes on the drawing: Fury *was typical of the between-the-wars destroyers built annually in flotillas of eight or nine vessels, in this case all laid down in 1933. The basic design did not change very much from the A class (which evolved from the Ambuscade and Amazon prototypes in 1925) through to the I class. The large Tribal-class destroyers were a departure from this mould but were superseded by a series of single-funnelled designs, the J to W classes and Z class (there was no X or Y class).*

At 0430 hours on 17 April, the group was attacked again by Ju 88s, and at 0750 hours *U-376* made an unsuccessful attack. Eventually, seven ships reached Murmansk on 19 April.

Convoy QP 10 was the 22-ship homebound counterpart to PQ 14. When it departed Murmansk on 10 April, it contained only 16 ships, but six joined from QP 14, having been damaged and turned back.

The first attack, Ju 88s as usual, managed to hit SS *Empire Cowper* with three bombs then a further two bombs, which sank it. Fortunately, three German destroyers failed to find the convoy, but in the early hours of 13 April *U-435* sank two ships, SS *El Occidente* and SS *Kiev*. Another air attack damaged SS *Harpalion*, which had to be scuttled by *Fury*. One ship was damaged by near misses and returned to Murmansk on 21 April.

Convoy PQ 15 was the first large convoy, with 26 ships. It was normal procedure to arrange large convoys across a wide front with short columns spaced a half-nautical mile apart (approximately 1,000 yards) and one-quarter of a nautical mile (500 yards) one behind each other. Thus, seven columns of three to four ships would cover an area of 3 miles by three-quarters of a mile: 2 and one-quarter square miles. With the escort spread ahead, beside and behind the convoy, out to a minimum distance of a mile in each direction, the footprint grew to around 15 square miles.

This convoy was a little different for many reasons. In late April, the Home Fleet received more escorts from Western Approaches Command. Many of the merchant ships were ones that had returned to Iceland in PQ 14. Two of the convoy's ships were ice-breakers – one Russian and one Canadian, gifted to the Soviets. The convoy was the first to have a CAM (Catapult Aircraft Merchant) ship, equipped with a catapult at its bow to launch a war-weary Hawker Hurricane Mk I on a one-way mission to shoot down a shadowing reconnaissance aircraft. Being out of range of land, the pilot would have to parachute or ditch into the sea when his petrol ran out. The pilot's role was thus almost suicidal in nature. A second Hurricane was stowed on board to be reassembled for a later repetition of this desperate measure. The final distinctive feature of the convoy was that an ex-Irish Sea ferry, *Ulster Queen*, was allocated to boost anti-aircraft defence via its three twin 4-inch guns and short-range weapons.

PQ 15 left the safety of Reykjavik on 26 April. Four days out and unmolested, it was spotted by a FW 200 Condor while still 250 miles south-west of Bear Island. Two days later, an unsuccessful attack was made by six Junker Ju 88 bombers. In the interim, the Luftwaffe had made attacks on the returning QP 11. In the early hours of 3 May, the first German aerial torpedo attack was made at wave-top by specially adapted Heinkel He 111s that had only been relocated to Bardufoss on 1 May. The change from bombing to low-level torpedoing tactics bore dividends. According to Woodman, three ships were torpedoed and sunk in this attack. Other sources claim that two were sunk and the third, *Jutland*, damaged and abandoned, later being sunk by *U-251*.

Bad luck continued to plague the escort, with the Tribal-class destroyer *Punjabi* run down in fog by the battleship *King George V* and sunk. Its depth charges had not been made safe and these exploded as the stern sank, adding to the death toll. The Polish submarine *Jastrzab* was then sunk by mistake. Navigation in these waters and in the prevailing conditions was extremely difficult, and it is possible that the sub was out of its assigned patrol position or the attacking two ships, a minesweeper and Norwegian destroyer, also mistook their position.

However, while PQ 15 made its destination without further incident, helped by a south-east gale from 4–5 May, there was more tragedy to come.

Convoy QP 11, a return convoy of 13 ships, departed Kola on 28 April. Scheduled Soviet air cover failed to arrive, but lurking German submarines did. On 29 April, the convoy was spotted by one of no less than seven U-boats (Wolfpack Strauchritter, 29 April–5 May 1942) that had been assigned to lie in wait across the convoy's expected route. *U-88* maintained a shadowing role.

Town-class light cruiser *Edinburgh* took up a position ahead of QP 11. Just after 1600 hours on 30 April, four torpedoes from *U-436* missed *Edinburgh*, but two from *U-456* found their mark, causing considerable damage. The presence of destroyers circling *Edinburgh* prevented the submarines from finishing off *Edinburgh*, but early on 1 May, three destroyers were dispatched from Kirkenes to take advantage of the situation.

On 1 May, QP 11 had made good progress, but when 150 miles from Bear Island was attacked by torpedo-carrying Ju 88s. While this attack was unsuccessful, it was followed up that afternoon by the three destroyers. The convoy turned sharply away behind a smokescreen and its motley collection of four destroyers – one A-class, two B-class and an even older ex-USN Town-class – prepared for engagement. Both sides opened fire and launched torpedoes without success, although the German ships had the upper hand with cruiser-type 5.9-inch guns versus the 4-inch and 4.7-inch British guns.

The convoy was now spread out, heading through drift ice, when a torpedo from *U-589* hit the Russian MV *Tsiolkovsky/Tsiolkovskj*. It was later sunk by *Z-24* and *Z-25*, two of the three German pursuing destroyers which had reappeared later that afternoon and probed in three more attacks without success. Between 1000 and 1200 hours on 2 May, PQ 15 and QP 11 passed in opposite directions. More submarine attacks ensued; a lone Heinkel He 115 floatplane kept watch for a while, but QP 11 arrived safely at Hvalfiordur on 7 May.

We must now return to *Edinburgh*'s plight. The cruiser had managed to make sufficient temporary repairs to work up to 8 knots, although directional issues were a concern due to a list and a contrary wind. This situation improved at midnight when a rescue tug arrived. However, the two Soviet destroyers which had been detached to refuel failed to make a rendezvous, but three German destroyers did, using *Edinburgh*'s trailing oil slick as a guide. Between snow showers, *Edinburgh* fired the first salvo and then its second one stopped the *Hermann Schoemann* dead in the water. In snowstorms and smokescreens for the next two hours, two sister-ships, destroyers *Forester* and *Foresight*, played deadly hide-and-seek with the two more heavily armed *Z-24* and *Z-25*. At 0650 hours, torpedoes from *Z-24* missed *Forester*, but 5.9-inch shells found their mark, forcing it to turn away while still firing at the stationary *Hermann Schoemann*. It was now *Foresight*'s turn, and having loosed a torpedo salvo at *Hermann Schoemann* it hit home with four shells, immobilizing the German destroyer. *Hermann Schoemann* sank at 0830 hours after most of its crew had been taken off by *Z-24*.

As fate would have it, and unbeknown to the Germans, who had retired, a torpedo fired by *Z-25* hit *Edinburgh* at 0702 hours on the opposite side to the damage it sustained earlier. Mortally wounded and in danger of breaking in two, the order was given to abandon ship, and this was accomplished by 0800 hours. It had to be sunk by the damaged *Foresight*, which set out for Kola

An unidentified Type 1936A destroyer of the Kriegsmarine. Note there is no radar apparent and the forward-facing 5.9-inch mount has been removed in favour of what looks like increased accommodation. (Public Domain)

Inlet with *Forester*, with Rear Admiral S. Bonham-Carter's flag hoisted in the diminutive, and overcrowded, minesweeper *Harrier*.

The actions involving PQ 15 and QP 11 were a victory for the Germans, although they were not aware of it until *U-456* arrived back in port on 3 May with the details of the battle.

On 6 May, Stalin sent the following telegram to Churchill:

> From Stalin to Prime Minister
>
> T.694/2 6.5.42
>
> I have a request for you. Some 90 steamers loaded with various important war materials for the U.S.S.R. are bottled up at present in Iceland or in the approaches from America to Iceland. I understand there is a danger that the sailing of these ships may be delayed for a long time because of the difficulty to organise convoy escorted by the British Naval Forces. I am fully aware of the difficulties involved and of the sacrifices made by Great Britain in this matter. I feel, however, [it is] incumbent upon me to approach you with the request to take all possible measures in order to ensure the arrival of all the above-mentioned materials in the U.S.S.R. in the course of May as this is extremely important for our front.[4]

Convoy PQ 16 was an even larger convoy, 36 ships making it the largest to date. Spread nine columns wide by four deep, it departed Hvalfiordur on 21 May. A dedicated anti-aircraft ship, the converted Bank Line's *Alynbank*, was to provide extra support in the form of four twin 4-inch dual-purpose guns plus two quad pom-poms. Conversely, the close escort was only a minesweeper, four corvettes and two submarines.

The far more substantial Close Support joined PQ 16 on 25 May just before a FW 200 Condor made its unwelcome appearance. Force Q detached at 1200 hours after refuelling the destroyers, and at 1400 hours QP 12 passed by in the opposite direction. The Condor was relieved by a BV 168 and at 1910 hours the first attack developed. The CAM ship launched its Hurricane against 19 Heinkel He IIIs. Quite why this dubious facility had not been used earlier to destroy, or at least chase off, the Condor is questionable. The Hurricane was shot down – quite possibly by

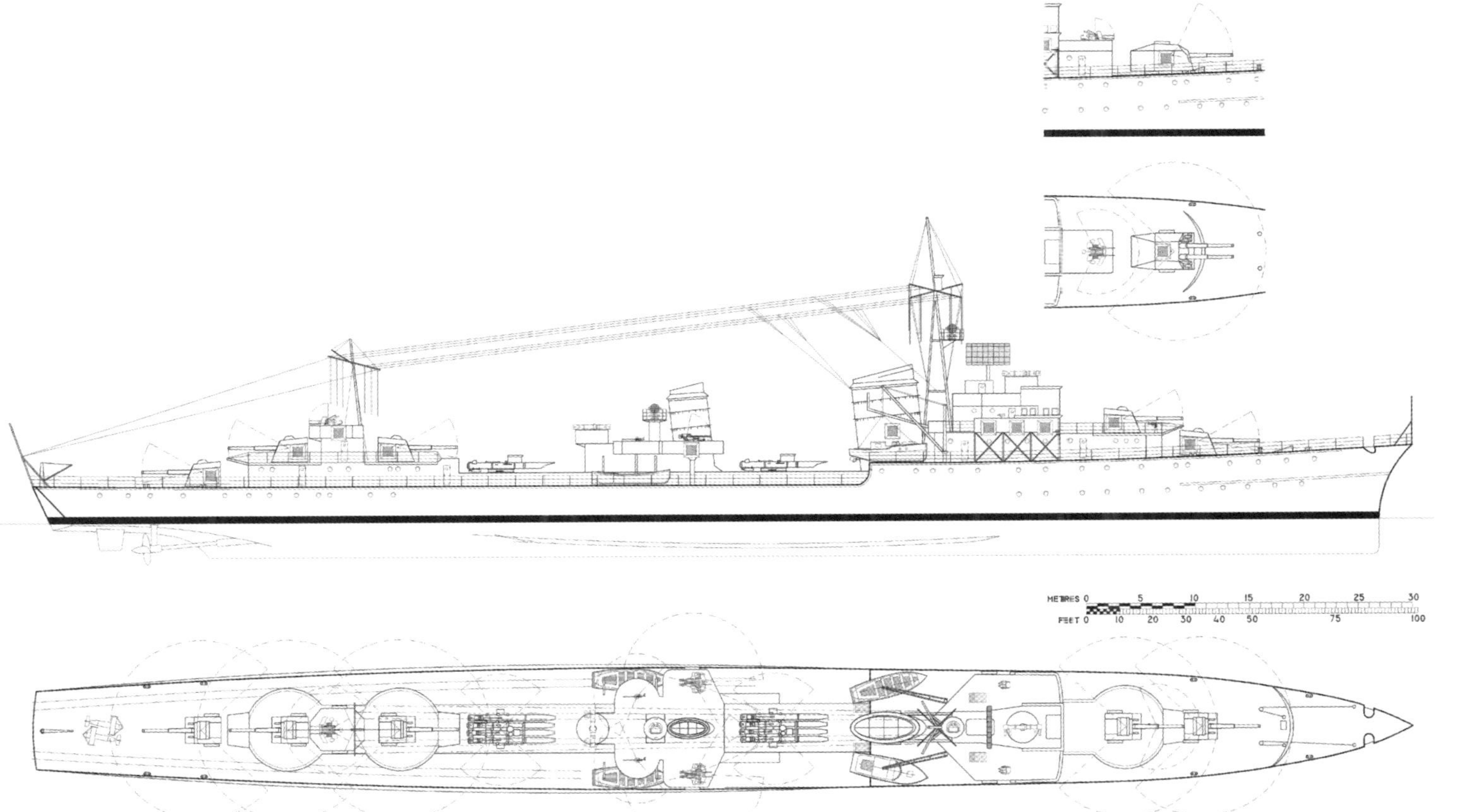

Notes on the drawing: *On the face of it, the Kriegsmarine's pre-war-built destroyers all look very similar, beginning with the 1934 Type Z-1, of which 22 were built in six batches with minor changes. The first major change was the 1936A, of which 17 were built. The German destroyers were poor sea boats. Despite having major surgery to their bows, they were 'wet' forward and squatted aft under power. The replacement of the forward 5.9-inch single mounts with a heavy twin mount did nothing to improve sea-keeping, nor did the addition of many extra close-range AA weapons. The insert drawing shows a typical arrangement. My drawing is not necessarily representative of any one Type 1936A, as there was little consistency and records tend to be vague as to just which destroyer had which mix of weapons and radar in July 1942.*

friendly fire – and the pilot saved. A dive-bombing attack by Ju 88s caused some near misses, and one ship, SS *Carlton*, had to be towed back to Iceland.

Another attack in the early afternoon damaged the SS *Alamar* and then the SS *Mormacsul*, which fell out of line, sinking. A similar fate befell the CAM ship SS *Empire Lawrence*. SS *Empire Baffin* was near-missed and damaged, as was SS *City of Joliet*, which was temporarily abandoned. It finally sank early on 28 May.

An attack around 2000 hours sunk SS *Empire Purcell* and then SS *Lowther Castle*, the latter being torpedoed. *Ocean Voice*, one of the 60 built to Thompson's design by Kaiser and the fore-runner of the Liberty ships, was hit by a bomb and set on fire, but managed to make it to Kola.

In the very early hours of 26 May, *U-703* torpedoed and sank SS *Syros*, and the close escort departed to join QP 12.

PQ 16 endured two unsuccessful U-boat attacks and two more air attacks from Ju 88s and He IIIs – dive-bombing and torpedo-bombing, respectively.

Early on 27 May, the presence of pack ice forced a change of course that brought the convoy closer to North Cape than intended. Low cloud assisted attacking German aircraft, which hit SS *Starii Bolshevik* and set it on fire. The ship dropped back, got the fire under control and rejoined the convoy.

On 24 May, while PQ 16 was still at sea, Stalin sent another telegram to Churchill:

> From Stalin to Prime Minister T. 755/2 24.5.42
>
> I have received your message which was delivered in Kuibyshev and in which you inform me that 35 ships carrying war materials for the U.S.S.R. are presently on their way to the Soviet ports. I thank you for your message on the sailing of the ships. On our part our naval and air forces will do their utmost for the protection of these transports on the section of the route which was indicated in your message to me on 9th May.[5]

Convoy QP 12 included the CAM ship from PQ 15. A Hurricane launched from it shot down a Ju 88 on 25 May, but the Hurricane pilot died from his injuries when his parachute failed to open properly. Heavy fog saved QP 12, which arrived at Iceland on 29 May, although one ship was forced to return to Kola, probably due to engine trouble.

PQ 16 (21–30 May) was the largest of the Russia-bound convoys to date, and although its 36 ships were well defended, it was the first to be heavily attacked. It lost seven merchant ships, one damaged and one returned to port damaged. Appalling as these losses were, they paled into significance compared with what was to follow.

PART 2

Fire and Ice

CHAPTER 4

Prelude to Disaster

Having looked at the 1941–42 convoys to date, it is now time to return to the focus of this book – the PQ 17 convoy.

As mentioned previously, the presence of *Tirpitz* played constantly on the mind of the Admiralty, Admiral Pound particularly, with the growing hours of summer's daylight and the risks they presented. Pound pushed frequently and forcefully for there to be a hiatus in the convoy schedule. Unfortunately, his words fell on deaf ears. Rear Admiral Bonham-Carter, with five ships sunk underneath him (including cruisers *Edinburgh* and *Trinidad*), also pushed for a cessation during the daylight period.

Perhaps as some sort of recognition by Roosevelt that these convoys must continue unabated, the USN attached the battleship *Washington*, aircraft carrier *Wasp* and heavy cruisers *Tuscaloosa* and *Wichita*, together with six to eight destroyers (officially Task Force 39), to the Home Fleet. However, without organic air cover from anti-submarine aircraft and fighters aboard one or more aircraft carriers attached to, or close by, the convoys, more battleships and cruisers were only of use if they happened to be in the right area at the right time if *Tirpitz* chose to venture out of its well-protected fjord.

RAF heavy bombers tried three time to sink, or at least severely damage, *Tirpitz* while in Norwegian waters in 1942 (30/31 March, 27/28 April and 28/29 April), but without success; indeed, at great cost, losing 12 aircraft.

To add insult to injury, Russian attitudes to the aid delivered at great cost were, at best, mildly appreciative and, at worst, simply dismissive. Attitudes matched the climate: cold to freezing. Their naval and air force contribution to protecting the approaches to Murmansk (and Arkhangelsk when not icebound) was patchy, often begrudging and seldom reliable. As Richard Woodman, merchant navy officer and naval historian, stated, 'neither the Soviet navy or its air force ever relieved the British Home Fleet of any appreciable share of the responsibility for the defence of an Arctic convoy'.[1] Britain expected more than the Soviets were willing or able to provide, but the Soviets either ignored or made only token efforts to provide the sort of protection to convoys – anti-submarine patrols and air cover – that was reasonably expected of them.

Frustration, indeed annoyance, extended from the RN to the War Cabinet due to the Soviet failure to provide their share of the merchant ships expected, plus their inability to handle cargoes in the quantities that did arrive, let alone the much greater quantities that Stalin kept demanding. While the quantities were not considered sufficient, frequently what was delivered sat where it was offloaded, was damaged in unloading and simply abandoned because the Russians did not have the ability, or the will, to make the necessary repairs, no matter how small.

A mission to Moscow was informed on 16 June that the Soviet navy promised all its resources would be concentrated on convoy protection. Previously, the Allies – mainly Admiral Tovey – had pressed the Soviet Northern Fleet for 'strong and continuous Russian patrol activity off the Kola Inlet, to make that area untenable by U-boats, and for short-range and long-range fighter protection.'[2] Tovey was of the reasonable opinion that the Soviets should be responsible for convoy protection in the White Sea and that their submarines should be employed against potential German surface ships. Both short-range (60 miles) and long-range (200 miles) fighter cover plus airborne anti-submarine patrols were critical for adequate convoy defence (in the absence of organic air cover from aircraft carriers) when the convoys were most susceptible to air attacks; this was within Soviet capabilities, especially in view of the aircraft being supplied to them. While the Soviets did, eventually, take responsibility for convoys once they crossed 18° east, they were either unable or unwilling – or both – to provide the quantity and quality of protection required, perhaps due to the more pressing issues fighting Hitler's invading armies.

Milan Vego, naval historian and professor of operations at the US Naval War College, summed it up this way:

> The Allies tried repeatedly to involve the Soviet Northern Fleet further in protecting convoys. Admiral Tovey in his messages to the Admiralty 'pressed for strong and continuous Russian patrol activity off the Kola Inlet, to make that area untenable by U-boats, and for short-range and long-range fighter protection... Tovey felt the Soviets should take over responsibility for defence of the convoys during the White Sea segment of the passage ... Although the Soviets repeatedly promised that they would provide adequate protection to the Allied convoys, they seldom did so in practice.'[3]

Recognizing the failure of the Soviets, in June 1942 some Consolidated PBY Catalinas of RAF 210 and 240 Squadrons were detached from their bases at Sullom Voe in the Shetlands and Castle Archdale, Northern Ireland, respectively, to Kola Inlet and Lake Lakhta near Arkhangelsk to provide long-range surveillance.

Facilities for crews resting between convoys or, worse, the crews of the minesweepers, oilers and heavy-lift ships based in Murmansk, were abysmal. Hospitals – necessary for the treatment of survivors suffering from immersion, exposure, frostbite, burns, scalds or wounds – were extremely primitive. Russians had priority to what little the hospitals at Vaenga and Sevroles offered. The situation was so bad that a fully equipped demountable hospital was offered but rejected by the Russians on 12 September 1942 as unnecessary, despite their own lack of basic drugs, antiseptics and anaesthetics.[4]

* * * * *

Unternehmen Rösselsprung (Operation *Knight's Move*) was the title given by the Germans to the proposed interdiction of PQ 17 by *Tirpitz* and *Admiral Hipper* (from Trondheim initially) and *Lützow* and *Admiral Scheer* (from Narvik), with escorting destroyers. This was by far the most detailed and comprehensive German tactical plan to date, and for *Knight's Move* to be successful, it was necessary for the movements of the major warships to go undetected, or at least detection be delayed. Furthermore, the combining of the two forces at the right place and at the right time was essential, not necessarily an easy task if radio communications were to be avoided.

KMS *Admiral Hipper* in dock. (Public Domain)

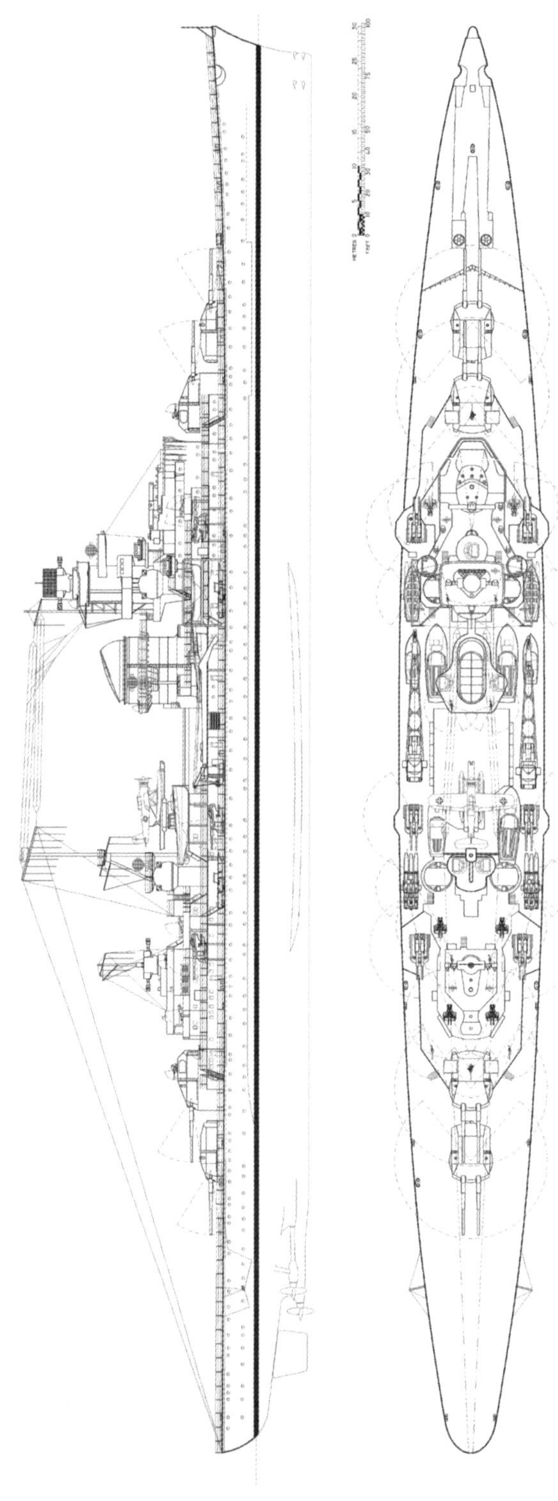

***Notes on the drawing:** The Admiral Hipper class of heavy cruisers paid lip service to the 10,000-ton restriction imposed by the Washington Naval Treaty and went closer to 15,000 tons. Five were planned but only three were completed as such.* Seydlitz *was scrapped incomplete and* Lützow *was sold incomplete to the USSR in November 1940, while* Blücher *was sunk by a Norwegian shore battery in April 1940. After the battle of the Barents Sea on 31 December 1942, Hitler decided, not unreasonably, that the Kriegsmarine's surface units were proving to be ineffective.* Hipper *was decommissioned; it was damaged by RAF bombers on 3 May 1945 and scuttled.*

On 4 June, operational instructions (*Operative Weisung*) were issued for the Trondheim and Narvik groups, named the 1st and 2nd Combat Groups respectively, that stated the next convoy was expected in the area of Jan Mayen Island on 20 June. While the Kriegsmarine and Luftwaffe prepared their operational plans and each service assumed close co-operation with the other, this was seldom achieved due to the nature of their command structures, which were far from efficient. In theory, the Luftwaffe was responsible for air reconnaissance and to provide close air support for the Kriegsmarine. The primary mission of the joint operation was not to engage the covering forces but the destruction of the merchant ships. It was not necessary to destroy these outright; neutralizing them was sufficient so that they could be captured or sunk later. The most favourable area for attack was judged to be east of Bear Island, between 20° and 30° east.

It was anticipated that U-boats would probably make first contact and, having done so, the Luftwaffe would maintain a continuous surveillance. It would concentrate its search activities in the Shetland–Faroes–Iceland–Jan Mayen sector and Reykjavik, Scapa Flow and the Firths of Forth and Moray too. When 1st and 2nd Combat Groups ventured out, the Luftwaffe was charged with monitoring out to 200 miles from Norway's coast, from 62° north to North Cape. When *Unternehmen Rösselsprung* was instigated, this was to be increased to 300 miles.

On 9 June, after meeting with Gross-Admiral Raeder, Commander in Chief of the Kriegsmarine, on 6 June, the Führer approved *Rösselsprung*, despite misgivings about the possibility of the Royal Navy deploying an aircraft carrier. He required that any carrier must be located prior to an attack, although the repositioning of 1st Combat Group to Altafjord (also known as Altenfiord and Altenfjord) was approved. However, the final order to attack was, typically, to come from Hitler.

On 10 June, three U-boats were stationed to the north-east of Iceland, with others to be stationed between Jan Mayen Island and Bear Island. By 1400 hours on 2 July, there were six U-boats in a patrol line halfway between the two islands.

On 11 June, three U-boats – the *Eisteufel* (Ice Devil) group – were directed to take up positions in the Denmark Strait, between Greenland and Iceland. Their mission was to detect and track, not to attack the convoy.

The first knowledge the Western Allies had of this intention came via the Swedes. Although technically neutral, Sweden played for both sides as and when it suited its interests. It supplied iron ore to the Germans via Norway and ball-bearings to the British via special diesel-engined, high-speed, adapted motorboats (Operation *Bridford*, which ran from September 1943 to March 1944) and via BOAC flights. Intelligence-wise, it was not known what useful information might have passed to Germany. What is known, however, is that the Swedes were tapping the German telegraph and teleprinter lines to northern Norway and had broken a number of German ciphers. The Royal Navy's attaché in Stockholm, Captain H. Denham, was tipped off by Sweden's C-Bureau secret intelligence agency that a fleet order, telexed on 14 June, stated the action proposed against the next Russian-bound convoy. Air reconnaissance was to locate the convoy at Jan Mayen Island, bombing attacks would follow from north Norway, *Lützow* and *Admiral Scheer* were to move to Altafjord, *Tirpitz* and *Hipper* to Narvik, action was to take place once the convoy had reached 5 degrees east, and simultaneous attacks from both surface groups, submarines and aircraft would be made on the Bear Island meridian.

As an opening move, on 11 June, three U-boats (*U-251*, *U-376* and *U-408*) were sent to position themselves in the Denmark Strait. They were not to attack any vessels but rather report and shadow them. They were only to attack if positive identification had been made. This seems to indicate that it was anticipated that German surface forces would be present in the area at the time.

Around the same time – precise dates are uncertain – Admiral Tovey, flying his flag on the battleship *Duke of York*, apparently received advice that the Kriegsmarine's main forces were going to be deployed against the next eastbound convoys. This may have been on 18 June after Captain Henry Denham, the British Naval Attaché in Stockholm, was able to send the following signal of German plans to the Director of Naval Intelligence (DNI):

```
MOST IMMEDIATE:
Plan to attack next convoy
1. Air reconnaissance to locate eastbound convoy when it reaches
   Jan Mayen. Bombing attacks will then be made.
2. Pocket battleships and six destroyers will move to Altenfjord
   and Tirpitz and Hipper to Narvik area. Both may be expected to
   operate once convoy has reached 6 degrees east. Simultaneous
   attack when convoy on meridian of Bear Island by two surface
   groups supported by U-boats and aircraft.
   Graded A3.[5]
```

This was followed by another signal giving Luftwaffe dispositions in northern Norway.

The First Sea Lord, Admiral Pound, spoke to Tovey by telephone when still anchored at Scapa Flow. Pound apparently told Tovey that in certain circumstances, the only course of action open to him (Pound) was to order the convoy to scatter to prevent its annihilation – a recognized tactic and one which had been used for HX 84 (see Chapter 2). However, the dispersion of HX 84 occurred in the middle of the Atlantic, where there was more room to manoeuvre and hide, well out of reach of enemy aircraft. When Pound told Tovey that he was thinking in terms of scattering the convoy if *Tirpitz* went after it, Tovey was horrified. He wanted to be able to turn the convoy around to the protection of the covering force. He told Pound that scattering the convoy was tantamount to 'sheer bloody murder'. But his comments failed to move Pound to reconsider his strategy, falling on deaf ears.[6]

Tovey argued that to lure these forces further west, where the Home Fleet and submarines could engage, it might be necessary to hold a convoy once it reached 10° east for between 12 and 18 hours, or until such time as it was known that the German forces were still in port, or that weather had precluded this from being firmly established or the same weather prevented the discovery of the convoy by German aircraft.

Tovey's proposal was rejected by the Admiralty, like so many if not all of his recommendations. Tovey, aware of the near-thing of PQ 12 and QP 8, feared that any convoy run in daylight was bound to involve a major disaster, sooner rather than later. He proposed that convoys be postponed until the darker months, but was overruled. Military logic, the fundamental tenet of the safe arrival of the convoy, was countermanded by the political need to keep the Soviets supplied, wherever and however deemed possible.

Yet, on the same day PQ 17 departed and the day after QP departed, the Admiralty issued instructions to be observed for a convoy being turned back on its order. It envisaged a scenario where an attack west of Bear Island should be met by surface forces, and one eastward of 10° east by submarines. Cruiser Squadron One should not go east of Bear Island unless the convoy was attacked by a surface force with which the cruisers could compete, but was not to go beyond 25° east.

Here is the signal, verbatim from the Admiralty to the Commander in Chief Home Fleet:

HUSH[7]

From: ADMIRALTY

To: C-in-C HF

Hush, YOUR 1355 AND 1727 25th AND MY 0221 25th

JUNE 1942

a) AFTER CONSIDERATION OF ABOVE TELEGRAM AND AS ADMIRALTY MAY BE IN POSSESSION OF FULLER AND EARLIER INFORMATION OF MOVEMENTS OF ENEMY SURFACE FORCES THAN OUR FORCES WILL BE AND AS YOU MAY NOT WISH TO BREAK W/T SILENCE IT APPEARS NECESSARY FOR ADMIRALTY TO CONTROL MOVEMENTS OF CONVOY AS FAR AS THIS MAY BE INFLUENCED BY MOVEMENTS OF ENEMY FORCES.

b) PARAGRAPH (a) WILL NOT PREVENT EITHER C-INC, HF, CS ONE, SENIOR OFFICER OF ESCORT OR COMMODORE OF CONVOY GIVING SUCH ORDERS REGARDING MOVEMENTS OF CONVOY AS LOCAL CONDITIONS MAY NECESSITATE.

c) SHOULD ADMIRALTY CONSIDER IT NECESSARY TO REVERSE COURSE OF CONVOY, THE TIME ON WHICH REVERSE COURSE IS TO BE HELD WILL BE SPECIFIED AND IT IS TO BE UNDERSTOOD THAT IT IS A TEMPORARY MEASURE UNLESS ADMIRALTY GIVE THE ORDER FOR CONVOY TO RETURN TO ICELAND.

d) ADMIRALTY MAY BE UNAWARE OF WEATHER CONDITIONS IN THE VICINITY OF THE CONVOY AND EVEN THOUGH ADMIRALTY MAY GIVE THE ORDER FOR COURSE OF CONVOY TO BE REVERSED IT IS AT THE DISCRETION OF SENIOR OFFICER PRESENT WITH CONVOY TO IGNORE THE ADMIRALTY ORDER SHOULD THE WEATHER BE THICK.

e) AS ADMIRALTY WILL BE EXERCISING CONTROL, IT IS ESSENTIAL THAT THEY SHOULD BE KEPT INFORMED NOT ONLY OF MOVEMENTS OF FORCES BUT ALSO OF ANY DAMAGE INCURRED. IT IS NOT INTENDED ABOVE SHOULD BE CARRIED WHEN SHIPS BY BREAKING W/T SILENCE WOULD GIVE AWAY THEIR POSITION, BUT ONLY WHEN POSITION OF FORCES MUST BE KNOWN TO THE ENEMY.

f) GENERALLY SPEAKING THE SAFETY OF THE CONVOY FROM ATTACK OF SURFACE SHIPS MUST BE MET BY COVERING FORCES TO WESTWARD OF MERIDIAN OF BEAR ISLAND AND BE DEPENDENT ON OUR SUBMARINE DISPOSITIONS TO EASTWARDS OF THAT MERIDIAN.

g) THE ADMIRALTY WILL KEEP ALL FORCES AS FULLY INFORMED AS POSSIBLE OF ENEMY MOVEMENTS.

h) THE MOVEMENTS OF THE BATTLE FLEET COVERING FORCE WILL BE AT THE DISCRETION OF C-IN-C HF BUT IT IS NOT EXPECTED THAT THIS COVERING FORCE WILL BE PLACED IN A POSITION WHERE IT WILL BE SUBJECT TO HEAVY AIR ATTACK UNLESS THERE IS A GOOD CHANCE OF BRINGING ADMIRAL VON TIRPITZ TO ACTION.

j) THE MOVEMENTS OF CRUISER COVERING FORCE WILL BE AT THE DISCRETION OF CS ONE SUBJECT TO INSTRUCTIONS FROM ADMIRALTY OR C-IN-C HF. IT SHOULD NOT INTENDED THAT CRUISER COVERING FORCE SHOULD PROCEED EASTWARDS OF BEAR ISLAND UNLESS CONVOY IS THREATENED BY THE PRESENCE OF SURFACE FORCES WHICH CRUISER COVERING FORCE CAN FIGHT. IN ANY CASE IT IS NOT INTENDED THAT CRUISER COVERING FORCE SHOULD PROCEED EASTWARDS OF MERIDIAN 25 DEGS. EAST.

k) OUR PRIMARY OBJECTIVE IS TO GET AS MUCH OF THE CONVOY THROUGH AS POSSIBLE AND THE BEST WAY TO DO THIS IS TO KEEP MOVING EASTWARDS EVEN THOUGH IT IS SUFFERING DAMAGE.

l) SHOULD THE PASSAGE OF THE CONVOY BE BARRED BY A FORCE INCLUDING ADMIRAL VON TIRPITZ IN WEATHER OF GOOD VISIBILITY AND TO EASTWARDS OF MERIDIAN OF BEAR ISLAND THERE WILL BE NO ALTERNATIVE BUT TO REVERSE COURSE OF CONVOY, ANYHOW FOR A TIME, THIS ACTION MAY BE TAKEN BY ADMIRALTY, BUT IF NECESSARY C-IN-C HF OR SENIOR OFFICER OF CRUISER FORCE OR SENIOR OFFICER WITH CONVOY MAY GIVE THIS ORDER.

m) ONCE CONVOY IS TO EASTWARDS OF MERIDIAN OF BEAR ISLAND CIRCUMSTANCE MAY ARISE IN WHICH BEST THING WOULD BE FOR CONVOY TO BE DISPERSED WITH ORDERS TO PROCEED TO RUSSIAN PORTS. IT IS AT THE DISCRETION OF EITHER C-IN-C, SENIOR OFFICER OF CRUISER FORCE OR SENIOR OFFICER OF ESCORT OF CONVOY MAY GIVE THIS ORDER CS ONE PASS TO KEPPEL AND DESTROYERS OF ESCORT AND COMMODORE OF CONVOY.

0157B/27[8]

In a) we can clearly see the micro-management tendency of the First Sea Lord, Admiral Pound: 'It appears necessary for Admiralty [that is, Pound personally] to control movements of convoy as far as this may be influenced by movements of enemy forces.' Paragraph k) makes it clear that, despite the possibility of damage, the convoy is to keep moving east. Paragraph l), on the other hand, gives the option to *reverse the convoy's course*, such an order coming from the Admiralty or, if necessary, the Commander in Chief Home Fleet, the senior officer of the Cruiser Force or the senior officer of the convoy escort. Thus, there was a flexibility built in there. Unfortunately, as we shall see, the Admiralty – via Pound – came to judgement prematurely without the facts.

CHAPTER 5

Days 1–7, Saturday, 27 June–Friday, 3 July 1942

Return convoy QP 13 left Arkhangelsk on 26 June and collected more ships from Murmansk on 28 June, bringing the total up to 35. Murmansk had been bombed regularly and, over time, possibly as many as five ships that had arrived there safely were too badly damaged to ever leave. Two I-class destroyers – the last class built before the Tribal class – *Inglefield* and *Intrepid*, were in the convoy's escort, having made a dash to Murmansk with anti-aircraft ammunition to top up empty or near-empty magazines on the ships that had been so heavily attacked in PQ 16. Another destroyer was the G-class ORP *Garland* of the Polish navy, partly crewed by survivors of *Edinburgh* replacing those injured or killed when *Garland* was near-missed by bombs on 27 May. Readers will note the irony of Polish servicemen coming to the aid – albeit somewhat indirectly – of the country that conveniently annexed a significant portion of Poland's eastern territory from 17 September 1941 and murdered almost 22,000 Polish servicemen in the infamous Katyn massacre.

QP 13 sailed into bad weather, which was a discomfort for some but a welcome event for others as it helped avoid detection, in this case until 30 June.

On 2 July, QP 13 and PQ 17 passed each other, and the RFA oiler *Gray Ranger*, with its escort the destroyer *Douglas*, left PQ 17 and joined QP 13. *Gray Ranger* had been expected to proceed to Murmansk and take up the duty of supply oiler to escorts, but was badly damaged when hitting submerged ice (commonly called a 'growler') on 29 June. Its bow was buckled and the forepeak flooded to such an extent that oil had to be pumped aft to compensate. The ship was replaced by the larger but now ill-fated RFA *Aldersdale*.

Day 1, Saturday, 27 June

The number of ships in PQ 17 is subject to debate. Woodman and Vego both state 36,[1] whereas Hague says 39.[2] The website www.convoyweb states 41. By deducting non-merchant ships (that is, oilers, anti-aircraft auxiliaries, rescue ships; five in total), I believe that the total was 36 merchant ships, of which three turned back, *West Gotomska*, *Richard Bland* and *Exford* (see Chapter 11 & Appendix B). Figures quoted in many sources, including Roskill, show there were 297 aircraft, 594 tanks, 4,246 military vehicles and 156,492 tons of weapons and other supplies loaded in the convoy.[3] While it is unlikely (due to different ship sizes and capabilities), though logical, that the ships would have been combat-loaded – that is, with the cargoes equally distributed amongst

RFA *Gray Ranger.* What is not obvious in this photograph is that the funnel is offset to port. (Public Domain)

the ships – if we divide these aircraft, tanks and vehicles by 36 ships, then each ship left Iceland carrying the equivalent of eight aircraft, 17 tanks, 118 assorted vehicles and 4,347 tons of supplies.

The 36 merchant ships of Convoy PQ 17 did not get away to a smooth or uneventful start from Reykjavik's nearby Hvalfjörður (Hvalfjord). *West Gotomska*, an emergency war construction for the Emergency Fleet Corporation (EFC) of the Robert Dollar type (design #1013) and completed in August 1918, turned back with engine problems. One hundred and eleven of these were built with either geared turbines or three-cylinder Vertical Triple Expansion (VTE) engines.

The Liberty ship SS *Richard Bland* ran aground before clearing the Icelandic coast. The efforts of a local tug, *Adherent*, and A/S trawler *Northern Gem* which were sent to assist, were not in sufficient time to allow *Richard Bland* to catch up to the 8-knot convoy.

While *Richard Bland* had the apparent good fortune to thus avoid the travails of PQ 17, its luck came to an end when it was torpedoed not once but twice as a member of Convoy RA 53 from Kola Inlet. On 2 March 1943, the first torpedo from *U-255* passed clean through its empty No. 1 hold – in one side and out of the other – and failed to explode. Eight days later, damaged but afloat, having strayed from the convoy in bad weather, one of a spread of three torpedoes from the persistent *U-255* disabled the *Richard Bland*, then another blew it in two, forward of the superstructure. The stern sank and the bow section was taken in tow by the tug *Horsa*, which in turn was wrecked near Akureyri and the remains of the Liberty ship were blown ashore. Six fired torpedoes seems a high price for the Germans to pay for one Liberty ship returning in ballast.

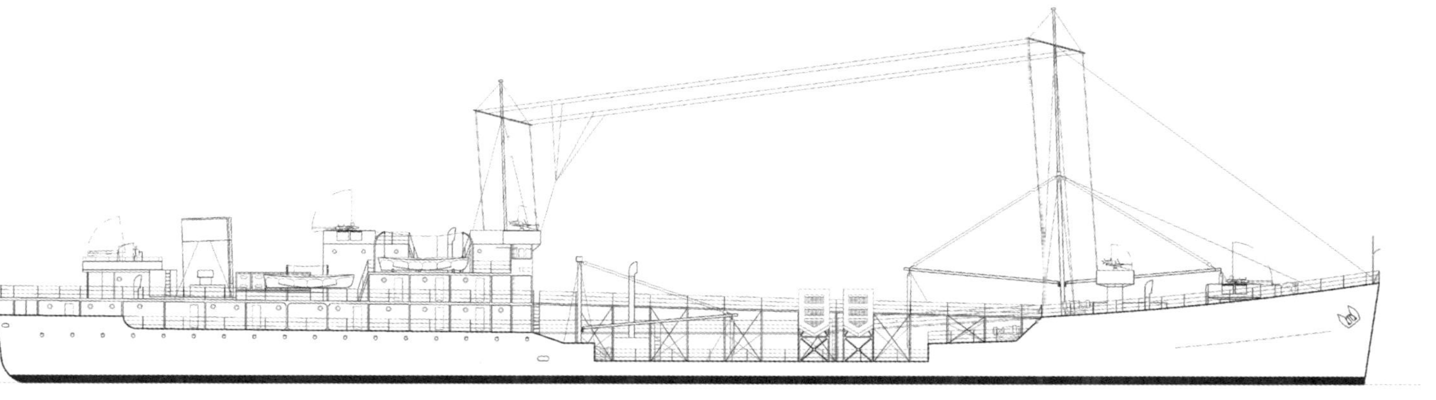

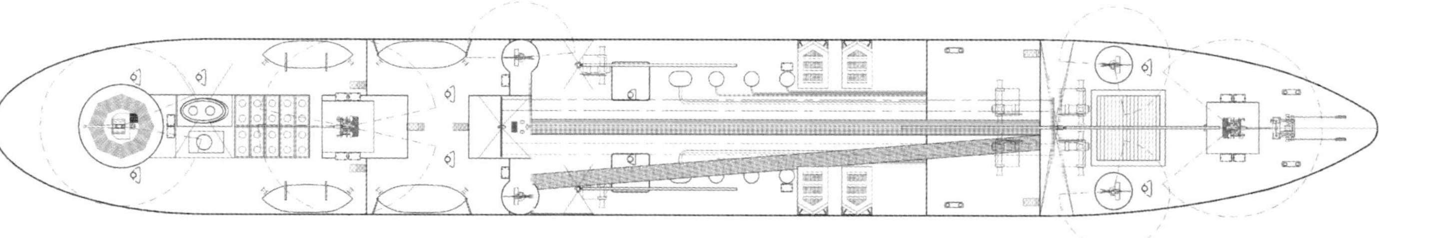

Notes on the drawing: *The many refuelling points within the British Empire meant that Admiralty policy was to flood special ballast-type tanks with seawater to compensate for oil fuel consumed and thus maintain the trim and stability of ships. This contrasted with the USN's practice of letting seawater into oil fuel tanks as it was consumed, which resulted in more fuel tankage available and, therefore, greater range. The RN failed to develop an efficient refuelling at seas (RAS) system; RFA ships like* Gray Ranger *were built with an over-the-stern system which was slow, cumbersome and inefficient.* Gray Ranger *was drawn from a series of photographs of ships of its class. Unfortunately, no detail was found as to the arrangement of pipes, hatches, pumps and the like on its decks, so my deck plan should not be taken as anything but a guess.*

The convoy's route was around the western and northern coasts of Iceland, through the Denmark Strait, past the east coast of Jan Mayen Island proceeding north-east to approximately 75°N, 19°E, with a change of direction to east in order to pass north of Bear Island then south-east until crossing approximately 33° east, where the convoy would divide into Murmansk-bound and Arkhangelsk-bounds sections (1,500 and 1,900 miles from Iceland, respectively). This route had the disadvantage of being longer but the advantage of being a little further from German air bases.

While this day was day one for PQ 17, it was the second day for the return convoy, QP 13, which left from Arkhangelsk and picked up more vessels from Murmansk two days later, totalling 35 ships. Two of QP 13's destroyer escort, *Inglefield* and sister-ship *Intrepid*, had made a dash from Scapa Flow to Kola with spare parts and ammunition for the escorts. Homeward, they carried some of *Edinburgh*'s survivors, others of whom had volunteered to help make up the shortage in the crew of escorting Polish destroyer *Garland*.

Day 2, Sunday, 28 June

The second day was insignificant insofar as PQ 17 proceeded unmolested at its best speed of 8 knots. The ill-fated five-month-long German summer offensive in the Soviet Union, *Fall Blau* (Case Blue), commenced on this day. Its aim was to capture the vital oil fields of Baku in Azerbaijan, not just to supply the Wehrmacht but to deny the resource to the Soviets. The failure of the campaign, which led to the destruction of the Sixth Army at Stalingrad, was to have a significant effect on the outcome of World War II.

Day 3, Monday, 29 June

In order to try to divert attention away from PQ 17 and draw attention and enemy forces to it, Operation *ES* was conceived as a decoy convoy which was intended to proceed from Scapa Flow north-east into the Norwegian Sea to a position 61°30'N and 1°0'E – about 180 miles from Scapa Flow – before retiring. This position was selected to offer the minimum risk of the ships being attacked by German surface forces, although there was a significant risk of air attack.

The ships assigned to Force X of Operation *ES* departed Scapa Flow on 29 June. They comprised minelayer-cruiser *Adventure*, Dido-class light cruiser *Sirius*, C-class anti-aircraft light cruiser *Curacoa*, destroyers *Brighton*, *St Mary's*, *Nepal*, HNLMS *Tjerk Hiddes*, *Oakley* and *Catterick*, four A/S trawlers, auxiliary minelayers *Southern Prince*, *Agamemnon*, *Port Quebec* and *Menestheus*, and four colliers.

The maximum speed of advance of the convoy was no more than 10 knots, given the presence of the colliers, and was more likely that of a normal 'slow' convoy, 8 knots.

Day 4, Tuesday, 30 June

The Ocean Escort (Escort Group 1, or EG 1) led by Commander J. E. Broome in the destroyer *Keppel* joined PQ 17 at 1200 hours. At this time, the convoy was some 200 miles south-west of Jan Mayen Island.

The SS *West Gotomska* in dazzle camouflage post August 1918. (Public Domain)

HMT *Northern Gem*. Apart from trawlers designed and built to Admiralty specifications, there was little uniformity between the hundreds of trawlers taken over by the Royal Navy, except perhaps the basic armament of a 12-pounder HA/LA or a 4-inch LA mounted forward and some form of close-range AA weapon fitted aft. (Public Domain)

Broome made adjustments to the disposition of the escorts, moving the four A/S trawlers out beyond what might be regarded as the extreme corners of the convoy, where they could hopefully give the earliest warning of approaching submarines and aircraft. The low speed and restricted armament of the trawlers meant that they could not afford to chase submarine contacts, but were good sea-boats and could maintain station whatever the weather.

The destroyers were positioned in an *en echelon*-type arrangement across the convoy's broad front. The two AA (anti-aircraft) ships, *Pozarica* and *Palomares* (former 'Banana Boat'/ fruit carriers), were positioned within the body of the convoy between the first and second columns and the eighth and ninth columns. The three rescue ships[4] – *Rathlin*, *Zaafaran* and *Zamalek* – were in line abreast at the rear of the merchant ships, where they could deploy quickly to come to the aid of survivors. The two submarines, *P 614* and *P 615*,[5] followed in line astern behind the centremost rescue ship. The RFA oiler, *Aldersdale*, was at the rear of a column, where it could be accessed for refuelling. The solitary CAM ship, *Empire Tide*, was ahead of *Aldersdale*. It was a British emergency-build Type X and, unusually for the PQ 17 merchant fleet, was diesel-powered.

At 1640 hours, Convoy QP 13 was detected 200 miles north of North Cape by Luftwaffe aircraft. Force X of Operation *ES* reversed direction when it arrived at the predetermined point, without having been located by German reconnaissance.

Day 5, Wednesday, 1 July

Cruiser Squadron One (CS One), under Rear Admiral L. ('Turtle') Hamilton, put to sea: heavy cruisers *London* (Flag), *Norfolk*, *USS Tuscaloosa* and USS *Wichita*, with destroyers *Somali*, USS *Rowan* and USS *Wainwright*. Its area of operation was to be 73°0'N, 4°0'E by noon on day six, 2 July, until day eight, 4 July, staying out of the range of shore-based aircraft and likely submarine concentrations.[6]

Taking advantage of calm weather, the destroyers took the opportunity of refuelling as the convoy passed the vicinity of Jan Mayen Island.

At 1615 hours, *U-255* sighted PQ 17 and reported it to be 60 miles east of Jan Mayen Island.[7] There is a contradiction here, because in the next paragraph Milan Vego states that at 1200 hours the same day, aircraft shadowing PQ 17 were noticed and that the position was then 200 miles west of Bear Island.

Around midday, the first of many submarine scares occurred. PQ 17's position became known as *U-255* and *U-408* began to shadow the slow-moving – 8 knots – convoy. Two more submarines of Wolfpack *Eisteufel* (21 June–12 July) were ordered to join, and six more were deployed across the convoy's likely route to the east.

At about 1800 hours, when the convoy was at 73°30'N, 04°00'E, nine aircraft approached, but the torpedoes that some dropped exploded wide of the convoy without doing damage. The USN destroyer *Rowan*, *en route* from CS One to the convoy to refuel from *Aldersdale*, reportedly shot one down. Claims of aircraft shot down – particularly by anti-aircraft fire – are notoriously unreliable and tend to overstate the actual results.

This photograph of *Keppel* shows it equipped with a Hedgehog ATW in 'A' gun position. It is possible that the Type 271 radar (above the bridge) and Type 291 radar (top of the foremast) had not been fitted in July 1942 but probably in its December refit. The flat-sided funnels mark *Keppel* as a Thornycroft-built ship. (Public Domain)

Sister-ship to *Rathlin*, SS *Glengariff*. (Public Domain)

The convoy's departure from Reykjavik had not gone unnoticed. German agents in Iceland reported this information, as well as, most likely, the make-up of the convoy. This intelligence was confirmed around 1400 hours when a Blohm & Voss BV 138 flying boat made its unwelcome appearance. Its radio transmissions to home submarines on to the convoy's position

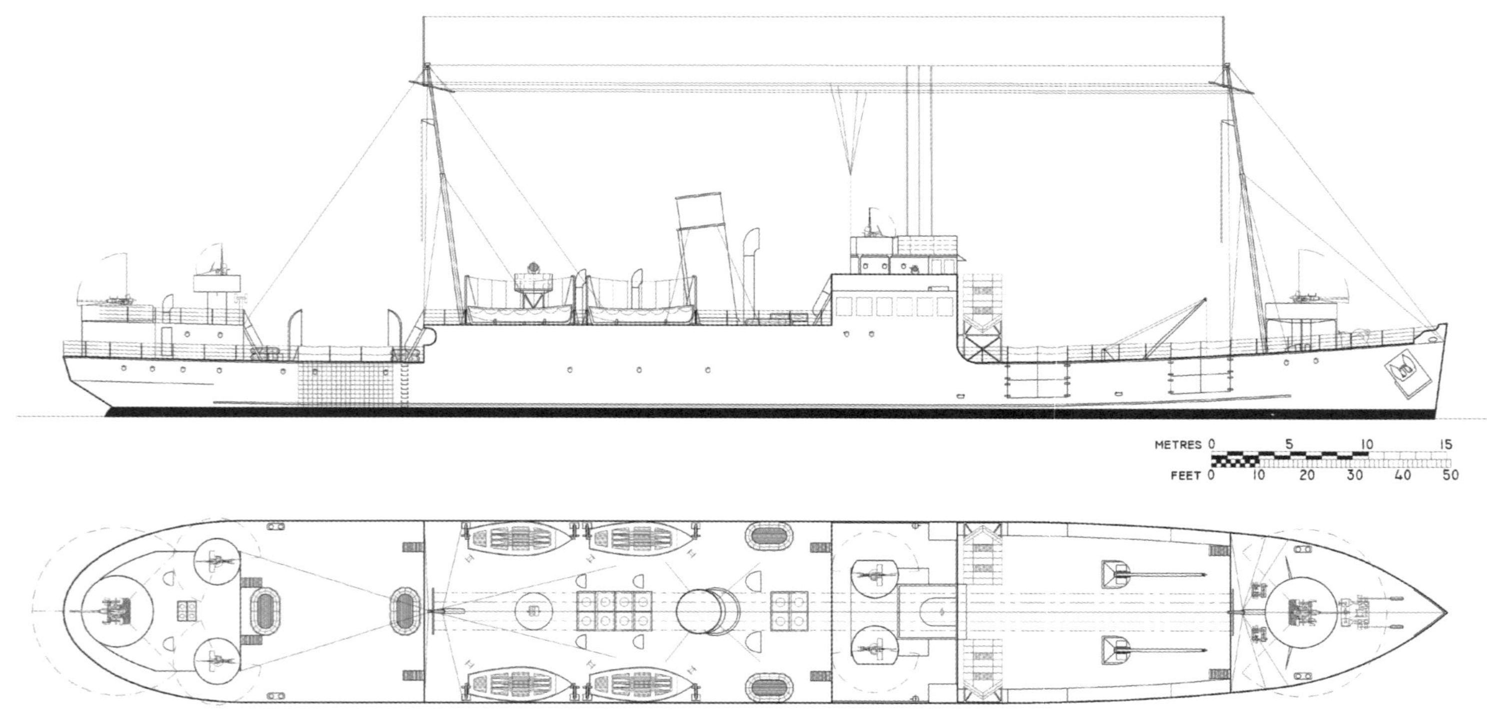

Notes on the drawing: *The best photograph available of SS* Rathlin *in profile was used as the basis of my drawing. Unfortunately, its overall length on record was almost certainly its LBP or PP (Length Between Perpendiculars) measurement and not its LOA (Length Overall). LBP is very much a shipbuilder's measurement: the distance between the main bow perpendicular member and the after surface of the sternpost or main stern perpendicular member. It cannot be determined without seeing its underwater shape; I had to make many calculated guesses in order to scale off the photograph, particularly as it appeared in plan. Similarly, its armament is a guess based on the size and location of the various gun tubs.* Rathlin *was selected rather than* Zamalek *and* Zaafaran *because I could find even less details of these two sister-ships to be able to make a drawing, and* Rathlin *served in the most convoys (47) and rescued the greatest number of survivors (634).*

The County-class heavy cruiser *Norfolk*. Note the Supermarine Walrus amphibian on its catapult aft of the distinctive three funnels. (Public Domain)

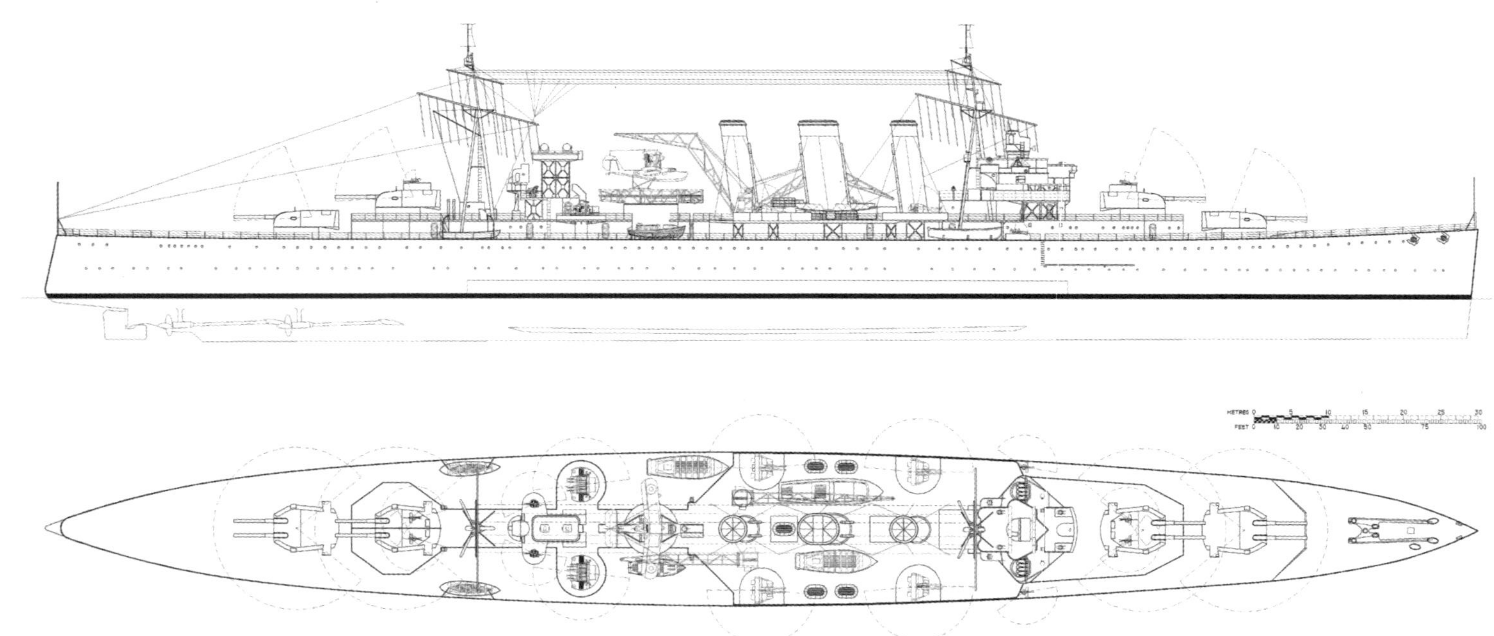

Notes on the drawing: *The County-class heavy cruisers were designed to fit the Washington Naval Treaty limit of heavy cruisers having a displacement of no more than 10,000 tons – the so-called Treaty cruisers. The class comprised three different sub-classes: Kent (five ships RN, two ships RAN), London (four ships) and Norfolk (two ships). Within these classes there were differences in armament and equipment as refits or modernizations took place. Despite their somewhat archaic appearance, with three raked funnels of even height, the County class was extremely successful. They were unique in that their 8-inch guns could elevate to 70º for anti-aircraft fire, but their slow rate of fire, traversing and elevation tended to make this inefficient.*

USS *Tuscaloosa* was contemporaneous with the RN's County class. (Public Domain)

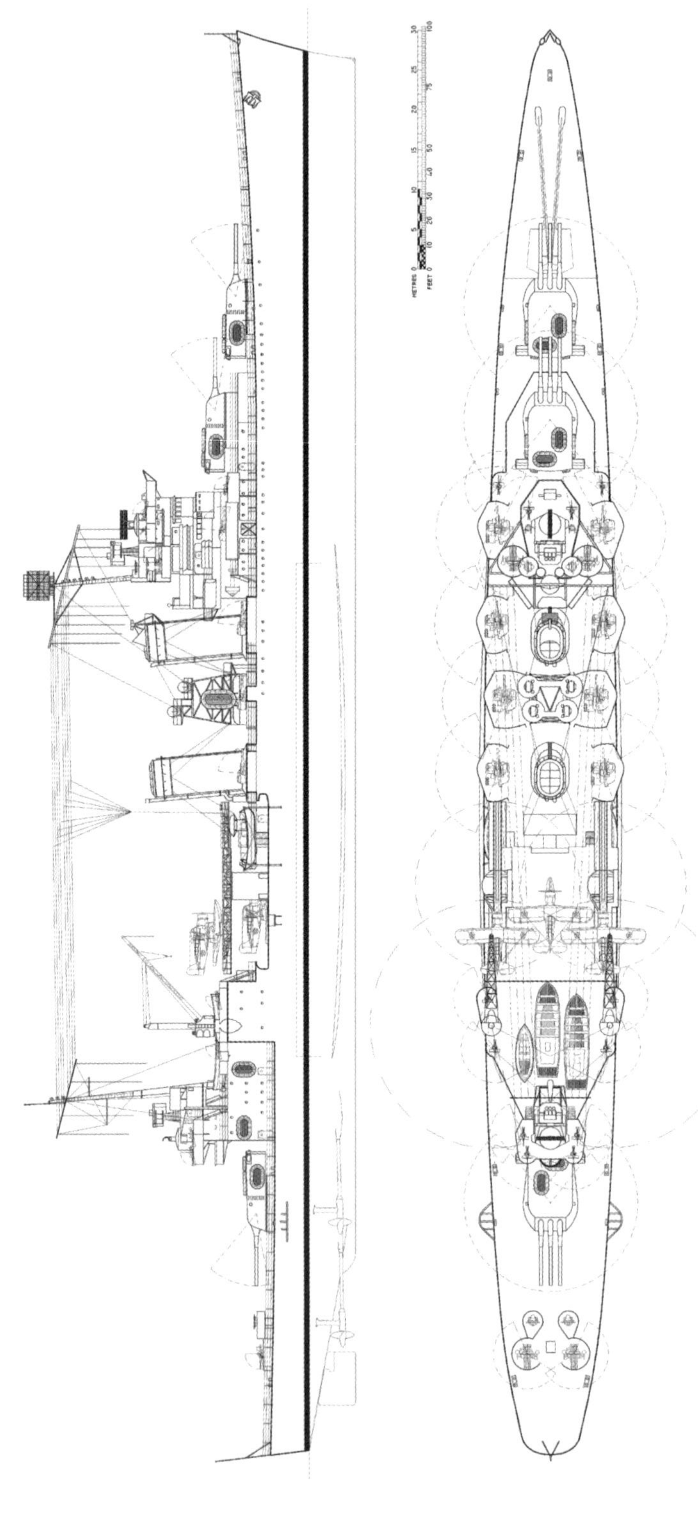

Notes on the drawing: USS Tuscaloosa *was one of two heavy cruisers that formed the second group of the six-ship* New Orleans *class, and was also designed to accommodate the 10,000-ton restriction of the Washington Naval Treaty. In the period before radar, its four scouting seaplanes were considered the most effective manner for extending reconnaissance range, especially considered necessary in view of the large expanses of the Pacific Ocean.*

were intercepted and decoded in the Submarine Tracking Room in London. It is difficult to know why the CAM ship did not scramble a Hawker Hurricane to intercept the BV 138. Had this happened, the convoy might have changed course and perhaps increased speed in order to confuse the Germans as to the convoy's location. However, there was a marked reluctance to use the 'one-shot' tactic, as commanders could never know when they faced the most serious peril during their voyage. Furthermore, the shadowing submarines could have been attacked to at least keep them submerged, where their slow speed and endurance might have caused them to lose contact with the convoy. Can this lack of activity be attributed to an air of predictability, of certainty or fatefulness, that, sooner or later, the convoy was going to have to endure submarine and air attacks rather than doing something to ameliorate these?

Late in the day, Admiral Tovey's Distant Cover Force was sighted: battleships *Duke of York* (Flag) and USS *Washington*, aircraft carrier *Victorious*, heavy cruiser *Cumberland*, light cruiser *Nigeria* and destroyers *Ashanti*, *Blankney*, *Escapade*, *Faulknor*, *Marne*, *Martin*, USS *Mayrant*, *Middleton*, *Onslaught*, *Onslow*, USS *Rhind* and *Wheatland*. The Battle Fleet, or Distant Cover Force, had expected to reach 65°56'N, 10°30'E at 0730 hours, and was due to be in the vicinity of 71°N, 0°E by the afternoon of day six, the next day, 2 July, and remain in that general area until day eight (4 July) without venturing north of 72°30'N.

At some stage, when the convoy was in the Denmark Strait, heavy loose ice was encountered and the American SS *Exford* turned back for Iceland, damaged, presumably without an escort. It joined PQ 18 more than two months later. *Exford* (ex-*Hog Island*, ex-*Express*), was an EFC Design 1022 Hog Islander, built to a standard design for the United States Shipping Board in 1919, but too late for World War I. Sixteen of the merchant ships in PQ 17 (when it departed) were predominantly either variations of this emergency programme or its World War II equivalent, the Type EC2-S-C1 Liberty ships, of which there were seven. An aspect of PQ 17 overlooked by historians is the significance of the number of American-built emergency wartime merchant ships: 16 of the various types ordered under the Emergency Fleet Corporation late in World War I (including one built in Japan) and the seven Liberty ships of the 2,710 ordered by the United States Maritime Commission. Therefore, 23 of the initial 36 ships that set off were the result of emergency-build programmes in the United States, to which must be added one of the American-built Ocean class, the predecessor to the Liberty ship – that is, 24 or two-thirds. One of the World War II British emergency-build ships for the Ministry of War Transport (MoWT) could be added, plus two of the World War I British emergency-build. This would then total 26, or 72.2 per cent, of PQ 17's merchant ships being the result of wartime programmes to produce standardized, simplified ships – often prefabricated – to replace ships lost mainly to submarines. PQ 17 would not have been possible – indeed many convoys would not have been possible – without these ships. America's contribution in *matériel* terms should thus be considered as being substantially more than the cargoes that these ships carried to aid the Soviet Union (see Appendix B for details).

Force X of Operation *ES* returned to the predetermined point and then changed direction, heading back to Scapa Flow – again without being spotted, which was the whole purpose of the exercise. Later that day, Force X divided in two. The minelayers, accompanied by *Sirius*, *Nepal*, *Tjerk Hiddes* and two other destroyers, headed for the minelayer base (Port ZA) at the Kyle of Lochalsh on the Scottish west coast, while the colliers and the remaining escort

This photograph is frequently attributed as being PQ 17 taken from a Luftwaffe reconnaissance aircraft – probably a Blohm & Voss BV 138 seaplane. The convoy looks to be quite disorganised as to columns and ships spaced within the columns. Perhaps it was taken during or after a change of course. (Public Domain)

This photograph is of the CAM ship SS *Empire Lawrence*, very similar to *Empire Byron*. Note how the catapult is angled to port with a Hawker Hurricane loaded. (Public Domain)

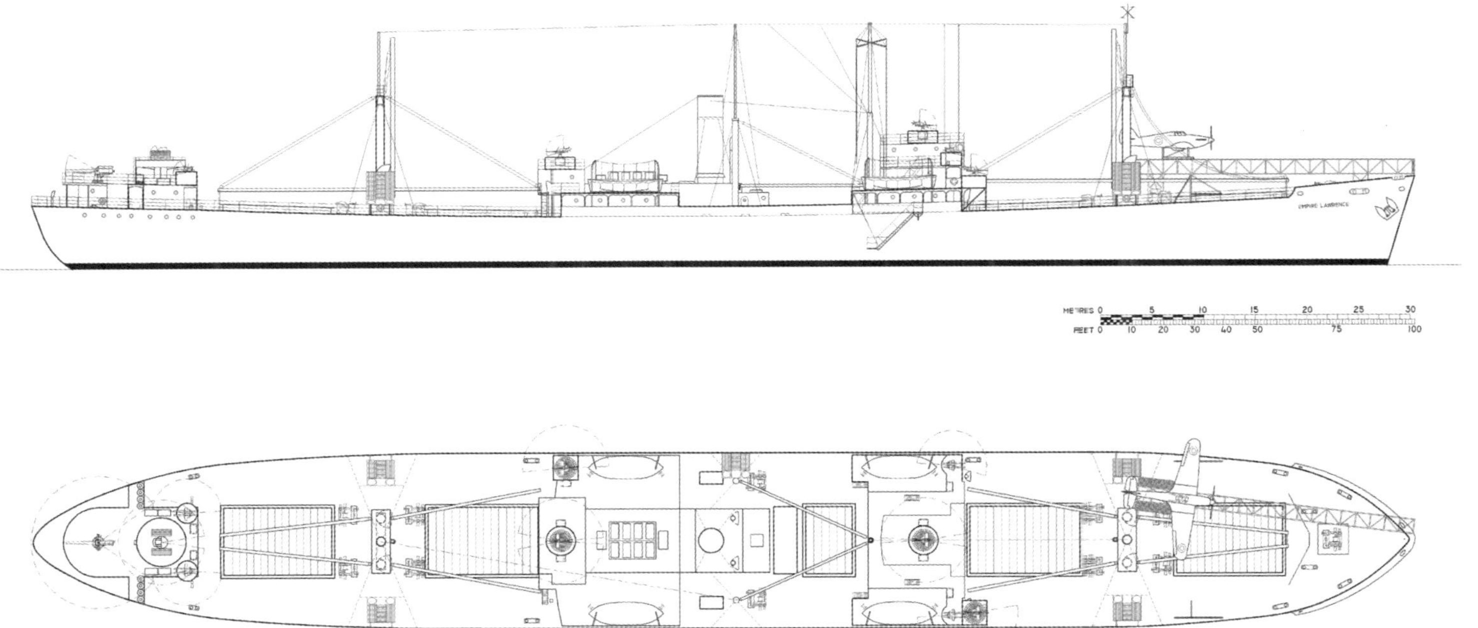

Notes on the drawing: *My drawing of the CAM ship* Empire Byron *assumes it was very similar to* Empire Lawrence, *although there was little uniformity as conversions were made on an ad hoc basis to different ships at different times. Note the asymmetrical layout and variety of the armament which included, in this instance, four twin water-cooled 0.5-inch heavy machine guns (ex-USN), only two 20 mm Oerlikons, the usual low-angle anti-submarine 4-inch gun at the stern and, above that, an anti-aircraft Unrotated Projectile rocket mounting of very dubious value. For some unaccountable reason, and despite the many opportunities, its Hawker Hurricanes (one on the catapult and one stored below) were never used to shoot down shadowing aircraft.*

A grainy yet worthwhile photograph of *Onslow*. Note that the strong wind is pushing the exhaust smoke well to port, despite its apparent speed, and the two forward gun mounts – in open shields, not turrets – would be difficult to operate in these conditions. (Public Domain)

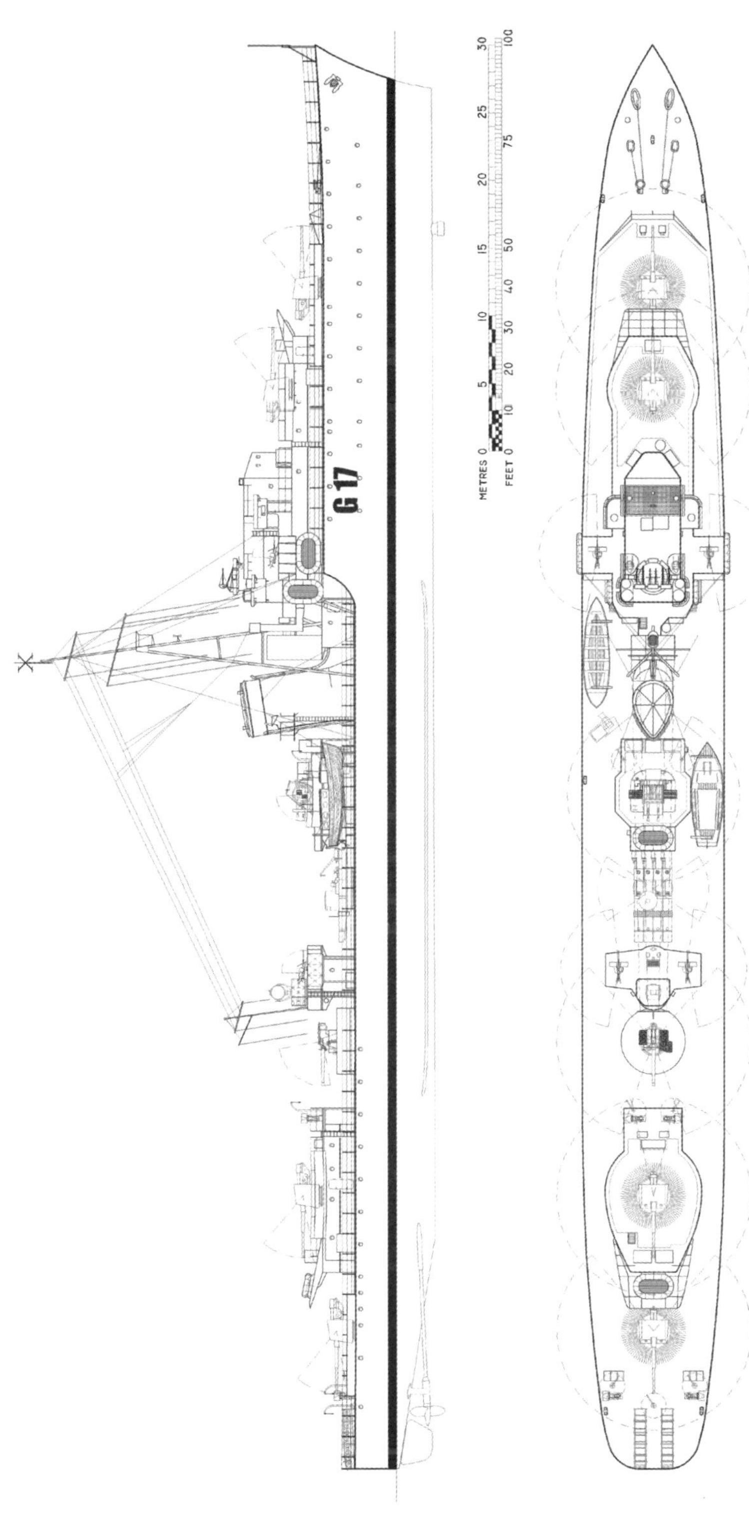

Notes on the drawing: Onslow *was a typical O-class fleet destroyer, retaining the low-angle 4.7-inch guns but removing the aft bank of torpedo tubes in favour of a 4-inch Mk V dual-purpose mount for AA fire. This was backed up by the ubiquitous quad 2-pounder pom-pom and four 20 mm Oerlikons for close-range defence. Note that the two depth-charge throwers are not mounted at main deck level but on the shelter deck aft.*

proceeded to Scapa Flow. Both convoys arrived at their intended destinations on 22 July. While Operation *ES* was a failure in that it achieved none of its limited aims, it does serve to show the extent to which the Admiralty was prepared to go, and the assets it was prepared to divert and risk to confuse the Germans, to attempt to disperse their efforts and reduce the pressure on the main convoy.

Day 6, Thursday, 2 July

Late on 2 July, the two convoys passed each other some 10 miles apart and divided into two sections: 20 ships proceeded to Loch Ewe and the remainder, mainly American, to Iceland. Vego says this was on the afternoon of 1 July at 73ºN, 3ºE.[8]

As previously noted, RFA *Gray Ranger* and escorting destroyer *Douglas* joined QP 13. *Gray Ranger* went on to Scapa Flow before proceeding to the River Tyne shipyards for repairs, which were not completed until 14 August.

Sometime in the afternoon, the destroyer *Fury* was missed by two torpedoes, and with escorts *Wilton* and *Lotus* counter-attacked without success. The U-boat involved has been reported variously as *U-255* and *U-456*, but www.uboat.net's comprehensive records do not show any U-boat of Wolfpack *Eisteufel* as being attacked on that day.

At 1800 hours, CS One was sighted by a Heinkel He 115 floatplane which made a lack-lustre attack, just as fog closed in. Fog was welcome as it prevented detection and attacks from aircraft, but was unwelcome too insofar as it made navigation and station-keeping difficult and threatened to cause any convoy to become scattered. Fog buoys would have been streamed astern of each ship on long floating lines, the idea being that the following ship kept the wake of the line and its buoy continually within sight, dead ahead. The bad weather also prevented RAF reconnaissance aircraft from visiting the Norwegian ports for several critical days.

German signals decoded at the Government Code and Cypher School (GC&CS – frequently unfairly referred to as the Golf, Cheese and Chess Society) at Bletchley Park, received from noon on 1 July to noon on 2 July, revealed that PQ 17 had been detected. Also, it was then known that that 2nd Combat Group had arrived at Altafjord and that *Tirpitz* had left Trondheim the previous night. It had, in fact, left Trondheim at 2000 hours for Gimsøystraumen, a strait between Austvågøya and Gimsøya, 75 miles from Narvik in the Lofoten Islands. It arrived there about 1400 hours and left the following afternoon. At midnight, the Narvik-based force sailed for Altafjord, only 80 miles from North Cape.

About midnight, the submarines and aircraft lost contact with PQ 17.[9]

Day 7, Friday, 3 July

The fog from 2 July did not prevent submarines from following the considerable propeller noise made by so many ships. Several unsuccessful attacks were made. Hamilton suggested to Broome that PQ 17 should change to a more northerly course, but Broome wanted to make

SS *Exford*, probably shortly after having been launched at Hog Island because no top-masts appear to have been fitted – standard procedure at that time to reduce visibility over the horizon. The tall mast forward of the funnel is for flag signalling. (Public Domain)

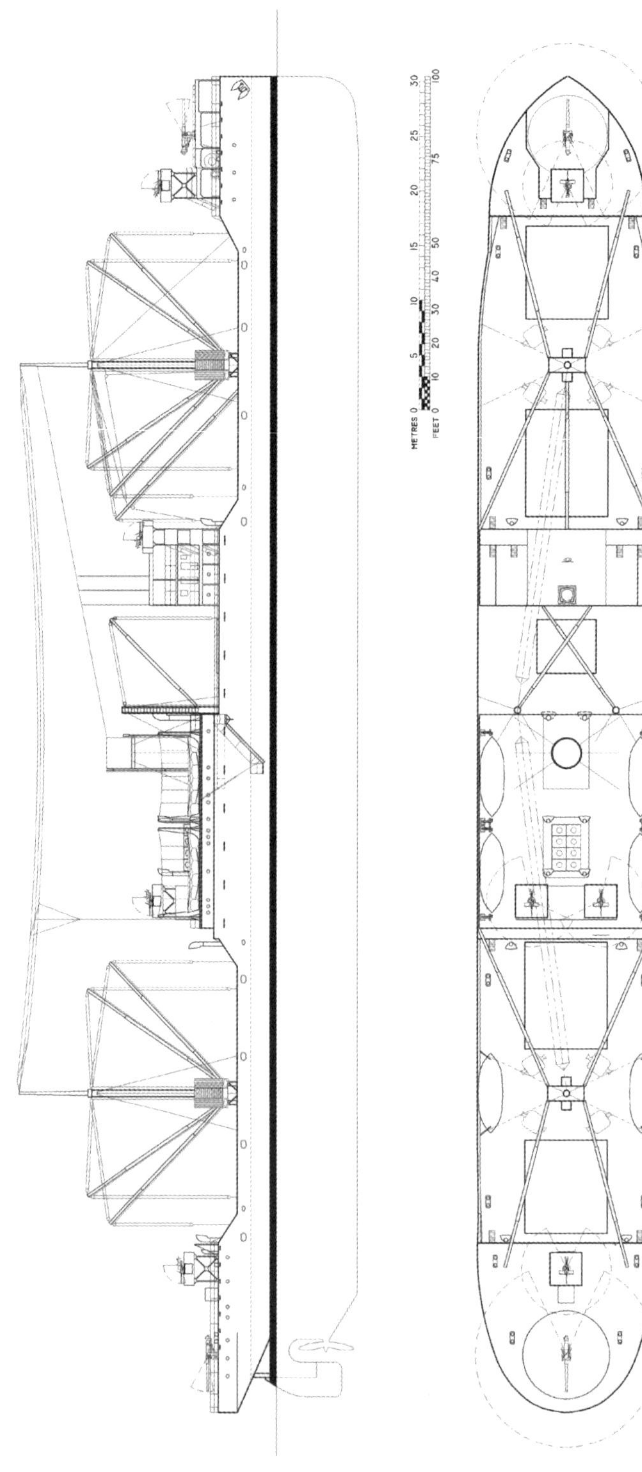

Notes on the drawing: *This drawing of an Emergency Fleet Corporation Design 1022 Hog Islander illustrates the type of economies built into the design. One thing not immediately apparent, due to the fitting of 4-inch low-angle guns fore and aft at the time of completion, was the design intention to make the ships looks so symmetrical that it was hoped that German submarines would not be able to easily determine a ship's direction.*

Note the angular, cost-saving measure of this World War I emergency-build N-Type. (www.collect.ons.tepapa.govt.nz)

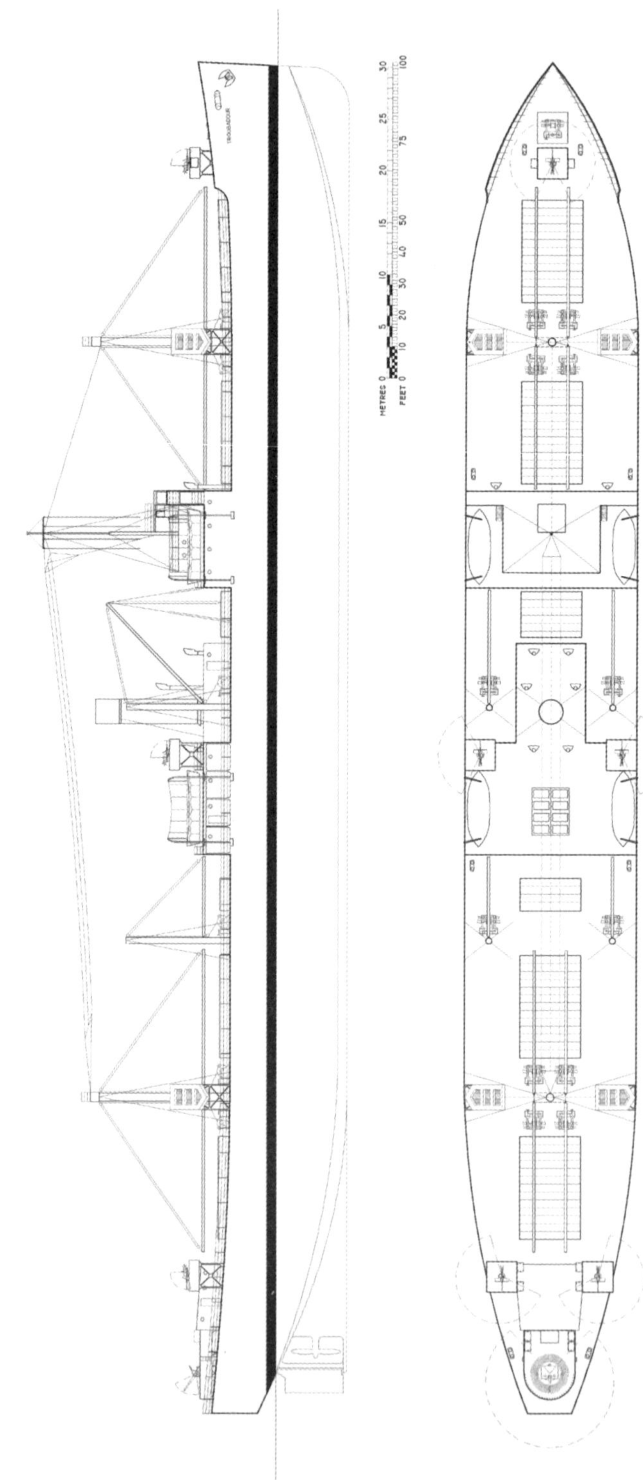

Notes on the drawing: *Contrast the EFC Design 1022 with the even more austere British N Type of the same period, which had had a multi-chined and a transom stern, both of which facilitated quick and simple construction. This illustration shows one as it may have appeared in wartime with armament.*

SS *Empire Iseult*, sister-ship to the very influential SS *Empire Liberty* – the progenitor of the 2,710-strong Liberty ships. (Public Domain)

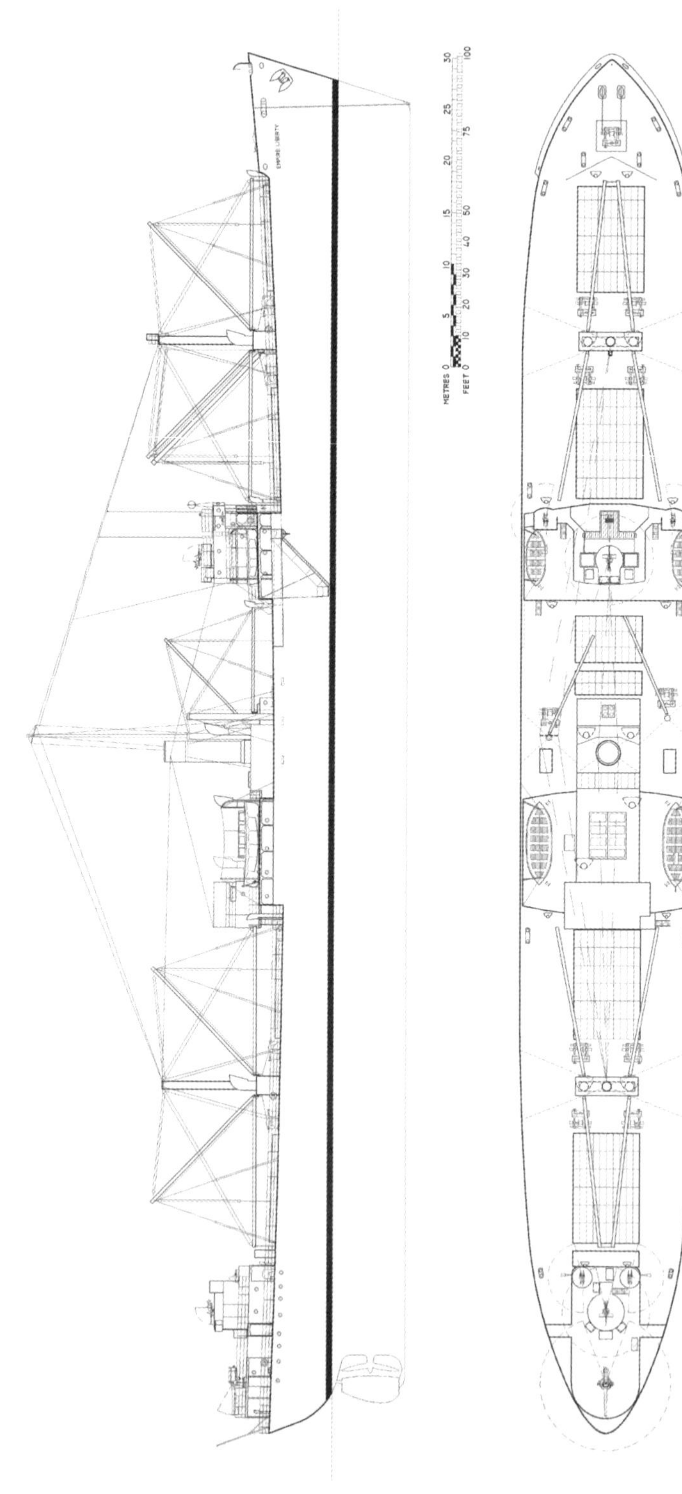

Notes on the drawing: Empire Liberty *was the progenitor of the famous Liberty ship. The design originated in the Joseph L. Thompson and Sons Limited shipyard in Sunderland, and was taken from Britain to the United States as the basis of an order for 60 Ocean-class ships to be built by Kaiser. Note the absence of special life rafts, usually fitted to frames abreast the masts.*

SS *Ocean Vanguard*, well loaded down, but its coal-fired boilers aren't producing any smoke. (Public Domain)

progress eastward. However, at 0700 hours, PQ 17 changed course to 021° in order to pass Bear Island.[10]

That morning, a signal had been sent from Flag Officer Submarines to all Allied submarines north of the 51st Parallel to the effect that PQ 17 was 'susceptible to surface attack'. Was 'susceptible to surface attack' simply stating the obvious likelihood, or did Flag Officer Submarines have more specific information which was not conveyed to Hamilton, Tovey or Broome? Irrespective, the submarines affected were dispersed: six Russian submarines in a patrol line off the Norwegian coast between North Cape and Vanna with, further offshore of this, a double cordon of nine submarines (U, S and T class), including the Free French *Minerve*. The next day, 4 July, they received orders to relocate to cover the approaches to the northern Russian coast. This order included *P 614* and *P 615* from PQ 17. Moving further north, away from where *Tirpitz* was expected to be located, seems counter-productive when the North Cape–Vanna cordon was already well north of Narvik and even further from Altafjord.

CS One was proceeding on a parallel course to PQ 17, about 40 miles to the north, using one of the cruiser's Supermarine Walrus seaplanes to maintain visual contact, presumably by avoiding the use of radio messages. One of *London*'s Walruses encountered a Blohm & Voss BV 138 – a 'Shagbat' versus a 'Clog', to use the popular if derogatory nicknames for these aircraft – without damage to either. The Clog was far better armed but lacked the manoeuvrability of the Shagbat.

This may have been the same Walrus that reported that the passage north of Bear Island had widened as ice had receded. The Admiralty suggested to Broome that PQ 17 should pass at least 50 miles north of Bear Island, but he preferred to keep within an area of low visibility and continue making ground east as much and as fast as possible, in accordance with his basic instructions. Burrough ordered Broome to alter course in order to pass 70 miles north of Bear Island, which would increase the distance from the German airfields at Banak to 400 miles.

If the receding ice was good news, it was balanced by bad news confirming that *Tirpitz* and *Admiral Hipper*, plus four destroyers and two torpedo boats (small destroyers), had departed Trondheim. This had in fact occurred on 2 July, but bad weather had prevented aerial reconnaissance seeing this. To compound the bad news, it was confirmed that *Lützow* and *Admiral Scheer* had departed Narvik with six destroyers. What was not known was that *Lützow* subsequently ran aground exiting Ofotfjord, while three destroyers attached to Trondheim also later met navigational hazards in Altafjord. The Knight's Move had not got off to a good start.

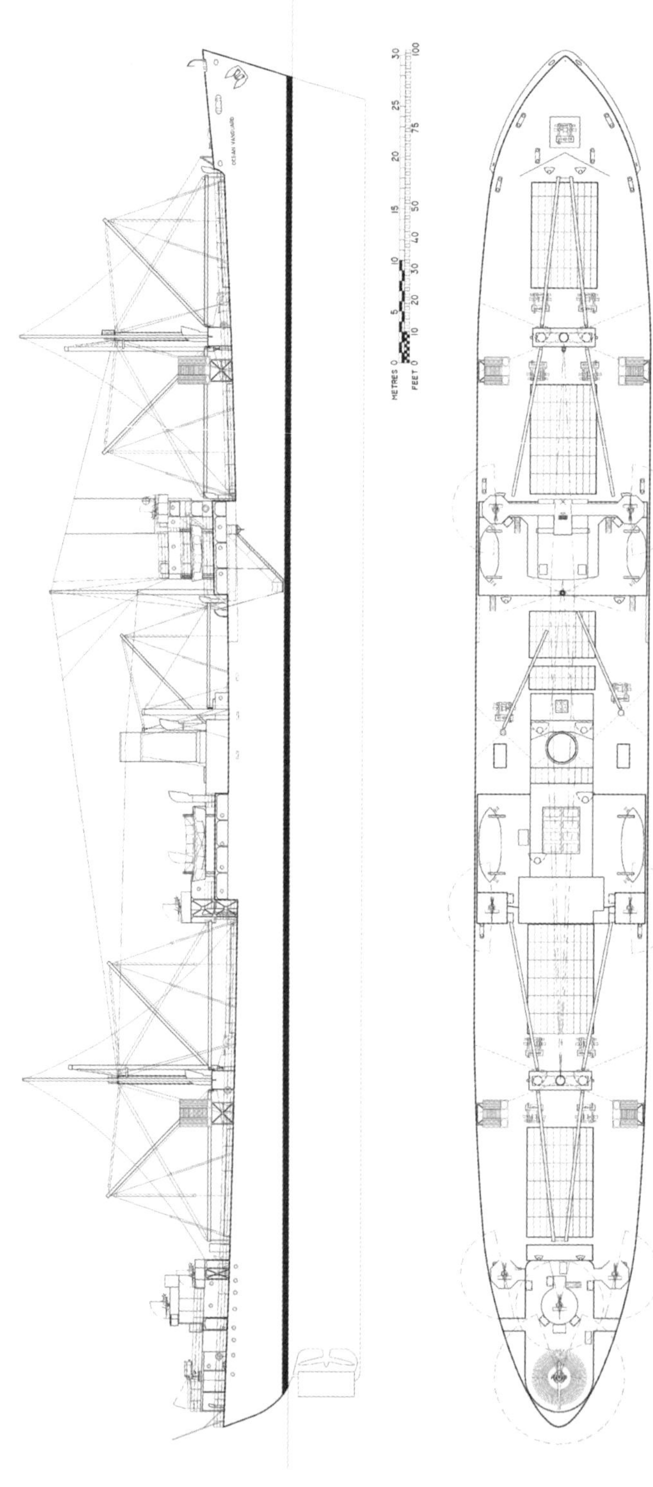

Notes on the drawing: Ocean Vanguard *was the first of the Kaiser-built Ocean class. They were coal-fired, since coal was a relatively plentiful resource in Britain, whereas fuel oil had to be imported. It is shown here with an armament fit-out of one vintage 4-inch low-angle gun at the stern and five 20 mm Oerlikons, although in some instances the super-firing one aft was either not fitted or the position was used for various types of anti-aircraft rockets. Note the life rafts fitted to frames abreast the masts for quick release.*

A typical Liberty ship: SS *Samuel Chase*. (Naval History & Heritage Command)

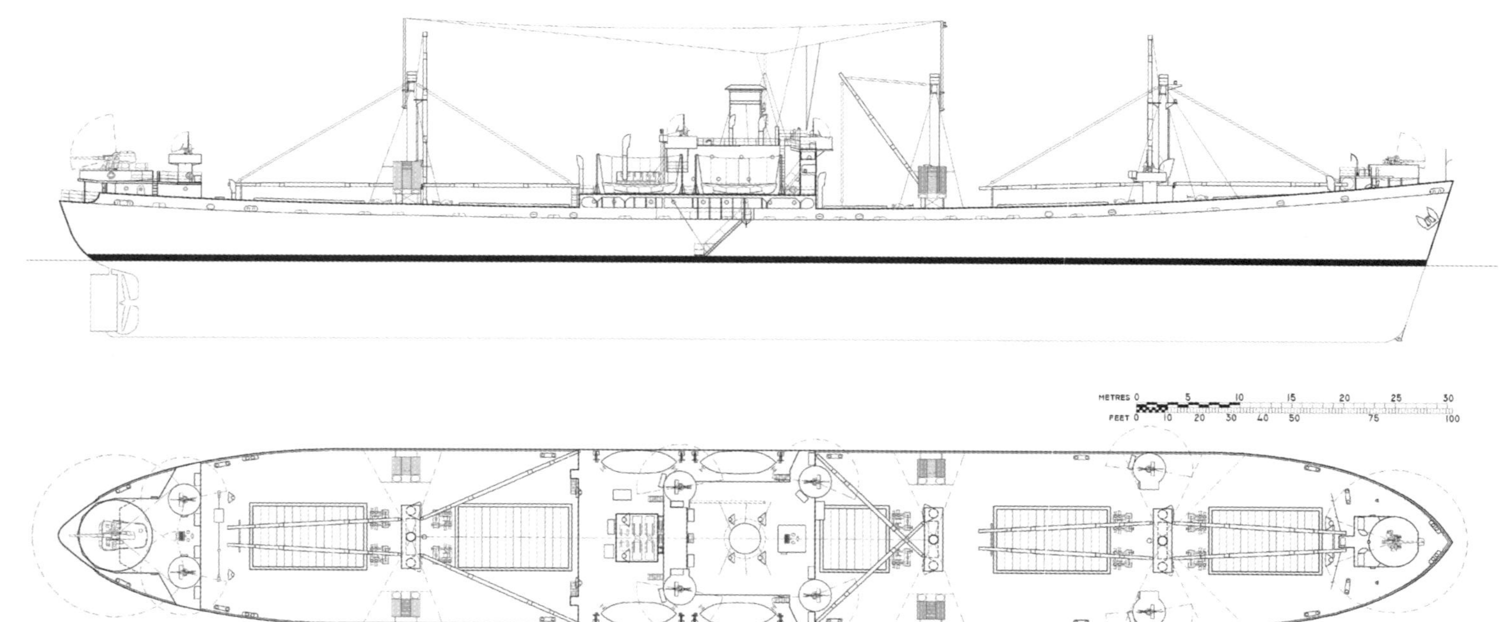

Notes on the drawing: *The 2,710 Liberty ships made a significant contribution to World War II, particularly the winning of the Battle of the Atlantic, since, eventually, they were being built faster than German U-boats could sink merchant ships. To speed the process of construction, they were prefabricated in sections and almost entirely welded. Machinery was identical to the British design on which they were based, but boilers were oil-fired and the superstructure was condensed into a central island. Armament, as illustrated, comprised a 5-inch dual-purpose gun aft, a 3-inch dual-purpose gun forward and eight 20 mm Oerlikons.*

Gray Ranger's escort, the Scott-class destroyer *Douglas*. This photograph probably post-dates its participation in PQ 17 as it is fitted with a HF/DF mast aft. (Public Domain)

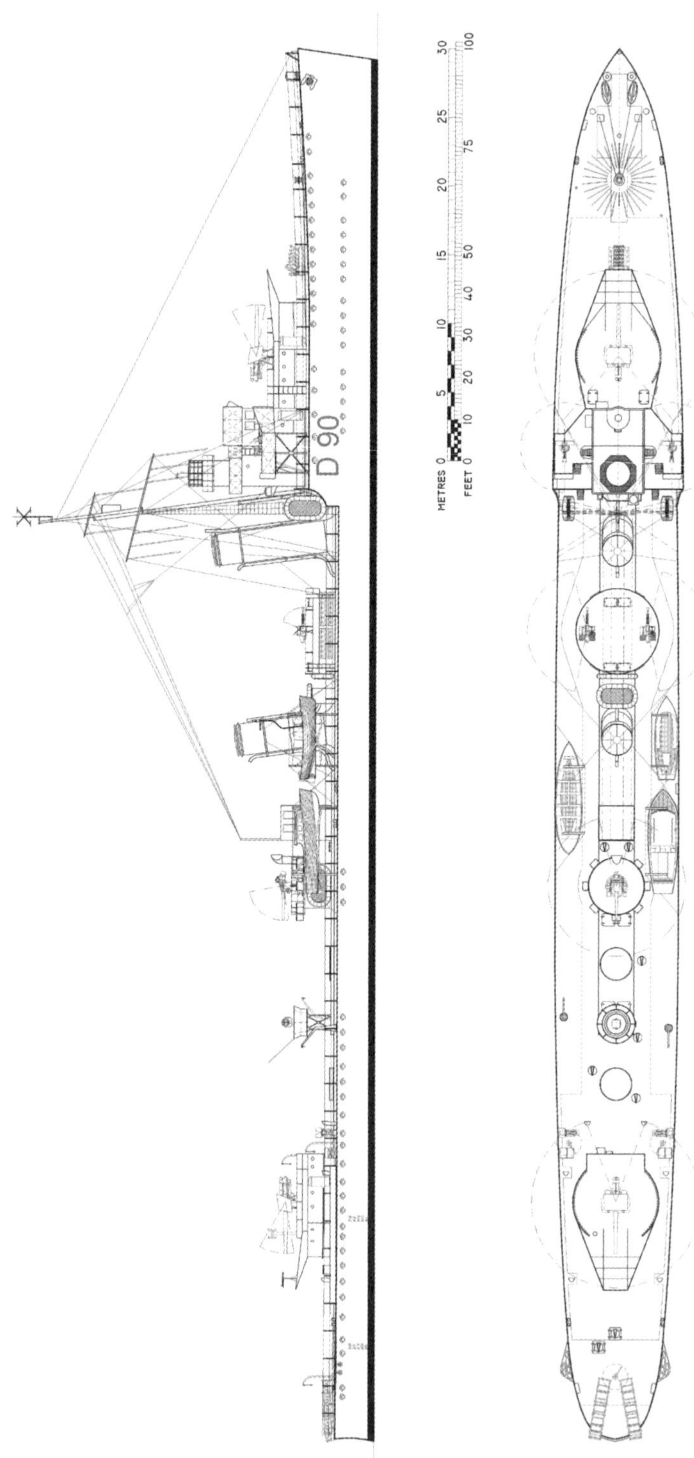

Notes on the drawing: Douglas *was one of eight flotilla leaders ordered under the 1916 War Emergency Programme and completed in September 1918. It was modified as a Short-Range Escort in early 1942 after a collision with* USS Mayo. *The modification involved,* inter alia, *the removal of A-mount and its replacement with a Hedgehog ahead-throwing A/S mortar.* Keppel *was similar.*

Leamington. (Public Domain)

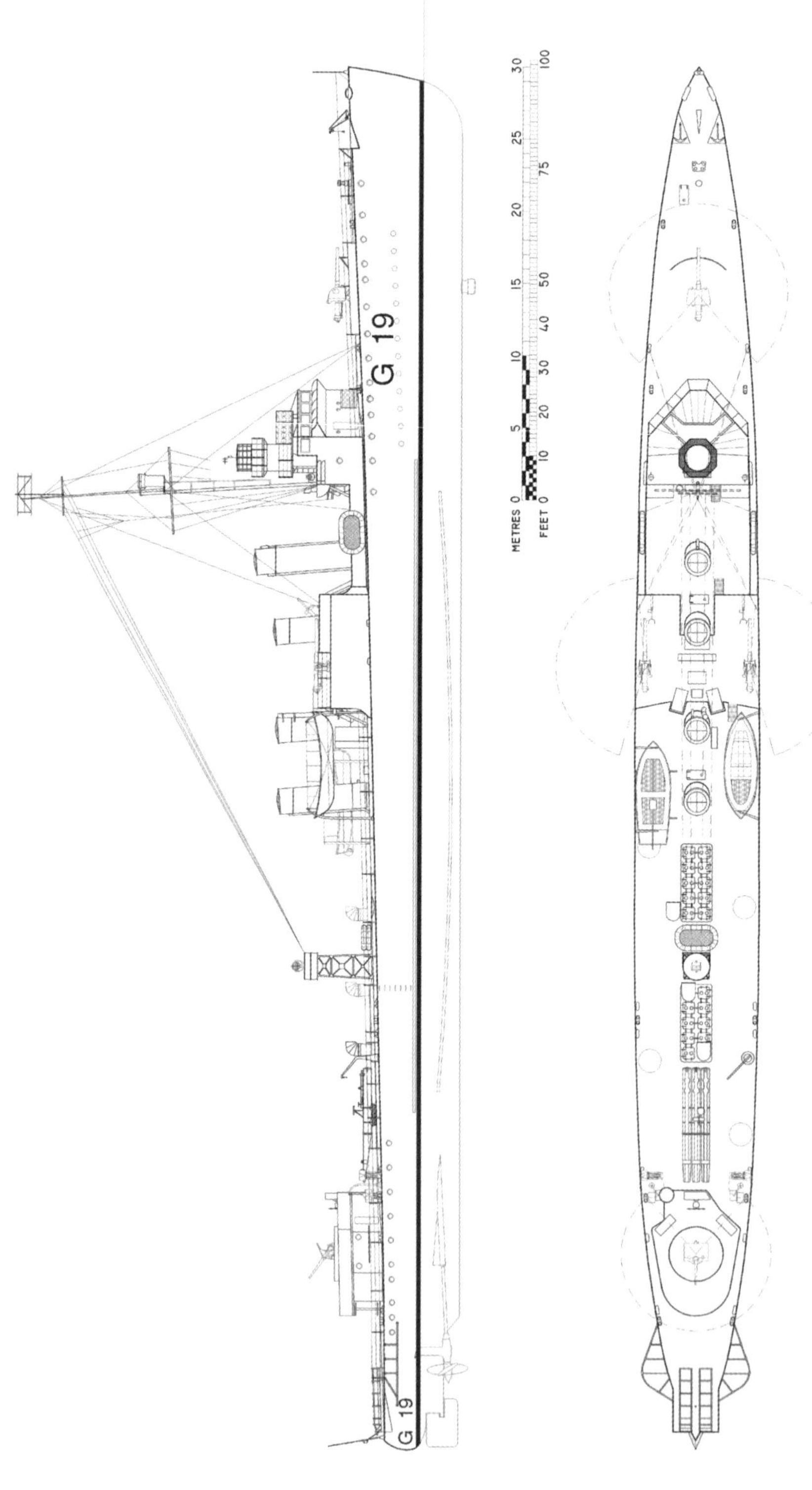

Notes on the drawing: Leamington *was one of 50 World War I-built destroyers (Wickes, Caldwell and Clemson classes) transferred from the USN to the RN in the Destroyers For Bases Agreement in September 1940. As a contemporary of* Douglas, *it is worth comparing the two navies' approach to destroyer design.* Leamington *(ex-USS* Twiggs*) was completed in July 1919.*

The Blohm & Voss Bv 138 was a diesel-engined seaplane nicknamed 'the clog' because of the shape of the hull. Sailors to and from the Arctic no doubt had less complimentary names for this aircraft that shadowed convoys. (Public Domain)

Although the Arado Ar 196 floatplane did not, apparently, play any part in PQ 17, it was the standard reconnaissance aircraft carried by *Tirpitz* and *Hipper*, seen here at the moment one left the athwartships catapult. (Public Domain)

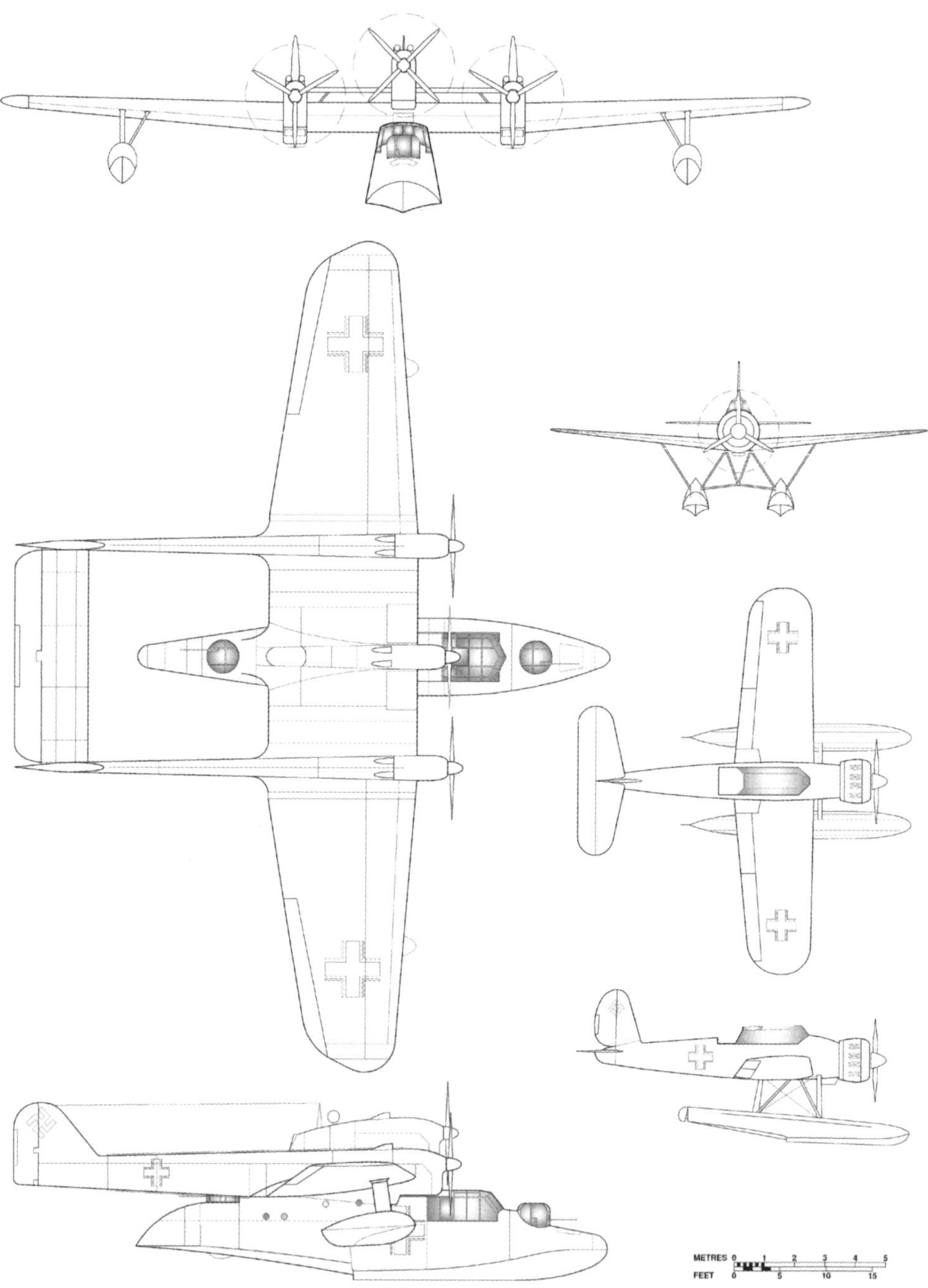

Notes on the drawings: *The Blohm & Voss was an unusual seaplane in many respects. Its ability belied its strange appearance, with three engines and a twin-boom configuration. Its diesel engines offered the necessary endurance to allow the aircraft to range far and wide, then loiter over a convoy, constantly reporting its position, course and speed. The Arado Ar 196 was a versatile floatplane intended for reconnaissance and the spotting of gunfire, and was the standard German ship-borne aircraft.*

The modified County-class heavy cruiser *London*. The boxy superstructure between bridge and fore-funnel contained a hangar for two Supermarine Walrus amphibians. (Public Domain)

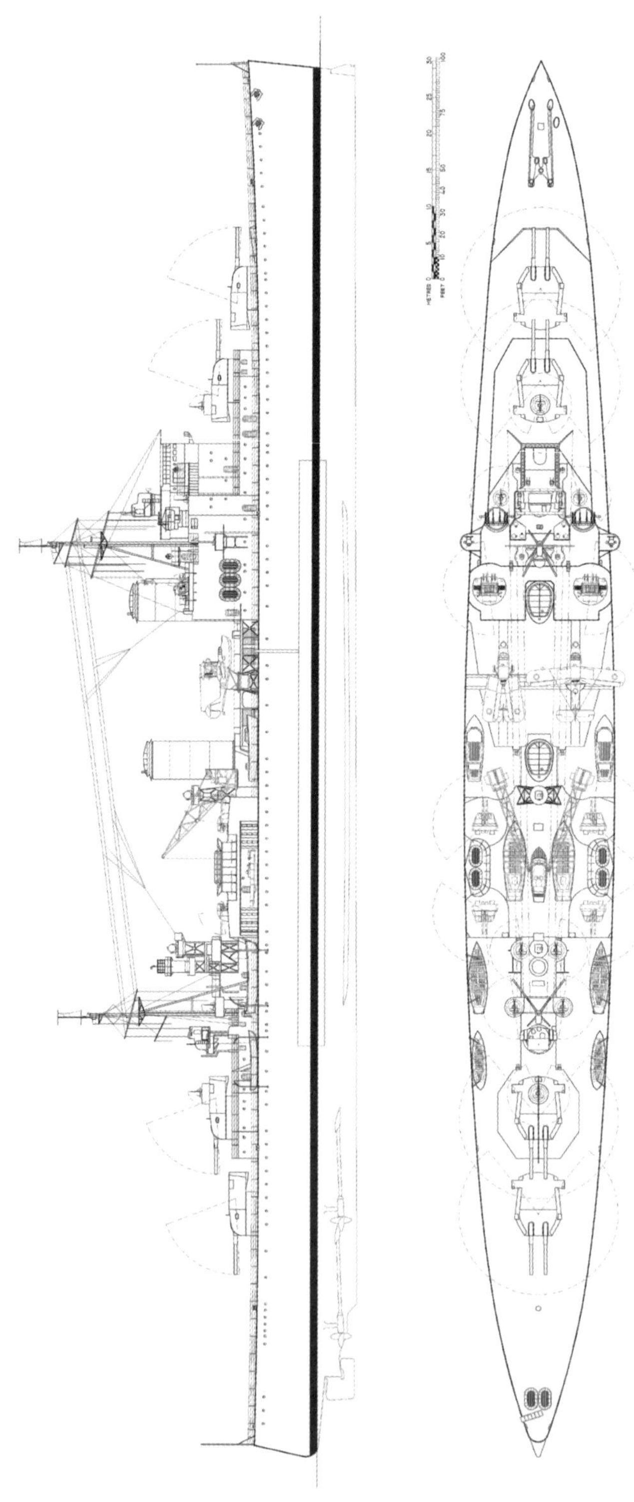

Notes on the drawing: London *was very much the odd one out in the County class of heavy cruisers, and from a distance is easily mistaken as being a Crown Colony-class light cruiser, the higher freeboard continued aft being a distinguishing feature.* London *underwent a major reconstruction commencing in March 1939, which took two years. It was intended that all of the County class would be similarly updated, but war intervened.*

Nigeria in 1943, after being repaired following serious damage in Operation *Pedestal* in August 1942. (Public Domain)

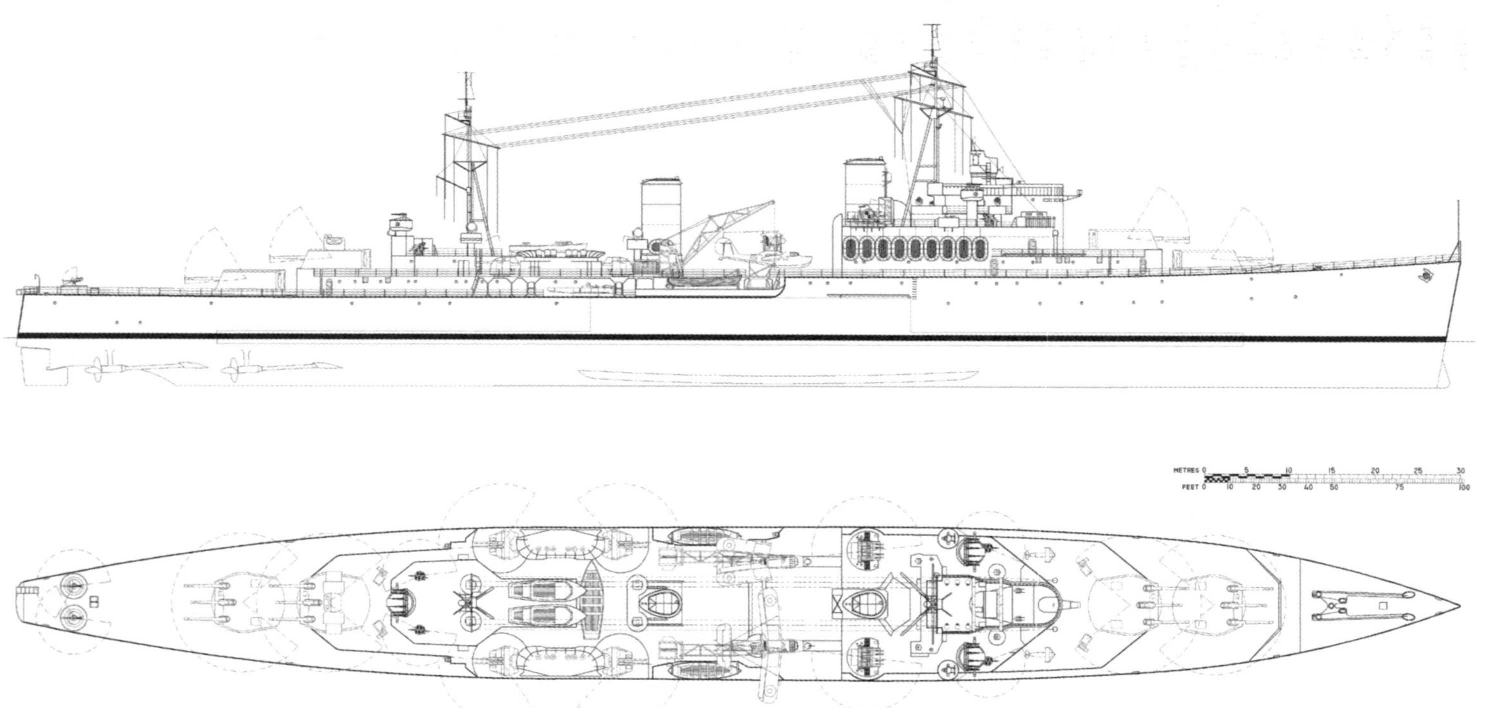

Notes on the drawing: Nigeria *was one of the 11 Crown Colony-class light cruisers, sometimes referred to as the Fiji class and built in two sub-groups of eight and three –* Fiji *and* Ceylon, *respectively. They were an improved version of the earlier Town class and can be identified by their vertical funnels and masts, whereas the 10 Town-class ships had raked funnels and masts.*

At 2325 hours, Bletchley Park sent the Admiralty the following message:

MOST IMMEDIATE

From: ________
To: Admiralty

FOLLOWING HAS BEEN RECEIVED FROM A MOST SECRET SOURCE. MY 1327 13th JUNE

1. GERMANS LOCATED WESTBOUND CONVOY FROM RUSSIA ON North CAPE MERIDIAN pm YESTERDAY JULY 2nd AND HAVE SINCE LOST IT IN FOG.
2. EASTBOUND CONVOY IS EXPECTED TO BE SIGHTED SHORTLY AND WILL BE ATTACKED IN ACCORDANCE WITH PLAN.
3. WARSHIPS ARE EXPECTED TO MOVE FROM TRONDHEIM AND NARVIK (?36) HOURS BEFORE CONVOY REACHES MERIDIAN 5 DEGREES EAST. MAIN ATTACK TO BE CONCENTRATED DURING PASSAGE BETWEEN 15th AND 30th MERIDIAN.
4. U-BOATS ALREADY ON STATION CLOSE TO ARCTIC ICE. A TWO REPEAT A TWO.

1642/3

DISTRIBUTION RESTRICTED TO DNI (4) ONLY[11]

On instructions from the Admiralty, as a result of this message, CS One was repositioned to the south, but was spotted by Luftwaffe reconnaissance just as fog came down, causing the shadowing aircraft to lose contact with the cruiser squadron.

On 3 July, the day after the two convoys passed, the destroyers *Inglefield*, *Intrepid* and *Garland* were detached from PQ 17's escort to make a sweep southward for *Tirpitz*. This ultimately proved unsuccessful, increasing anxiety as to *Tirpitz*'s location.

CHAPTER 6

Day 8, Saturday, 4 July 1942

The convoy was about 60 miles north of Bear Island when the fog that had given some protection from surveillance began to lift. At 0130 hours, PQ 17 changed course to 091°, thereby sailing into an area heavy with ice growlers. This may have been prompted by another Admiralty message advising of a possible attack by German surface forces between the 15th and 30th meridians. The information was derived from decrypted signals that confirmed *Admiral Scheer*'s arrival at Altenfjord and the departure of *Tirpitz* from Trondheim.

At 0415 hours, PQ 17 was detected by the Luftwaffe, north-east of Bear Island, about equidistant from Spitzbergen.[1]

At 0452 hours, a single Heinkel dropped out of the low cloud and headed for the anti-aircraft auxiliary *Palomares*, which took evasive action and opened up with close-range weapons. The Heinkel's torpedo missed, but hit the Liberty ship SS *Christopher Newport* in the engine room. It was heading the second column in from the convoy's right-hand side and its immediate loss of way and a dangerous swing put it into the path of the adjoining column. This caused mayhem as ships changed course to avoid a collision. The crew abandoned ship, prematurely, being picked up by the rescue ship *Zamalek*. Under other circumstances it would have been possible to take *Christopher Newport* in tow, but the decision was made to sink it. Yet that was easier said than done. A torpedo from the surfaced submarine *P 614* and then depth charges from the corvette *Dianella* were ineffective, and *Christopher Newport* was left abandoned and afloat. It was finally dispatched by *U-457* later that day.[2] It was somewhat ironic that the first casualty was an American ship on American Independence Day. The American ships took down their weather-battered ensigns and raised the Stars and Stripes, the act raising morale within the convoy. Quite what the ever-circling BV 138 seaplanes made of this visual act of defiance is unknown.

Flower-class corvette *Dianella* in 1943, probably after a refit judging by its apparent pristine condition. (Public Domain)

There is another irony here. On the day that marked the loss of the British colonies in America, 166 years earlier, British warships escorting American merchant ships were coming to the aid of what would become, in a matter of three years, their common enemy.

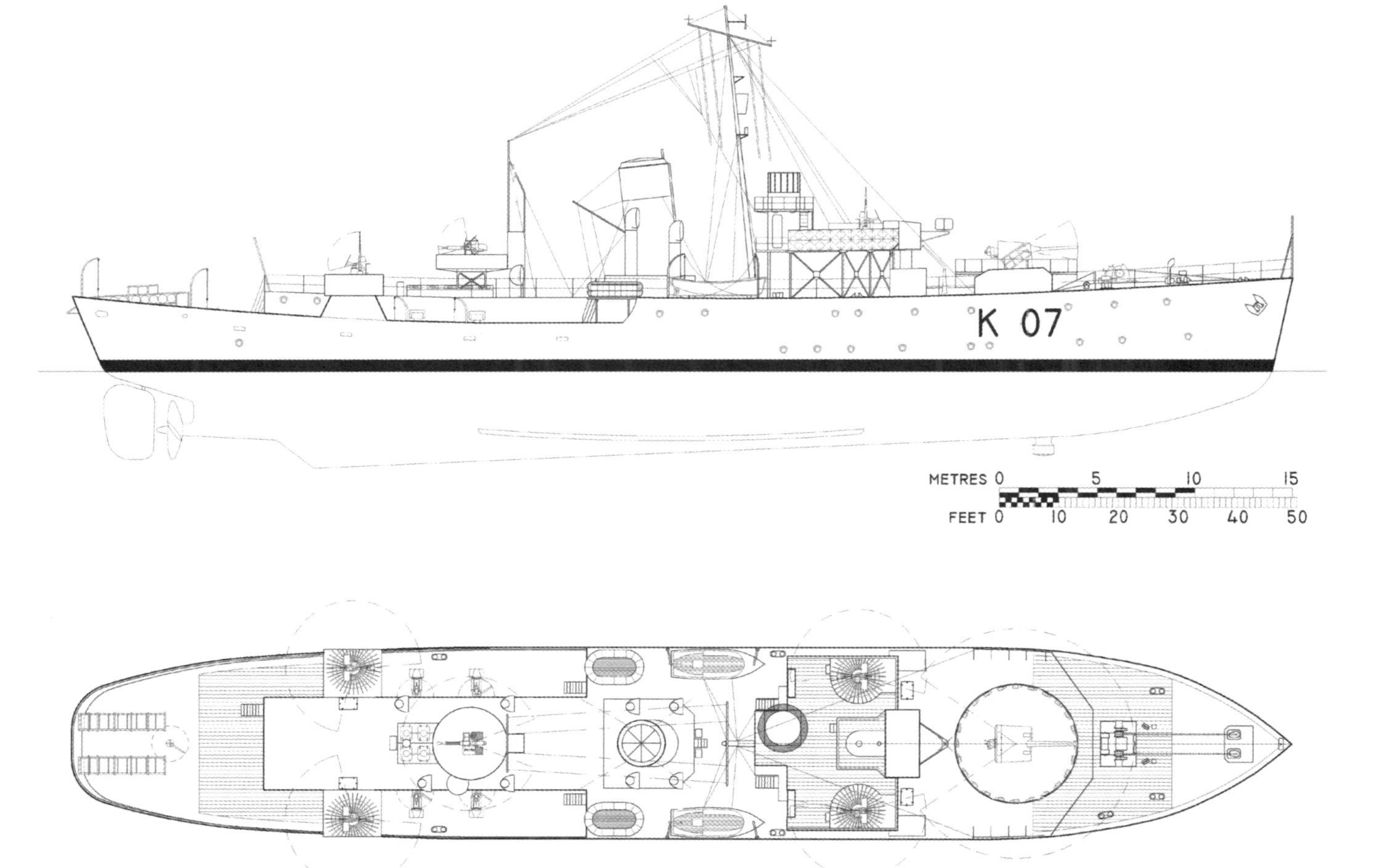

Notes on the drawing: Dianella *was one of 294 Flower-class corvettes built for the Royal Navy and Allied navies. Apart from the final iteration of the design (the Modified Flower class), there was little uniformity and there were many variations in the design, especially the earliest in service, as they were modified in an ad hoc manner depending on shipyards and what material, fittings and armament were available at the time. The 1943 photograph of* Dianella *would appear to be after a refit. Note the TBS communication antennae on the yardarm.*

Liberty ship SS *Christopher Newport* in two halves after being abandoned on 4 July and torpedoed by *U-457*. (Public Domain)

At about 1230 hours, Admiral Hamilton received a signal from the Admiralty giving him discretion as to whether or not he should proceed with CS One north of 25° east. This action was subject to Admiral Tovey not issuing orders to the contrary. However, Tovey did in fact issue an order at 1512 hours for Hamilton not to enter the Barents Sea unless there was confirmation that *Tirpitz* would not be there, being a vague command at best (just what are the precise boundaries of the Barents Sea?) and surely a dilemma for Hamilton. If *Tirpitz* was not going to be there, what was the point of CS One being there? CS One had been zigzagging some 12 miles ahead of PQ 17, which was thought to be 30 miles south of where Hamilton believed it to be; such is the variability of Arctic navigation and the need to use Dead Reckoning (DR) to try to establish position. Despite the merchant ships providing their daily estimates of position – which were more than often DR estimates – then averaging all of these with the averaged DR positions of the escort force, the convoy's estimate differed by 30 miles from the cruiser force's estimate. Moving more slowly, the convoy would have been subject to drift and unknown currents, whereas this would not have affected the faster-moving cruisers.

At 1330 hours, Hamilton closed towards PQ 17. Despite differences of opinion as to the convoy's position, Hamilton ordered Broome to head the convoy north-east via a 45-degree alteration of course. PQ 17 was to open the distance from German airfields to 400 miles by changing from 090° to 045°.

At 1520 hours, Hamilton signalled that CS One would stay with PQ 17 until the location of the enemy force was known or until 1200 hours on 5 July – whichever was the earlier.

Around the same time, the dogged *U-457* sighted CS One and reported, falsely and fortuitously, that it contained a battleship. The bulk and silhouette of the heavy cruiser *London* may have resulted in this mistake. Later, *U-457* also reported the presence of enemy aircraft, leading to the obvious speculation that the Germans' worst fears might be realized – that an aircraft carrier was present too. What *U-457* had almost certainly seen was one or more of *Wichita*'s catapult-launched Curtiss SOC-1 Seagull floatplanes on A/S patrol. This was another fortuitous overestimation.

During the day, there were many unsuccessful probing attacks by submarines, which could not break through the escort screen. Similarly, several attacks by He 115 floatplanes, BV 138 seaplanes and Ju 88s were beaten off by intense though inaccurate AA barrages.

At 1640 hours, Hamilton gave orders for a change of course to the convoy from 090° to 045°.

After advising the Admiralty at 1809 hours that he intended to withdraw westward at 2200 hours once his destroyers had refuelled, Hamilton received a message from the Admiralty 30 minutes later directing him to keep CS One with PQ 17.

At 1839 hours, Hamilton was advised to remain with the convoy (which was some 10–20 miles behind) pending instruction relating to further information being forthcoming.

The Operational Intelligence Centre received good news at 1900 hours that the decrypts from the previous 24 hours were expected soon. At 1930 hours, the Admiralty sent a message to Tovey that *Tirpitz* had arrived at Altafjord at 0900 hours on 4 July, that destroyers and torpedo boats were to refuel, and that *Scheer*, *Lützow* and *Hipper* were present. Some sources state that *Lützow*'s damage from grounding meant it had not made the voyage.[3] The decrypts also revealed that at 1623 hours on 3 July, two U-boats had been informed that their main task was to shadow the convoy.[4]

The Heinkel He 111 – probably the H-6T variant, specially adapted to carry two torpedoes. (Public Domain)

At 1918 hours, Tovey was informed of the substance of a recent decrypt to the effect that the Commander in Chief of the German force had arrived at Altafjord at 0900 hours on 4 July in *Tirpitz*, that *Admiral Scheer*, *Hipper* and *Lützow* were present, and that destroyers and torpedo boats had been ordered to refuel immediately. Pound decided, against advice, to add to the signal that evidence suggested *Tirpitz* was still in Altafjord. That 'evidence' included the lack of signals from Naval Group Command North to *Tirpitz*, a lack of any reports from the British submarines and no evidence from Bletchley Park that the Germans had detected the covering force, with no warning transmitted to U-boats to keep clear of the convoy.

At 1930 hours, Hamilton received a signal from the Admiralty telling him that 'further information may be available shortly'.

At 2020 hours, a patrolling Curtiss SOC Seagull from USS *Tuscaloosa* sighted *U-457* on the surface at 75°57'N, 27°50'W. The submarine promptly crash-dived, but not in sufficient time to avoid minor damage.[5]

Also at 2020 hours, auxiliary anti-aircraft ship *Palomares* picked up large formations on its Air-Warning radar: 25-plus He 111s and Ju 88s, this time torpedo-equipped. USS *Wainwright* had earlier dropped back to refuel from RFA *Aldersdale* and had been attacked, suffering some near misses off its port bow. The refuelling was aborted, and without specific orders, Captain D. P. Moon swung *Wainwright* around and headed for the threat at 32 knots, turning broadside on to give his guns the best firing arcs. They immediately downed a Heinkel He 111 which had already launched its two torpedoes. Wainwright's four single 5-inch guns elevated to 85 degrees, compared with the British 4.7-inch with only 40–50 degrees. Only the diminutive Hunt-class escort destroyers and the auxiliary anti-aircraft ships could provide a worthwhile barrage with their multiple 4-inch dual-purpose guns. Poor fire discipline from within the convoy, however, saw two merchant ships hit by low-angle fire: *Empire Tide* and *Ironclad*. CS One, zigzagging ahead of the convoy, turned back to add its gunfire to the barrage.

Despite the weight of anti-aircraft fire, SS *William Hooper* was torpedoed. It too was abandoned prematurely and had to be sunk by gunfire later. Next, a damaged He 111, losing height and in flames, managed to release its torpedoes, one of which fatally struck SS *Navarino*. Russian tanker *Azerbaijan*, with a cargo of linseed oil, was next, and looked doomed when it disappeared in a sheet of flame and dropped astern. The stoic Russian crew, mostly comprising women, managed to get the fire under control, made repairs, and it soon regained its position in the convoy. In contrast to the crews of the *Christopher Newport* and *William Hooper*, who abandoned their ships prematurely, only one small group launched a lifeboat; later, *Azerbaijan*'s skipper refused to accept them back on board, having been rescued by the *Zamalek*.

The long, slender fuselage of the Heinkel He 115 floatplane had a bomb bay capable of holding a torpedo, seen here being loaded from a special pontoon. (Public Domain)

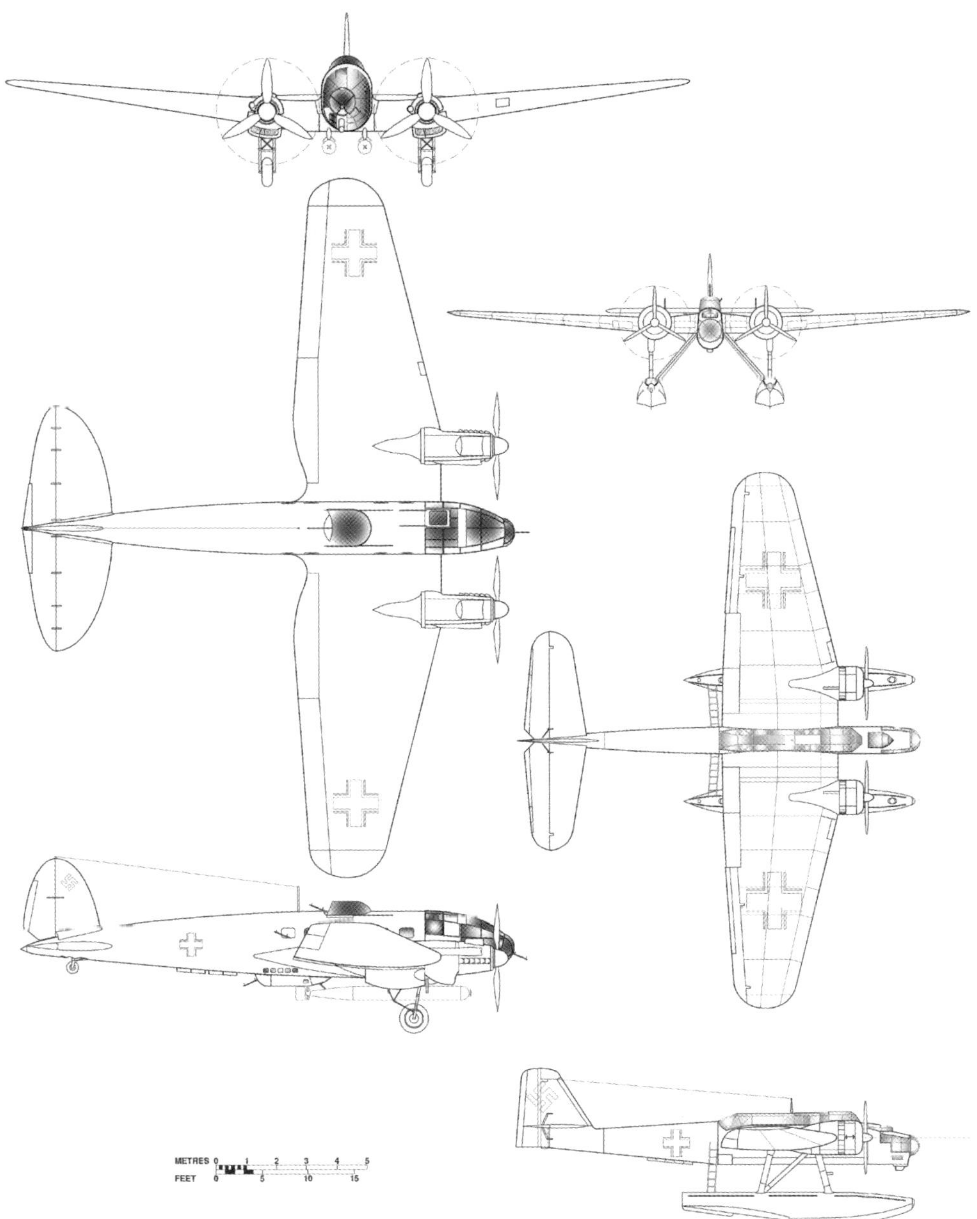

Notes on the drawing: *By the time of PQ 17, the Heinkel He 111 was beginning to show its age, and fitting two heavy torpedoes under the fuselage did nothing to improve its performance. The Luftwaffe's Bomber B project failed to deliver a superior replacement, and while construction stopped in September 1944 the He 111 soldiered on until war's end. The Heinkel He 115 was used for reconnaissance, minelaying and as a torpedo-bomber, despite its mediocre performance. One was shot down, but another landed and rescued the crew while a destroyer sped to the scene. Quite where the downed crew fitted in the very narrow fuselage is unknown.*

This photograph of USS *Wainwright* was taken on 22 March 1942. Its two forward 5-inch guns are trained to their maximum: number one to port and number two to starboard. (Public Domain)

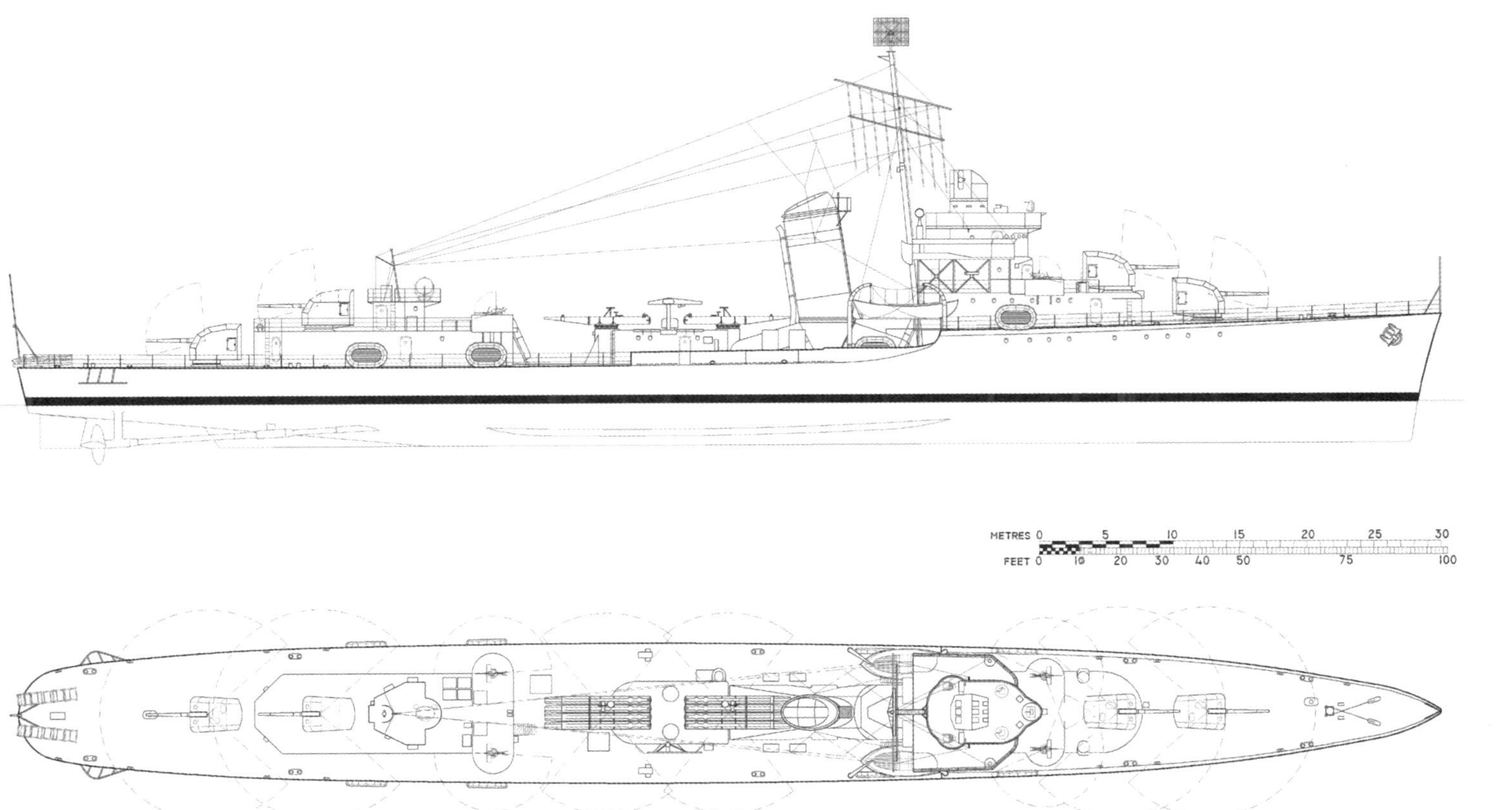

Notes on the drawing: Wainwright *was one of the 12-strong Sims-class destroyers – the last of the single-funnelled Somers, Gridley and Benham-class destroyers, all of which had featured heavy torpedo armament (12–16). Topweight was a problem, and* Wainwright *not only dropped one 5-inch mount (#3 mount), its super-firing aft mount only had a canvas roof and there were two quad torpedo tubes. The class introduced the Mark 37 Gun Fire Control System, but its extra topweight was more than compensated by the improvements to fire control due to its tachymetric computer below decks.*

The Hunt-class Type II escort destroyer *Ledbury* with its three pairs of 4-inch guns trained to starboard as it appears to overtake a fleet carrier, judging by the shape and type of 4.5-inch guns in the foreground. (Public Domain)

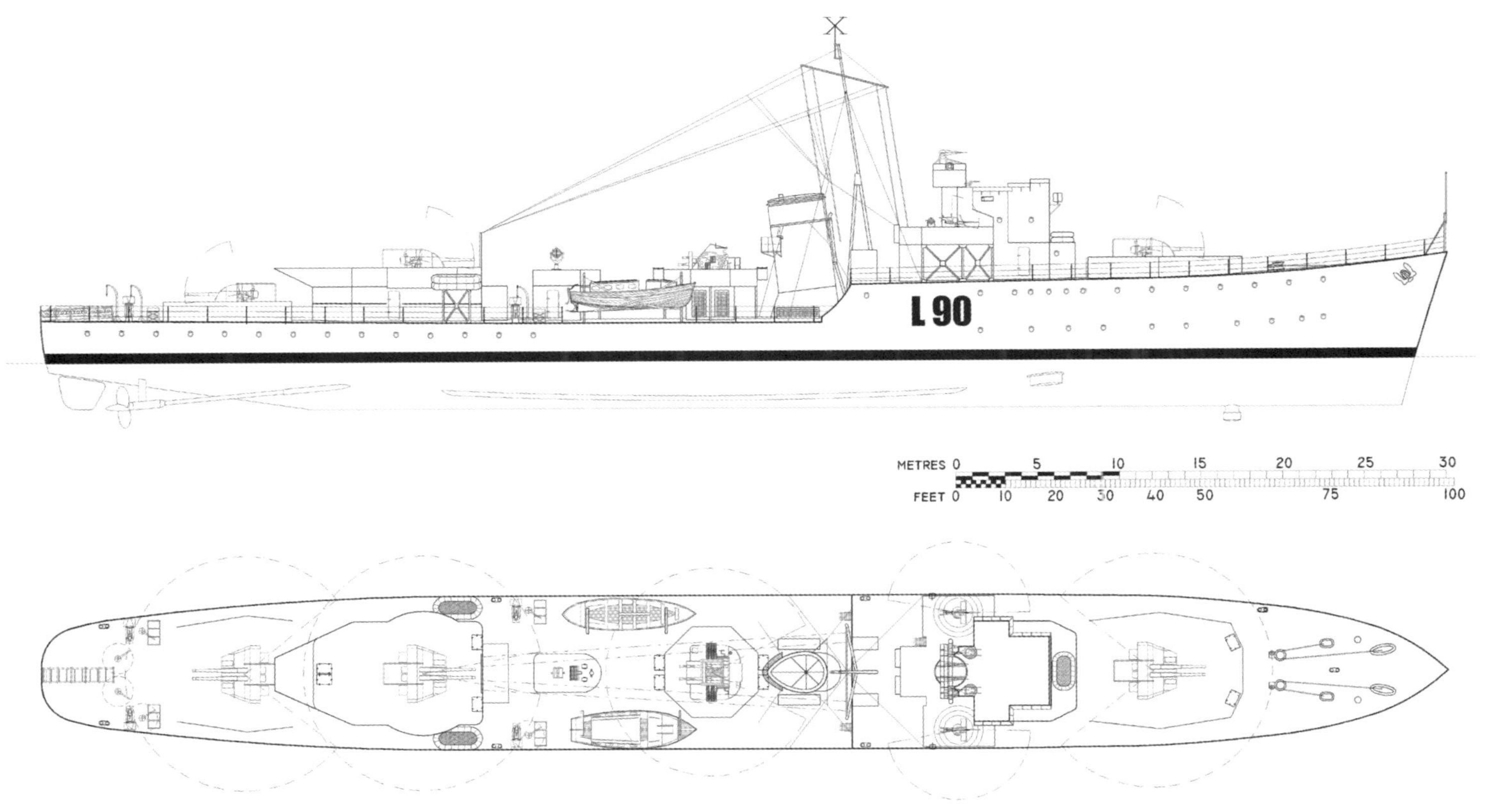

Notes on the drawing: *The Hunt-class destroyers were designed as escort destroyers, as distinct from fleet destroyers, and were well suited to the task, especially in the anti-aircraft role. There were four distinct versions: Type I proved to be tender due to a design error and only had two twin 4-inch mountings, Type II had three twin mountings, Type III deleted one mount in favour of a twin torpedo mount and Type IV, a Thornycroft initiative, had the third 4-inch mounting plus a triple torpedo tube mounting. In many instances, stabilizers were removed in favour of increased bunkerage.* Ledbury *gained fame in August 1942 for its actions in Operation* Pedestal.

The auxiliary anti-aircraft vessel *Palomares*. (Public Domain)

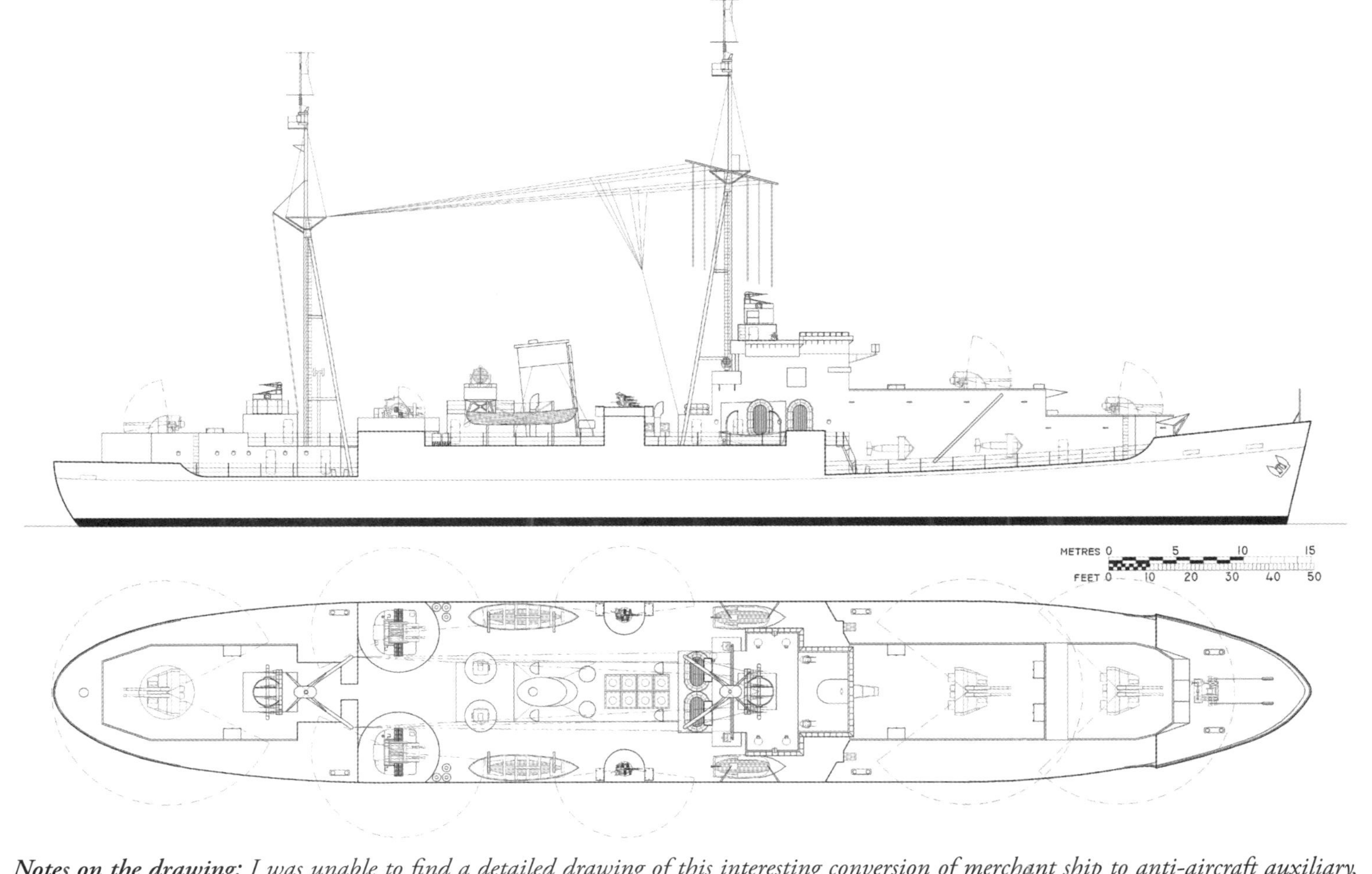

Notes on the drawing: *I was unable to find a detailed drawing of this interesting conversion of merchant ship to anti-aircraft auxiliary, so relied on the photograph for scaling and used other photographs for details. While the overall length of* Palomares *(and* Pozarica*) is very similar to a Black Swan-class sloop, which has the same main armament of six 4-inch Mk XVI guns (3 × 2), the auxiliaries had duplicated fire control systems (HACS), their wider beams offered a more stable base and there was an additional quad 2-pounder mounting.*

Liberty ship SS *William Hooper* sitting high in the water and without weapons in its gun tubs – probably shortly after launching. (Public Domain)

Considering the convoy was then 300 miles from Banak, steaming north-east, and Bear Island was now some 130 miles astern, two ships lost and one damaged was a reasonable state of affairs, the anti-aircraft barrage having been relatively successful. On the face of it, PQ 17 was coping quite well. As naval intelligence historian Patrick Beesly stated, 'The convoy and its escort were in good heart and confident they could fight their way through to their destination provided their ammunition lasted.'[6] CS One was covering the convoy some 10 miles to the north-east, with orders to keep doing so until ordered otherwise. Some 350 miles to the west, too far away to have been truly effective, was the Home Fleet, cruising south-west of Spitzbergen.

At 2011 hours, CS One sent a visual message to *Keppel* that the convoy was to steer 045 degrees until further orders. It must have come as a shock, therefore, when Hamilton's CS One sent another message to *Keppel* at 2040 hours:

> Due to proximity of surface forces report when convoy is on 45 degrees.

At 2111 hours, an even more ominous signal was received from the Admiralty by Admiral Tovey, now around 350 miles west of PQ 17, and by Hamilton on *London*:

> Secret, Most Immediate:
> Admiralty to CS One, (repeated) Commander-in-Chief
> Cruiser force withdraw to westward at high speed.

This signal was based on information not shared with Tovey and Hamilton. There was no explanation. The only conclusion to be drawn from these foreboding messages, so closely following each other, was that not only was the *Tirpitz* and supporting forces at sea, but likely to appear on radar sets at any moment. But would it be from the east, with the cruisers to avoid action, or from the west, in order for them to engage?

Twelve minutes later, at 2123 hours, a signal from the Admiralty was received by Broome in *Keppel*, repeated to Tovey and Hamilton, that put the matter beyond doubt:

```
Immediate:
Admiralty to escorts of PQ 17 (repeated) Commander-in-Chief, CS One.
Owing to threat from surface ships convoy is to disperse and proceed
to Russian ports.
```

At 2136 hours, just 13 minutes later, an even more disturbing message was received:

```
Secret. Most Immediate:
Admiralty to escorts of PQ 17 (repeated) Commander-in-Chief, CS One.
Convoy is to scatter.
```

How did this happen? How did a situation arrive where PQ 17 had beaten off attacks from the air and had suffered comparatively few losses, but could be suddenly put in this drastic situation? What had transpired that was not conveyed to Tovey, Hamilton and Broome? Who was responsible for issuing these orders, and why? To answer these questions, we must leave PQ 17 for a moment and look to the Admiralty.

CHAPTER 7

Admiral Pound and the Operational Intelligence Centre

The Admiralty, established by King Charles I in 1628 – replacing an earlier iteration established in 1524 – is the organization responsible for the leadership, command and control of all aspects of the Royal Navy. At the time of PQ 17, the First Lord of the Admiralty (the political head and a cabinet member and chairman of the Admiralty Board) was A. V. Alexander, and Admiral of the Fleet Sir Dudley Pound was First Sea Lord, the professional head of the Royal Navy. The Second, Third, Fourth and Fifth Sea Lords were responsible for manning, construction, supplies and transport and aviation, respectively.

Admiral of the Fleet Sir Alfred Pound, GCB, OM, GCVO (29 August 1877–21 October 1943), was appointed First Sea Lord of the Admiralty and Chief of the Naval Staff in June 1939. His career to that point had been as follows: 25 November 1890, placed first out of 57 candidates for cadetship; 1896, promoted to sub lieutenant and two years later to lieutenant; by 1909 he was Assistant to the Director of Naval Ordnance (rank unknown, presumably lieutenant commander, because he was a commander later that year; five years later, in 1914, promoted to captain and in command of the battleship *Colossus* in 1915 at the battle of Jutland; followed by being made a Companion of the Bath after war's end in 1919; then Director of Planning Division in 1923; in 1926 promoted to rear admiral and Assistant to the Assistant Chief of the Naval Staff; followed by a sea-going role as commander of the Battle Cruiser Squadron in 1929 and a year later promoted to vice admiral; by 1935 he was a full admiral and in 1936 was Commander in Chief of the prestigious Mediterranean Fleet, his final promotions comings in June 1939 as First Sea Lord serving on the Combined Chiefs of Staff Committee, which he later chaired, rising to Admiral of the Fleet in July 1939 until his resignation in September 1943.

When attached to the Admiralty, in 1928–29, Pound had been a strong advocate for the expansion of the Fleet Air Arm, and later a critic of the failure of the RN to adopt better anti-aircraft weaponry and control (the generally ineffective HACS system).[1]

Pre-war, Pound was not considered to be a potential First Sea Lord. The most suitable candidate, Admiral Sir Bertram Ramsay, resigned in 1936 after a disagreement with Admiral Sir Roger Backhouse, who for a short time (June–September 1939) was First Sea Lord until bad health forced his resignation. Admiral Sir William Fisher had died in 1937 and Admiral of the Fleet Sir Ernle Chatfield, the First Sea Lord at the start of 1939, was appointed Minister for the Coordination of Defence. Pound's appointment was almost a case of the last man standing.

History has not been kind to Pound, as we shall see, when it came to PQ 17. However, consider that he was First Sea Lord for four years in wartime, whereas his immediate predecessors held the position in a time of peace, no matter how fragile it was prior to Pound's appointment. He had to make many difficult decisions – remember, these were not decisions by consensus of votes of a committee: the sinking of the French fleet at Mers-el-Kébir (July 1940), the (disastrous) Norwegian campaign (April–June 1940), the dismissals of Admirals North and Forbes,[2] sending the battleships *Prince of Wales* and *Repulse* on the ill-fated deployment to Singapore (December 1941) and the embarrassing German success of the Channel Dash (February 1942).

Admiral of the Fleet and First Sea Lord Sir Dudley Pound in lock-step with Prime Minister Winston Churchill, figuratively but not in reality. (Public Domain)

History records that even at the time of his appointment as First Sea Lord, Pound was not in good health. He had an arthritic hip in a time when the anti-inflammatory medicines which in the 21st century are taken for granted were not available. He often gave the impression of dozing off in meetings, and his deafness was probably due to his passion for shooting game. He died in October 1943 – just a month after his resignation – after suffering two strokes brought on by a brain tumour that had been diagnosed by the Fleet Medical Officer but deliberately kept quiet. His second stroke was in August 1943 during the Quadrant Conference in Quebec. As Robin Brodhurst states in his book *Churchill's Anchor: Admiral of the Fleet Sir Dudley Pound*, it appears that his fatal brain tumour maybe only appeared, or perhaps came on to blow, a couple of months before Pound's untimely demise. One can only admire Pound for his remarkable fortitude and sense of duty under these circumstances.

The always conservative and objective Imperial War Museum in London produced a video documentary, via Rob Rumble, titled *Why Convoy PQ 17 Was Doomed to Failure*, which pulls no punches. The video transcript stated:

> Admiral Pound wasn't in a space such as this on the bridge of a ship[;] he was working in the Admiralty thousands of miles away from the action. Although he had all of the intelligence reports coming in from Bletchley Park, he didn't have the minute-to-minute intelligence from reconnaissance aircraft, radar that his Fleet Admirals in the Arctic were receiving. This meant that there was a bit of an intelligence gap. The information he was receiving didn't paint the entire picture of what the German fleet was doing. … From 9 pm on the 4th of July, Pound gave a series of increasingly alarmed instructions to his forces. First, he ordered the cruiser squadron to withdraw to the west, before 10 minutes later ordering the convoy to disperse. 10 minutes after that he gave his final order 'convoy is to scatter'. The convoy commanders took those orders to mean that an attack from the Tirpitz was imminent. The merchant ships quickly dispersed, while most of the escort ships joined the cruiser squadron withdrawing to the West. But Pound's decision would have disastrous consequences. This would seem an utterly insane thing to do, a monumental mistake and even his colleagues in the Royal Navy thought

> so. He was trying to put himself into the shoes of his German counterparts. Major German battleships and cruisers had been deployed to Norway and Pound was convinced that these were going to be used. That's what he would have done. And he chose to discount other intelligence that contradicted this. He was also seriously ill during this period. Unknown to even him at that time he had a terminal illness, a fatal brain tumour which caused him huge amounts of fatigue and exhaustion. In fact, his colleagues used to mock him for falling asleep during meetings and it's possible that the exhaustion and fatigue caused by his illness may have impaired his judgment at this time.[3]

History tends to record Pound's shortcomings rather than the unassailable fact of having an absolute dedication to the Royal Navy, of being in a difficult position for four years and of having to deal with Churchill's frequent flights of fancy (such as Operation *Catherine*[4]) with new schemes or interfering in ones already committed. Churchill was First Lord between September 1939 and May 1940, and took a leading role in operational matters. Pound did not see eye to eye with Churchill as to how, when and where the Royal Navy should be used, and was frequently brow-beaten by Churchill. As if this sort of interference was not enough, Pound also had to deal with interference from Admiral Keyes (Director of Combined Operations) and Admiral Dreyer (Chief of Naval Aviation), as well as from the USN's Anglophobic Admiral King and the Air Ministry's Air Chief Marshal Portal, and the hostile lobbying of the Russian ambassador, Ivan Maisky.

Pound was described as reserved, an autocrat, who kept his own counsel and did not reveal his thought processes. Pound did tend not to delegate, believing if something was within his capabilities then he should do it. Today, we would probably label him a micro-manager. He tended to interfere in naval operations with orders from the Admiralty, cutting across established lines of authority instead of leaving it to the man, or men, on the spot. This did not endear him to commanders. The burden of such self-inflicted over-work led to bad decisions, which is an appropriate point from which to segue to PQ 17.

Captain Jack Broome's autobiography *Convoy is to Scatter: The Story of PQ 17* paints an interesting picture of Pound. Co-incidentally, Pound had been captain of the old battleship *Colossus* when Broome first went to sea on it as a midshipman. Their paths were to cross 26 years later. In Broome's book, the naval historian Arthur Marder is quoted as having this to say about Pound: Pound was said to have the qualities of an efficient human computer, but Marder did not consider him an ideal choice for the job of Head of the Planning Section of the Operations Division due to Pound's 'rigidity', because he was 'too much a master of detail' and a 'supreme centralizer who did not know how to employ assistants'.[5]

* * * * *

The Royal Navy's Operational Intelligence Centre (OIC) was established in 1937 and was the eighth section of the Naval Intelligence Division (NID). Its purpose was the analysis of a mass of intelligence from a number of sources including, particularly, decrypts from Bletchley Park, then pass on the results of its analyses and advice for operational exploitation. The OIC was housed in cramped conditions in London within the Admiralty Building's 'Citadel' – a bomb-proof, windowless concrete monolith which still exists – and was staffed by non-executive naval officers, RNVR personnel and civilian graduates under Rear Admiral J. H. Godfrey, Director of Naval

Intelligence (DNI). Paymaster Lieutenant Commander Norman Denning was entrusted by the then DNI, Rear Admiral J. A. G. Troup, to establish the OIC in June 1937.

By 1942, the then-Commander Denning was a most influential and well-regarded intelligence analyst, going on to become Director of Planning for the Admiralty, Director of the Royal Naval College, Greenwich, Deputy Chief of Naval Personnel (Training), Director of Manpower, Director of the NID and Deputy Chief of the Defence Staff for Intelligence, ending his career as Vice Admiral Sir Norman Denning KBE.[6]

Kriegsmarine signals were not decrypted in real time. Usually, they were decrypted in 48-hour batches, but often with gaps between these batches which might vary from four to 48 hours. The OIC knew that when Kriegsmarine ships put to sea, they observed radio silence and received a steady stream of instructions and information issued from their relevant shore command, in this case Gruppe Nord (Group North). Therefore, the absence of such signals was a reasonable, but not infallible, indicator that ships like *Tirpitz* were not at sea.[7]

By the afternoon of 3 July, the decrypted signal traffic for the period from noon 1 July to noon 2 July, then noon 2 July to noon 3 July, confirmed the move from Narvik to Altenfjord and the departure of *Tirpitz* the previous night, later confirmed by an RAF PRU (Photographic Reconnaissance Unit) overflight.[8]

From 1100–1700 hours on 4 July, there were no reports from air reconnaissance. However, Bletchley Park did know from Luftwaffe signals traffic that the Home Fleet had not been located by their reconnaissance. This led to the quite reasonable belief that the Kriegsmarine would not risk its ships without knowing the whereabouts of the Home Fleet, especially its aircraft carrier or carriers. In addition, there had been no reports from the submarines stationed off Altenfjord, nor had anything been heard from a Norwegian agent stationed at the entrance to Altenfjord.

At 1900 hours, the OIC was informed of a breakthrough in the 24 hours ending at noon that day, and this was the basis of the 1930 hours 'further information may be available shortly' signal to Hamilton, referred to previously. This signal may have originated from the Director of Operations (Home), Captain Eccles, prior to Admiral Pound being involved.[9]

When Pound visited the OIC to see the intelligence for himself, Bletchley Park had teleprinted the news that *Tirpitz* and *Hipper* had joined with *Scheer* in Altenfjord that morning, and had not proceeded in the direction of PQ 17. It was also known that the escorting destroyers had been detailed to refuel, but what was not known was how long that might take.

Commander Denning, his immediate superior, Rear Admiral Jock Clayton (Deputy Director OIC), and Professor Harry Hinsley (Naval Section at Bletchley Park) were convinced that the German ships had not sailed.

Unfortunately, Pound did not give Denning an opportunity to explain the reasons for his convictions or those of Clayton and Hinsley. As Pound was Admiral of the Fleet and First Sea Lord, it was not possible for Denning to force his views on Pound; nor, for that matter, was Clayton. In the very structured, class-conscious and hierarchical Royal Navy of the time, it was simply not the done thing to venture strong and contrary opinions to its most senior officer. Denning, in his memoirs, regretted bitterly that he did not speak up more forcefully.

Historian Correlli Barnett had this to say about Pound in his book *Engage The Enemy More Closely*: 'It is not unjust to see in all of this a combination of Pound's old-fashioned naval authoritarianism and his well-known stubborn closed-mindedness – coupled with that lack of imaginative talent which is the mark of great commanders.'[10]

In Patrick Beesly's book *Very Special Intelligence; The Story of the Admiralty's Operational Intelligence Centre 1939–1945*, he quotes from Donald McLachlan's book *Room 39*, this conversation between Commander Norman Denning and Admiral Pound (apparently after a 2030 hours staff meeting and before the 2123 hours signal) based on the recollection of two witnesses:

> Pound: Do you know if Tirpitz has put to sea?
> Denning: If Tirpitz has put to sea you can be sure that we would have known about it very shortly afterwards, within four or six hours.
> Pound: Can you assure me that Tirpitz is still at anchor in Altenfjord?
> Denning: No. I shall have firm information only when Tirpitz has left.
> Pound: Can you at least tell me whether Tirpitz is ready to go to sea?
> Denning: I can at least say that she will not leave in the next few hours. If she were on the point of sailing the destroyer escort would have preceded her and made an anti-submarine sweep. They have not been reported by our submarines patrolling off Altenfjord.[11]

Milan Vego is of the opinion that, 'On this question [firm information only when *Tirpitz* has left], in fact, hung the entire future of Convoy PQ17.'[12] It is difficult to dispute this view.

After Pound left to visit the Submarine Tracking Room, Clayton and Denning were 'profoundly anxious that a decision which they both considered unnecessary and mistaken was about to be made. The First Sea Lord wanted positive evidence; all they had to offer was negative intelligence'.[13] In one of the great 'what-ifs' of World War II, one can only wonder what the result might have been had Denning and Clayton not been so reticent to speak up.

Pound's visit to the Submarine Tracking Room (where a two-storeyed wall map kept track of known and suspected U-boat locations) was run by the very astute Commander Rodger Winn, RNVR. Winn had a most incisive mind and was able to glean useful intelligence from seemingly innocuous U-boat signals. Winn was able to tell Pound that the situation developing with regard to CS One's operation was 'very serious indeed'. This information resolved Pope to withdraw CS One to the west.[14] However, while Pope's visit confirmed known information, it did not reveal the critical information to suggest that U-boats should expect their own surface units in their area – a fundamental precaution. A signal informing U-boats that surface units were not in their areas of operation was decrypted, but not until after Pound had left.

At 2000 or 2030 hours, depending on sources, a staff meeting called by Pound reviewed the situation as it was understood at that time. His advisers were opposed to dispersal. Nonetheless, after listening, eyes closed – some thought him asleep – he asked for a signal pad, wrote on it, then announced that the convoy was to be dispersed. This signal was sent at 2123 hours (refer to Chapter 6).

The Vice-Chief of the Naval Staff, Admiral Moore, then expressed the view that if the convoy was to scatter, then orders to do so must be issued promptly. Pound responded by issuing the second signal to scatter at 2136 hours. Contrary views seem to have fallen on deaf ears. Pound had weighed the evidence and concluded that it was insufficient to dismiss the possibility that *Tirpitz*, and others, were at sea, and that an attack on PQ 17 could occur in the early hours of 5 July. Clayton left the meeting depressed and discussed it with Denning, who tried to persuade him to approach Pound to change his mind. One factor perhaps influencing Pound's mind was that this was the first Anglo-American operation and it was under RN command. If the worst was to happen and the Home Fleet with Task Force 39 was to become involved in combat that went pear-shaped, and the USN suffered significant losses, could this result jeopardize that alliance? Well, maybe. But that is what the combined force had been conceived to do, not sail around, going through the motions of being an effective deterrent, and never come to action. That was hardly in the spirit of Nelson's Trafalgar message, 'Engage the enemy more closely!'

In hindsight, Pound was wrong – gravely wrong. To his credit, Pound accepted that it was a decision of such grave consequence that it was unfair to expect anyone else to share in accepting responsibility for it. His decision to withdraw the cruisers – which had already ventured further east than was intended – may have been justified, as they would have been no match for the heavier German forces and their return passage was threatened by the build-up of submarines, hence their ordered speed.

The question is: what else could have been done? One option would to have been to turn the convoy around, either as a temporary measure or to head back to Iceland to make another attempt and possibly draw *Tirpitz* on to the aircraft and guns of the Home Fleet, backed up by CS One's presence as a screening force. This option was mentioned in the HUSH signals of 25 June from the Admiralty to Commander in Chief Home Fleet mentioned in Chapter 4. Why go to so much trouble spelling out this option in detail and then ignore it? Why could this not have been ordered? Why else were two submarines attached to PQ 17, if not to threaten possible German attackers? Had *Tirpitz* and others been at sea, they may have been lured into a trap, possibly turning a British disaster into a German one.

Admiral Kuznetsov did not hold back in his memoirs:

> As I have pointed out our Allies had no reason to avoid an encounter with the Tirpitz. If necessary, they could have engaged her. During such discussions reference was made to cases, when our fighting ships left separate transport vessels without adequate cover. Of course, from a purely military point of view circumstances sometimes compel the commanding officer to sacrifice both transport vessels and fighting ships to avoid heavier losses. But the moral and ethical aspect cannot be ignored. We invariably adhered to the principle that it is wrong to leave comrades in trouble, particularly if they are unarmed. I reported the tragic case of Convoy PQ-17 to J.V. Stalin. He was displeased with the behaviour of the British naval command. It was inconceivable for all the fighting ships to abandon a convoy. It should be mentioned that the British command took this step though it enjoyed a tremendous superiority in forces. Stalin asked me: 'Was it necessary to abandon the convoy?' I replied that as far as I knew there were no serious reasons for that. Of course, the British had reasons to be wary of German battleships, particularly after the Bismarck had sunk the Hood. But this time just caution grew over into extreme caution. *Admiral Pound was unwilling to risk his capital ships for the sake of a convoy bound for the Soviet Union. It is a fact that in those days some of the Allied military leaders most reluctantly offered us aid.*[15]

However, the bigger question was: what was so special, what was so substantially different about PQ 17, as compared with PQ 13, that prompted the order to scatter? What happened to the received wisdom that a convoy always stuck together? When HX 84 scattered, it had a very weak escort and no backup. PQ 17 had a strong escort, a cruiser force and the Home Fleet nearby!

In PQ 13's case, *Tirpitz* was already at sea; it was a clear and present danger to PQ 13, and QP 8 particularly. Why was it that a surmised breakout of *Tirpitz*, in the mind of Pound alone, was enough to issue the order? Was the defence structure for PQ 17/QP 13 any less than that for PQ 13/QP 8? Admittedly, the Home Fleet/Distant Cover Force was, perhaps, a bit too distant at 2230 hours in the approximate position 75'N 3'E, which was about 450 miles west of the convoy and steering north-eastward, but this is easy to say with the benefit of hindsight.[16] Yet it had an aircraft carrier in its complement. Although Hitler's appreciation of naval matters took a back seat to his interference with army and air force issues, he had sufficient knowledge of them to understand the threat posed by carrier-borne aircraft, even if he was not fully aware of the inadequacies of the Royal Navy's obsolete aircraft (as regards their range, speed and armament) and their small number.

CHAPTER 8

Day 8, Saturday, 4 July 1942

According to the First Cruiser Squadron's operation orders, the primary objective was to deliver PQ 17 to Russia. Beyond that, the objective was to bring the enemy to action with the Battle Fleet/Distant Cover Force and the Cruiser Covering Force. To increase the chances of both objectives being successful, PQ 17 could reverse direction having reached approximately 10° and lure the German force away from their bases and into the Allied submarine zones.

But Hamilton had his orders. Whether he approved of them or not was irrelevant; they had to be obeyed. There was no room for a to-and-fro discussion on the subject. Despite the fact that *Norfolk*'s Walrus was making use of the long daylight to be aloft scouting, at 2230 hours Hamilton wheeled his force, passed ahead of PQ 17 and down its eastern flank at 25 knots heading west, positioning it between the convoy and the presumed direction of the enemy.

Hamilton was concerned what effect this apparent desertion would have on the morale on board the merchant ships. The scarcity of real information from the Admiralty as to the position and strength of the German ships did not explain the scattering of the convoy. Indeed, it only falsely intensified the anxiety, particularly with Commander Broome, who believed – quite reasonably – that Hamilton must have been in possession of more detailed information. He wasn't. Hamilton had simply obeyed orders, even though his instinct was to remain in a covering position while the convoy dispersed.

Broome had his orders too, to alter course by 45 degrees and head the convoy north-east, although they were less clear than Hamilton's. The way in which such a dispersal was to be put into effect was not some extemporized procedure; it was the subject of a detailed convoy manual. Upon the 'Execute' signal, each ship was expected to divert 10 degrees outwards from its inner neighbour and increase to maximum speed in doing so. In effect, the convoy would open up like a fan, with the very centre column alternating – odd numbers to starboard, even numbers to port. Their direction was still basically east.

At 2215 hours, when the convoy was at 75°55'N, 27°52'E, Broome hoisted the requisite signal (presumably predetermined in the convoy's sailing instructions). Some sources refer to this as a white flag with a red diagonal cross; the letter 'V'. Normally, this code flag, hoisted on its own, signals 'I require assistance'. Broome needed more than assistance; he needed a miracle if PQ 17 was to survive.

Other sources say that this was a numeral pendant/pennant (that is, a long, truncated V-shaped flag), which would make it numeral '8'. In the International Code of Signals, a numeral pendant/

pennant is not a message on its own. Coupled with, for example, 'W' plus 'Y', it means 'the state of the sea is very high'.[1]

Broome flashed a 'join me' message to all his escorts. The convoy commodore on SS *River Afton*, Dowding, hoisted his answering pennant to the dip (below the yardarm), indicating he had acknowledged Broome's signal flag but did not understand it. *Keppel* closed and drew alongside *River Afton* so they could confer by megaphone. Broome then confirmed the order. He finished by shouting across to Dowding, 'Sorry to leave you like this. Goodbye, and good luck. It looks like a bloody business', then wheeled away with five destroyers to join up with Hamilton and CS One. Dowding, no doubt dismayed and reluctant, ordered the pennant to be hoisted close-up, then lowered smartly – the signal to execute the dispersal. He was no longer commodore of PQ 17; it did not have one. It was every ship for itself, every man for himself.[2]

CHAPTER 9

Day 9, Bloody Sunday, 5 July 1942

At 1517 hours, the Home Fleet was in approximate position 73°35'N, 2°0'E, steering south-westerly, when the Admiralty signalled again. It was presumed by the Admiralty that enemy ships were north of Tromsø, but it was by no means certain that they were at sea. However, by then, the distance between the warships heading west at some 20-plus knots and the merchant ships heading in a generally east direction at best possible speed, would have been well over 120 miles. Broome's destroyers were ordered to refuel from *London* and *Norfolk*. By 1630 hours, all destroyers had been topped up, a necessary precaution if battle was to be joined.

At 1740 hours, an FW 200 Condor reported CS One's position as 74°30'N, 07°40'E. Knowing that his force had been spotted, Hamilton broke radio silence at 1830 hours and informed the Home Fleet – repeated to the Admiralty – that he was being shadowed and of his position (74°22'N, 06°40/53'E), speed (19 knots) and course (230°), plus advising that all destroyers were now in company. Admiral Tovey is reported to have queried how the destroyers from Broome's First Escort Group happened to be there.[1] Yet where did Tovey expect them to be: scattered piecemeal amongst a scattered convoy? Given the current perception of the German threat, surely they were adjudged to be far more use as a cohesive group attached to Cruiser Squadron One. On the other hand, one could argue: which was more important, protecting merchant ships from submarine and/or air attack – getting the convoy through – or bolstering naval assets considered to be at a somewhat indeterminate risk?

The Home Fleet had spent 4 July cruising about 150 miles north-west of Bear Island and had turned south-west during the morning of 5 July, heading for Scapa Flow, and was then some 120 miles south-west of CS One.

Around midnight, 4/5 July, *U-456* reported the convoy's dispersal and, more ominously for the convoy, the withdrawal of all warships. Would *Unternehmen Rösselsprung* be put into effect? Indeed, was there now any need for it? To settle the issue for the Germans, aerial reconnaissance revealed the Home Fleet was moving north-east to cover Hamilton's withdrawal, meaning the threat to *Rösselsprung* from carrier-borne aircraft had disappeared. Nonetheless, permission had to be sought from Raeder, who had to convince Hitler. In anticipation of a favourable response, *Tirpitz*, *Scheer* and *Hipper*, along with seven destroyers and two torpedo-boats, were out at sea by 1500 hours.

Then three things happened that changed the dynamics of the situation.

The U-class submarine *Unshaken* underway in April 1942. (Public Domain)

First, at 1700 hours, the Russian submarine *K 21* reported that it had sighted *Tirpitz* and *Scheer*, plus eight destroyers, at 71°25'N, 23°40'E, steering 45°. Despite the submarine commander's opinion to the contrary, no hits were received from the two torpedoes launched at *Tirpitz*.

Second, at 1816 hours, a patrolling RAF Consolidated PBY Catalina reported 11 strange ships at 71°31'N, 27°10'E, course 65°, speed 10 knots.

Finally, either the small U-class submarine *Unshaken* or the larger T-class *Trident* (depending on sources) also made sightings at 2029 hours of *Tirpitz*, *Scheer* and *Hipper*, along with six destroyers and eight aircraft, at 71°30'N, 28°40'E, making 22 knots on a course of 60°. *Trident*'s actual message is quoted by Broome, so I am inclined to accept this source.[2]

Hitler's permission to launch the *Rösselsprung* had apparently been confirmed earlier that day at 1137 hours (sources vary). When it became apparent that CS One was moving west and the Home Fleet was some 450 miles from the convoy and U-boats, and that aircraft were taking a heavy toll of the scattered merchant ships, there seemed no point in continuing the operation. The 'return to harbour' orders were given at 2132 hours, and at 2152 hours, when at 71°38'N, 31°05'E, the force headed for the safety of Altenfjord. Observant readers will note the disparity of times and the course of *Tirpitz* and others. Even if there was some inaccuracy as to the precise complement of the force, one factor was constant – the 60–65° course was towards Norway, not in the direction of PQ 17.

In chess terms, *Unternehmen Rösselsprung* was less a Knight's Move than it was a pawn's *en passant.*[3] It was simple in concept but difficult to execute. It required a quick massing and concentrated employment of German forces over a short duration, preferably neutralizing the merchant ships sufficient to be finished off at will by submarines and aircraft without exposing the force to carrier-borne aircraft.

Almost inevitably, PQ 17 broke up into small groupings upon receipt of the order to scatter. It would have been difficult, and foolish, to go it alone. There was still some safety to be had in small numbers – providing, of course, that everyone could keep up the pace of the fastest ship. The anti-aircraft *Palomares* had the most senior RN officer now present (Acting Captain J. H. Jauncey) on board. He took the Walrus that had run out of petrol in tow and ordered two Halcyon-class minesweepers, namesake *Halcyon* and *Britomart*, to follow. This was an order I am sure their captains would have accepted readily, considering the warning radar and anti-aircraft firepower of *Palomares*. One corvette, *Dianella*, was to stand by the two surfaced submarines, P 614 and P 615, and corvettes *Poppy* and the French *La Malouine* were directed east. The captain of *Palomares*'s anti-aircraft auxiliary sister-ship, *Pozarica*, Acting Captain E. D. W. Lawford, tried to re-form part of the convoy, against the spirit of the 'scatter' order. The Admiralty gave a specious approval, indicating that the most likely surface attack would be

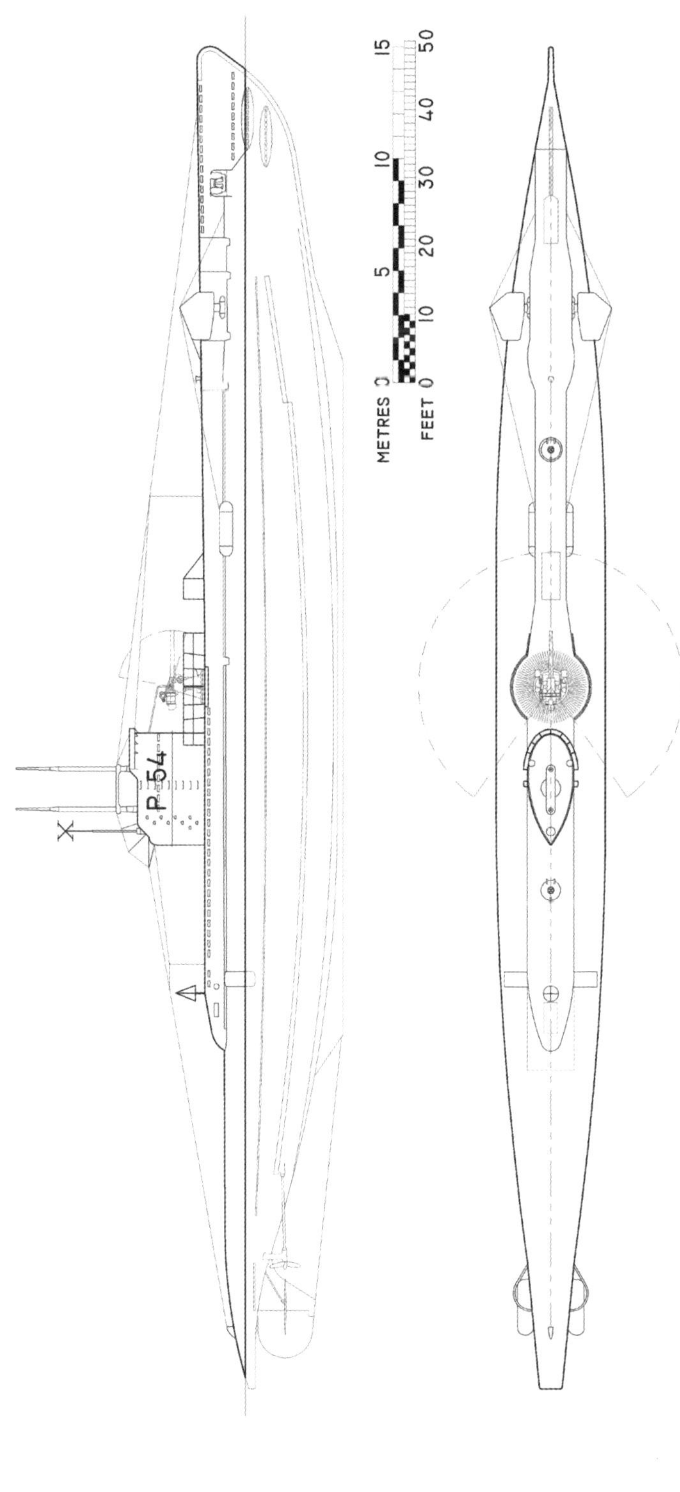

Notes on the drawing: *The U-class submarines were designed as training submarines but proved so adept that they were used successfully as fleet submarines, particularly in the North Sea and Mediterranean. A total of 49 were built in three separate groups, reflecting improvements resulting from operational experience.*

A typical S-class submarine. Note the prominent jumping wires fore and aft to assist submarines to pass under defensive nets. (Public Domain)

almost 24 hours later on the night of 5 July or morning of 6 July. Lawford collected the rescue ship *Rathlin*, corvettes *Poppy* and *La Malouine* and made for Nova Zemlya. The American SS *Bellingham* (ex-*West Himrod*) belligerently declined and proceeded independently.[4] Four other American ships formed themselves into a tight group with *Palomares*: *Benjamin Harrison*, *Daniel Morgan*, *Fairfield City* and *John Witherspoon*.

Another little group coalesced around the A/S trawler *Ayrshire: Ironclad*, *Troubadour* and, later, *Silver Sword*, all heading into the comparative safety of the ice pack and as far as possible away from aircraft attack – around 20 miles into the ice according to some sources.[5] *Ayrshire*'s commanding officer, Lieutenant L. J. A. Gradwell, showed remarkable leadership despite being a hostilities-only RNVR officer. He sent his second-in-command across the ice with orders for the three merchant ships. Decks were cleared for supplementary armament, white paint from *Troubadour* was applied to the starboard sides of all ships and this hasty camouflage – taking about five hours – helped prevent reconnaissance aircraft to the south spotting this grouping. Fires were ordered banked and,

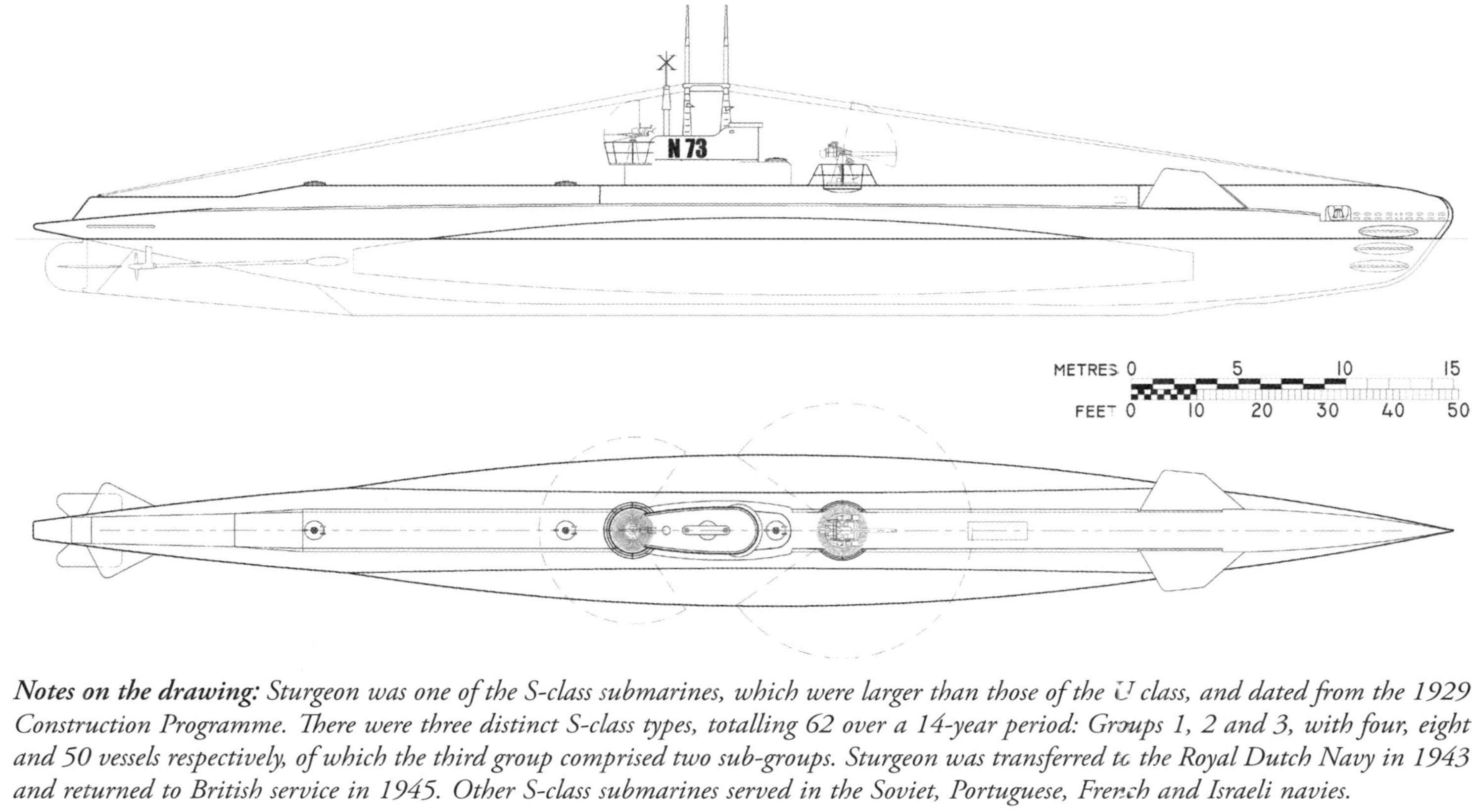

Notes on the drawing: *Sturgeon was one of the S-class submarines, which were larger than those of the U class, and dated from the 1929 Construction Programme. There were three distinct S-class types, totalling 62 over a 14-year period: Groups 1, 2 and 3, with four, eight and 50 vessels respectively, of which the third group comprised two sub-groups. Sturgeon was transferred to the Royal Dutch Navy in 1943 and returned to British service in 1945. Other S-class submarines served in the Soviet, Portuguese, French and Israeli navies.*

Auxiliary anti-aircraft vessel *Pozarica*. (Public Domain)

according to some accounts, guns on some of the American M3 tanks were manned.[6] I find the last-mentioned hard to believe. First, I am not at all sure that it would be standard operating procedure for tanks to be shipped with ammunition aboard. Second, even if this was the case, what expertise would merchant seamen have in operating the guns; a 3-inch main weapon in a casement with limited travel and a 37 mm gun in a turret?

In contrast, the crew of *Samuel Chase* stopped their ship about 1030 hours and abandoned it, believing they were being overhauled by a U-boat. Having stood off for two hours, the crew reboarded, hoisted the lifeboats, raised steam and proceeded somewhat sheepishly. The crew of *Alcoa Ranger* discussed capitulation after a FW 200 Condor circled but flew off. *Alcoa Ranger* (ex-*Sarcosie*) was what was commonly called a Hog Islander, being one of the 122 emergency war cargo ships built

One of the hastily camouflaged merchantmen in the group with HMT *Ayrshire*. Note the hastily applied white paint and the lifeboat swung out, ready to be lowered. (Public Domain)

to design 1022 for the United States Shipping Board and completed on 9 May 1919, too late for the conflict.

A much-enlarged photograph of what is believed to be HMT *Ayrshire* in Icelandic waters. (Public Domain)

Pan Kraft (ex-*West Kader*, ex-*New York*) was also a standard war emergency design, number 1019, of 5,721 GRT for the Emergency Fleet Corporation and completed in 1919. It was abandoned after being damaged in a high-level bombing attack, and was subsequently set on fire by a Ju 88.

At sometime late on 4 July, *Empire Byron* – a recently completed Type Ba standard tramp ship – was torpedoed by a Heinkel He 111 bomber of KG 26, but managed to keep going at reduced speed. Its end came at 0827 hours when torpedoed by *U-703* on its fifth attempt. Survivors were picked up by the corvette *Dianella* and landed at Arkhangelsk on 16 July, except for one passenger, a British Army captain who was taken prisoner by *U-703* as he had knowledge of the operation of the Churchill tanks that were either being delivered or scheduled to be delivered.

Carlton was pursued by *U-88* for three hours. At 1015 hours, the submarine fired a torpedo which hit *Carlton* but failed to detonate. A second torpedo struck amidships and the 5,000 barrels of oil exploded, collapsing bulkheads. It sank on an even keel within 10 minutes, taking 37 American-built tanks with it. Ten hours after the attack, having been spotted earlier by a Heinkel He 115, other Heinkels and a larger Dornier Do 24 flying boat took 26 of the survivors to Billefjord, the others choosing to sail for the Murman coast. They made landfall at Tufjord in northern Norway 19 days later.

Four ships in the *Palomares* group had become detached. About 1500 hours, *Daniel Morgan* was attacked by Ju 88s; another five attacked at 1800 hours, with three near-misses causing number four and five holds to flood and the ship to list to starboard. At 2252 hours, *U-88* hit *Daniel Morgan* with two torpedoes and it sank stern-first soon afterwards. The survivors were picked up around 0800 hours on 6 July by the Russian tanker *Donbass*, which dropped anchor at Ioanka two days later and then proceeded for the White Sea and Molotovsk.[7]

Around mid-afternoon, *Honomu* (an EFC Design 1079 built by Skinner and Eddy in 1919) was to the west, proceeding independently, when it was discovered by three submarines: *U-88*, *U-334* and *U-456*. *U-456* struck *Honomu* with two torpedoes: one around number three hold and another near number four hold. Nineteen crew were killed; of the 37 survivors, the vessel's master, Captain Frederick Strand, was taken prisoner on board *U-88*. *Honomu* (ex-*Edmore*, ex-*Grays Harbour*) was a 6,800-ton war emergency order by the United States Shipping Board.

Around the same time (records are imprecise), the British *Earlston* entered into a gun duel with a tailing submarine, forcing it to submerge, where its underwater speed could not keep up with *Earlston*. However, the ship's luck did not hold. It was bombed by ubiquitous Ju 88s, and near misses were so damaging that they shifted its engine off its mountings. A torpedo from *U-334*

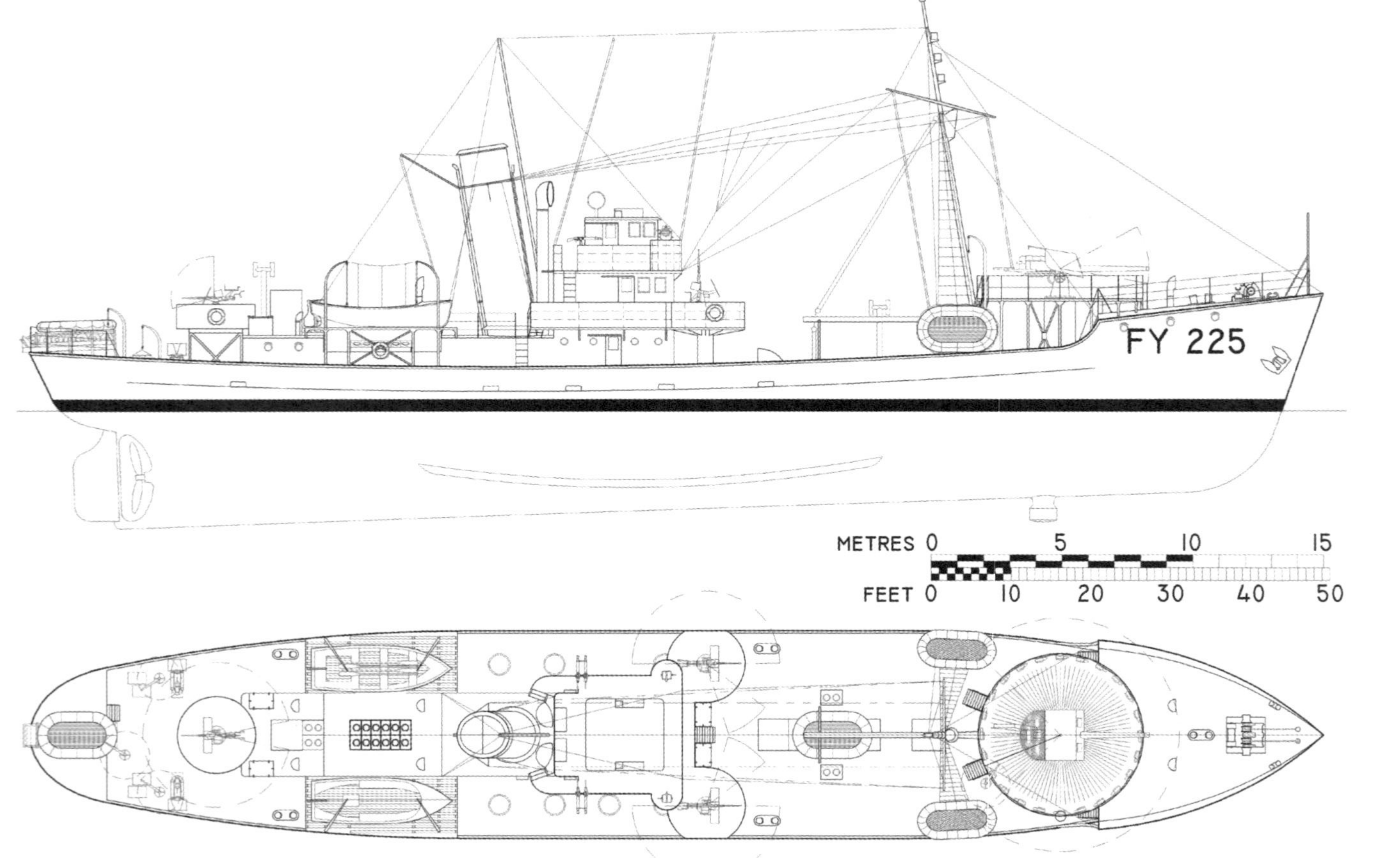

***Notes on the drawing**: I could not find details about HMS or HMT* Ayrshire, *let alone a drawing to work from, no matter how basic. The only photograph attributed to* Ayrshire *is the IWM's #FL 1284, 'Underway off Iceland', and it's a long-distance photograph at that. This illustration is based upon a drawing of the trawler* Bedfordshire, *built in 1935 and 443 tons as compared with* Ayrshire *built in 1938 and 540 tons (Denton & Colledge), with adjustments, modifications, armament added etc., as was fairly typical for trawlers taken up from trade and used as ASW (anti-submarine warfare) escorts.*

A sister-ship to both *Pan Atlantic* and *Pan Kraft*, SS *Norranus*. (Public Domain)

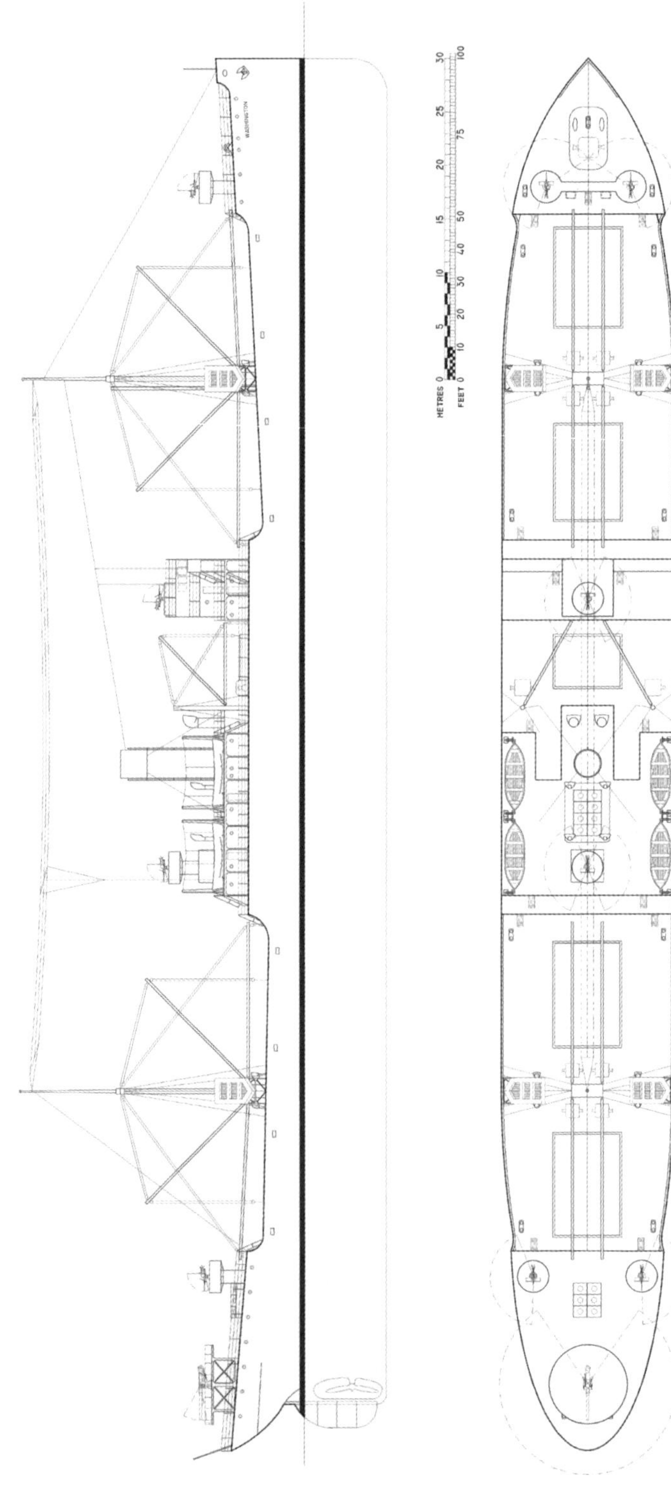

Notes on the drawing: Pan Kraft, Pan Atlantic *and* Washington *were all examples of the United States' emergency merchant shipbuilding project carried out by the Emergency Fleet Corporation on behalf of the United States Shipping Board, in this case design 1019 and usually referred to as being the Ferris Standard Type. Details of its defensive armament were unavailable and I have drawn it as fairly typical of the times, the aft deckhouse not leaving room for a 4-inch LA (low-angle) gun.*

This is one of SS *Empire Byron*'s eight sister-ships, *Empire Ballad*, post-war. The original slim funnel has been replaced by a more substantial one. Five of the nine ships were sunk and two badly damaged in World War II. (Public Domain)

The painting of SS *Carlton*'s hull with the upswept dark colour could not hide the absence of sheer on this Hog Islander. (Public Domain)

SS *Honomu*, taken when it was known as *Edmore*. (Public Domain)

SS *Fairfield City*. (Public Domain)

struck number two hold and *Earlston* broke in two. Again, the master, the Norwegian H. J. Stenwick, was taken prisoner.

Fairfield City also fell victim to the Ju 88s that attacked *Daniel Morgan*, despite a spirited defence from its Armed Guard. At 1645 hours, two or three bombs struck the port side near number two hatch and it sank at 1740 hours. Thirty-four survivors of the attack got away in three of the four lifeboats, and at 1850 hours they set off for Novaya Zemlya, about 250 miles distant.

Peter Kerr, a Japanese-built Type 1127 for the EFC, had evaded torpedoes from no less than seven attacking He 115 floatplanes by judicious use of rudder and engine speed. As they flew off around 1700 hours, they were replaced by four hunting Ju 88s of KG 30, and this time three bombs scored direct hits and others near misses. On fire and sinking by the head, *Peter Kerr* was abandoned just before the flames took hold and it exploded. It was built by Osaka Iron Works in Japan and completed in June 1920 as *Eastern Sailor*.

Washington (ex-SS *West Cayote*, a Design 1019, Ferris type, World War I EFC emergency-build ship) had been bombed and damaged earlier. About 30 minutes after the attack on *Peter Kerr*, *Washington* was subjected to strafing followed by a bombing, which disabled its steering and increased the leaks sustained earlier. Fortunately, the decision to abandon ship was made and effected before 350 tons of TNT exploded.

Bolton Castle and *Paulus Potter* were the next targets when east-north-east of Bear Island, attacked by Ju 88s of KG 30 and suffering direct bomb damage and near misses. *Bolton Castle* caught fire and then sank when a bomb entered number two hold and exploded a cargo of bombs it was carrying. *Paulus Potter* was abandoned after sustaining two bomb

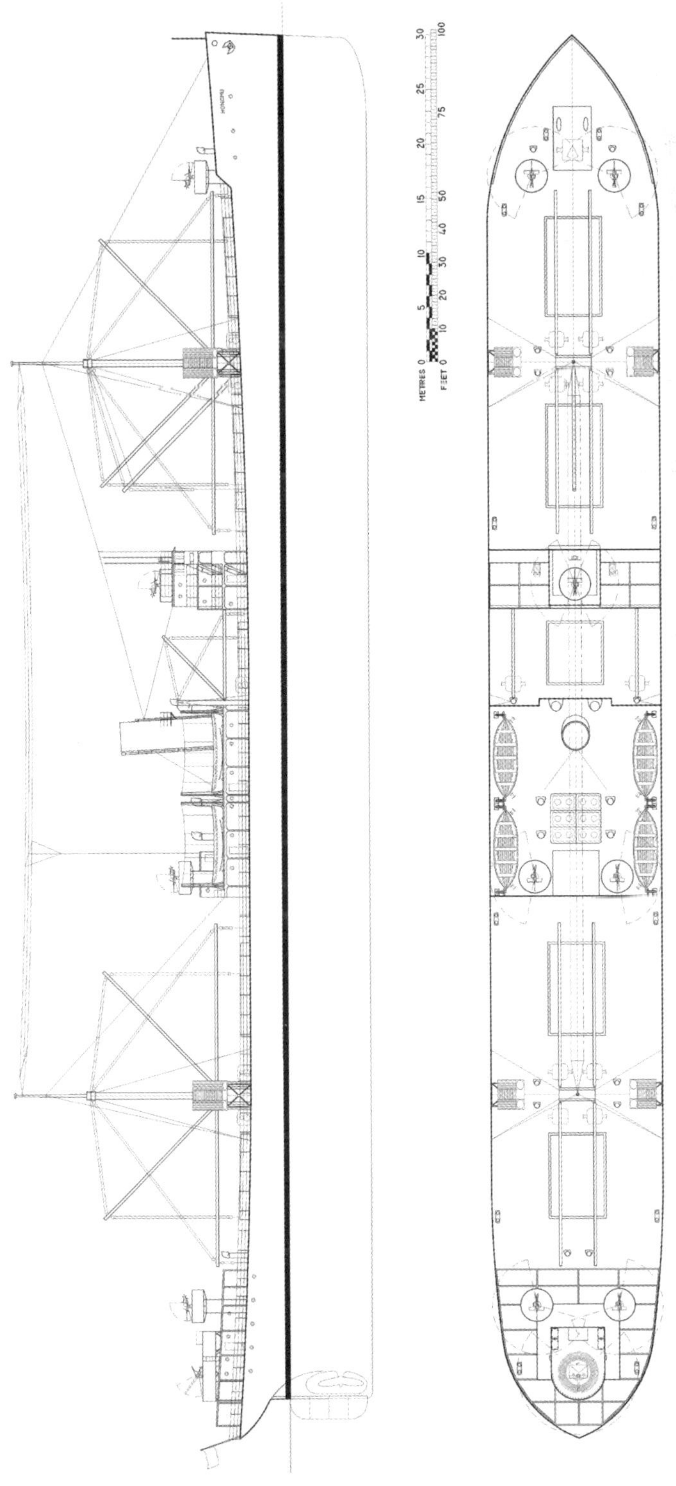

Notes on the drawing: Honomu *was another EFC design, 1079, one of 19 built by Skinner & Eddy, with a further 39 cancelled at war's end. It was completed in 1919 as* Edmore *and then* Grays Harbor *in 1937 for the Matson Line. A raked funnel was untypical of the time.*

SS *Eastern Admiral*, sister-ship to *Eastern Sailor* which was renamed *Peter Kerr* in 1923 due to a change of ownership. (Public Domain)

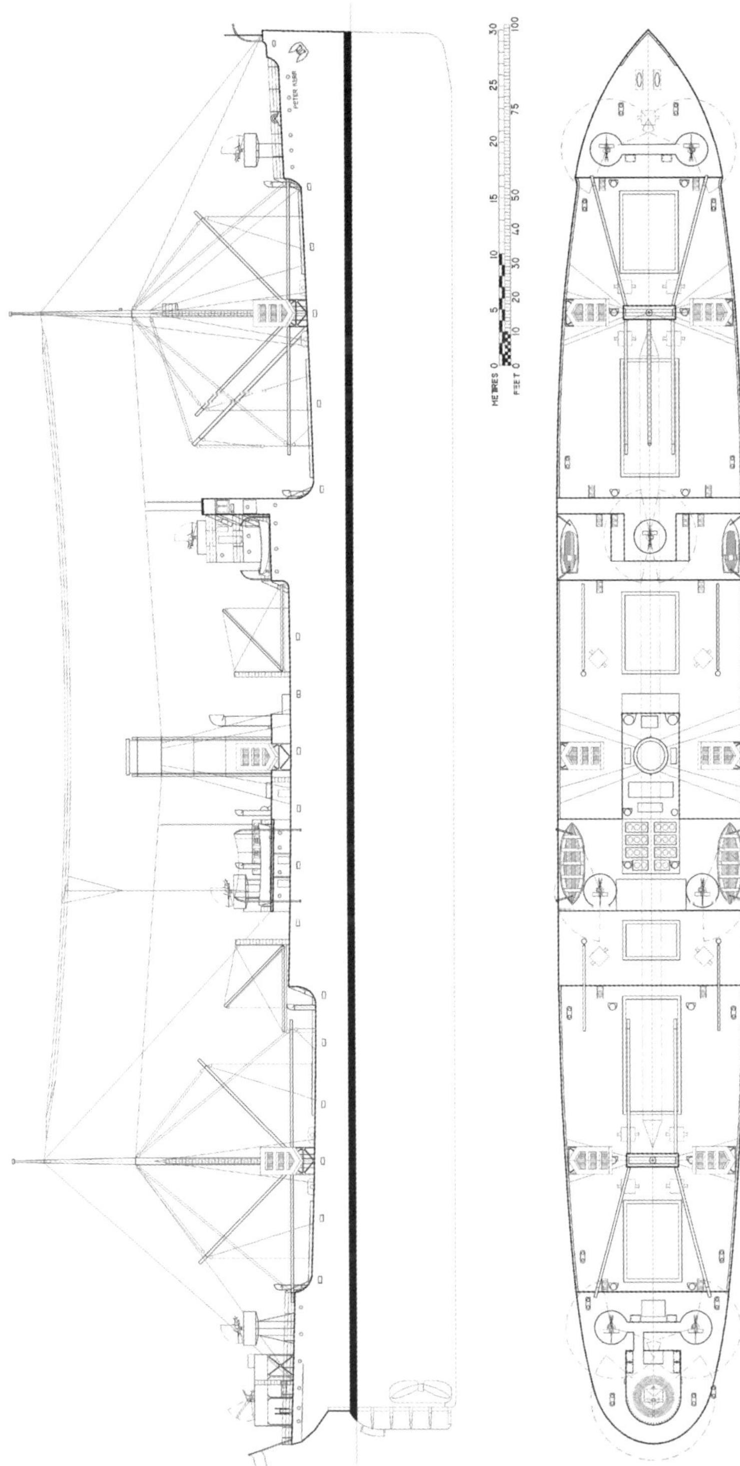

Notes on the drawing: SS Peter Kerr *was built in Japan for the EFC Design 1127 and is often referred to as the Osaka type, after the builder. There is nothing particularly significant about its design, following the then-common layout, except that the second and fifth holds (forward of the bridge and aft of the superstructure) are larger than normal and there is a small number four hatch served by goal-post derricks aft of the engine casing.*

The EFC Design 1019 SS *West Norranus*, a sister-ship to SS *Washington* (ex-SS *West Cayote*). Photo taken circa June 1920. (Public Domain)

SS *Lancaster Castle*, sister-ship to SS *Bolton Castle*. (Public Domain)

Photograph taken from *U-255* of the abandoned Dutch ship SS *Paulus Potter*. (Public Domain)

This photograph shows the last moments of one of PQ 17's merchantmen still flying its barrage balloon. (Public Domain)

The rescue ship MV *Zaafaran* in commercial service before being converted. (Public Domain)

This photograph is of one of RFA *Aldersdale*'s sister-ships, RFA *Bishopdale*. Although taken post World War II, note the gun-tubs are still in place on the forecastle, on the bridge and fore and aft of the funnel. (Public Domain)

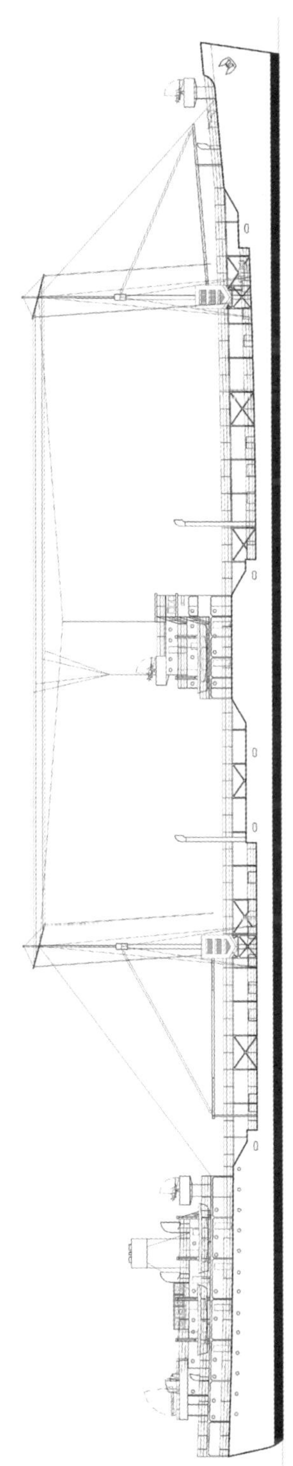

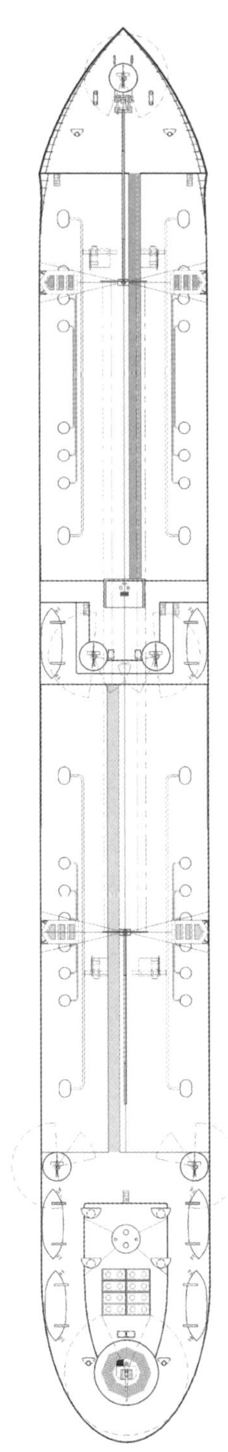

***Notes on the drawing:** RFA* Aldersdale *was a Dale-class freighting tanker, according to the comprehensive Royal Fleet Auxiliary site www.historicalrfa.org. Like its 18 sister-ships, it was originally built for commercial use but was requisitioned by the MoWT. This drawing is based on photographs which, alas, provide no detail as to the deck layout of the various pipes, valves, pumps and hatches related to its use as a tanker.*

hits as the crew believed that it would soon sink. The 76 survivors reached Novaya Zemlya on 10 July. On 14 July, they met up with survivors from *Washington* and headed south, finding the abandoned *Winston-Salem*, from where they were rescued on 17 July and arrived at Arkhangelsk on 24 July. *Paulus Potter* was found drifting on 13 July by *U-255*. After trying unsuccessfully to get the engines started, *Paulus Potter* was sunk by a torpedo from the U-boat at 0825 hours.

Olopana had been attacked earlier and had ignited smoke floats to give the impression of being on fire. Unexpectedly, various lifeboats from *Bolton Castle*, *Paulus Potter* and *Washington* all refused the offer of rescue, preferring the known risk of ice and cold to head for Novaya Zemlya. *Olopana* (ex-*Bearport*, ex-*Golden Mountain*) was an emergency war construction for the EFC to design 1015, commonly called the Moore & Scott type.

At 2102 hours, *River Afton* – a veteran of no less than 42 convoys – was torpedoed in the engine room by *U-703*. The ship exploded and broke in two after torpedoes at 2105 and 2122 hours. Twenty-three of the crew were lost, but 33 survivors, including Commodore J. C. K. Dowding, were picked up by the corvette *Lotus* and landed at Matochkin, Novaya Zemlya.

Fleet oiler RFA *Aldersdale*, in company with the rescue ship *Zaafaran*, *Ocean Freedom* and the minesweeper *Salamander*, was heading doggedly east when it was bombed by three Ju 88s from astern. *Aldersdale* was carrying a part-cargo of aviation petrol. The first and second aircraft scored some near misses, which shook but did not stop the ship, and strafed the decks. The third Ju 88 came in at an even lower angle of attack, and a terrific explosion appeared to lift the ship out of the water. Its engines were wrecked and immediately stopped. *Aldersdale* rapidly started taking in water and was abandoned by the crew. Fifty-four of the survivors were picked up by *Salamander*, but the oiler refused to sink; after some farcical attempts to sink it, it was left afloat. Between 1140 and 1300 hours on 7 July, *U-457* shelled *Aldersdale* and at 1456 hours torpedoes broke it in two, with both parts sinking 20 minutes later.

Convoy rescue ship *Zaafaran* was straddled by bombs which disabled its engines and, reluctantly, was abandoned. Sister-ship *Zamalek* managed to collect the survivors.

Illustrating the perils of submarine warfare, *U-334* was severely damaged on the evening of 5 July when off North Cape by bombs from a Luftwaffe Ju 88 and had to be escorted to nearby Neidenfjord by *U-456*.

CHAPTER 10

Days 10–15, Monday, 6 July–Saturday, 11 July 1942

Day 10, Monday, 6 July

During the night of 5/6 June, the Admiralty sent two Most Secret Immediate signals – at 2106 hours on 5 July to Commander in Chief Home Fleet and at 0230 hours on 6 July to PQ 17 escorts, repeated to Commander in Chief Home Fleet. Then at 0630 hours on 6 July, the Commander in Chief Home Fleet signalled Most Secret Immediate to CS One, all signals underlining a firm belief that *Tirpitz* would attack.

At 0700 hours, CS One was at 75°40'N, 16°00'E and reduced speed to 20 knots, and at 0930 hours set course heading for Jan Mayen Island in response to the Commander in Chief's signal of 0730 hours to

```
join me with destroyers.
```

It was suggested that if the Home Fleet was sighted by the Germans heading eastward, then it might deter *Tirpitz* and also place the aircraft of *Victorious* within range. At 0645 hours, course was altered to the north-east and an hour later a German reconnaissance aircraft passed overhead, above the clouds. Despite gunfire to attract its attention, the Home Fleet was not detected.

The *Pozarica* group, now with the rescue ship *Rathlin* in company but having difficulty keeping up, came across *Samuel Chase* the following morning, 6 July. Then it ran into fog. Contrary to the logic I expressed earlier, there was a certain feeling in the corvettes that had been ordered to join *Pozarica* that in doing so they were attached not to a protecting ship but rather one that was the most obvious target in any attack, by submarine or aircraft. The corvette *Lotus* had been ordered to turn back and scout along the ice-edge. This proved fruitful when it came upon three A/S trawlers and the *Pan Kraft*, still ablaze. *Lotus* was about to sink *Pan Kraft* by gunfire when it was warned of the 5,000 tons of TNT on board and wisely stood off. Raging fires finally disposed of *Pan Kraft* when it exploded at 0600 hours on 7 July.

At 0600 hours, the *Pan Atlantic* – sister-ship to *Pan Kraft* and built for the United States Shipping Board to design 1019 of 5,721 GRT in 1919 for its emergency war shipping programme – was heading independently for Cape Kanin at the head of the peninsula leading into Arkhangelsk, making a steady 12 knots with *U-88* and *U-703* in pursuit. A solitary Ju 88 then attacked, stowed ammunition blowing off the ship's bow. *Pan Atlantic* sank in three minutes, taking 26 crewmen with it.

The Russian tanker, *Donbass*, rescued the survivors of *Daniel Morgan*.

The Novaya Zemlya archipelago separates the Barents Sea from the Kara Sea. Matochkin Strait, between Novaya Zemlya's Severny Island and Yuzhny Island, is one of the largest fjords in the world and acted as a ship magnet. Using fog banks and sea-smoke, the *Alcoa Ranger*, *John Witherspoon*, *Empire Tide*, *Winston-Salem*, *Bellingham*, *Hartlebury* (Vice Commodore's ship) and *Olopana* all headed for the Strait.

At 1040 hours, CS One joined the Home Fleet, and at 1230 hours CS One and eight destroyers were detached to Seidsfjord (Iceland) and the Home Fleet turned south, both groups reaching harbour on 8 July. Earlier, at 0725 hours, when in visual range and when the fog lifted, Broome signalled Hamilton informing him of his last orders from the Admiralty and requesting that they should be amplified or amended as necessary.

At 1638 hours, *John Witherspoon* was torpedoed 20 miles from Novaya Zemlya by *U-255*, having been spotted by a FW 200 Condor on the morning of 5 July. One torpedo struck between number four and five holds, followed a minute later by one under the bridge. At 1655 hours, the submarine delivered the *coup de grâce*, breaking *John Witherspoon* in two, after which the ship was quickly abandoned. Some of the 50 survivors were picked up by *La Malouine* on 9 July and others by *El Capitan*, about which we will hear more later.

Late in the afternoon, the minesweeper *Britomart* rounded Cape Stolvoboi, the headland on the southern entrance to the western end of Matochkin Strait. Later, five other ships arrived and dropped anchor: *Palomares* (still towing the fragile Walrus amphibian), *Halcyon*, *Salamander*, *Zamalek* and *Ocean Freedom*. They were followed by three more: *Pozarica*, *Poppy* and *La Malouine*. That evening, Lawford ordered *La Malouine* to make a search for stragglers and it found *Hoosier*, *Benjamin Harrison*, *El Capitan* and *Samuel Chase*.

The corvette *Lotus* came upon three of the navy trawlers – *Northern Gem*, *Lord Middleton* and *Lord Austin* – which were all now running low on coal and gave them directions to Matochkin, where it arrived, loaded down with survivors, just before midnight. Unaware of the fact that *Tirpitz* was now at sea, they headed for the relative safety of the Lagerni anchorage in Matochkin Strait, where they arrived at dawn on 7 July.

At 2100 hours, Lieutenant Gradwell RNVR of *Ayrshire* forced it out of the encircled ice, far to the north-north-west from where the other dramas were playing out. Followed by *Ironclad*, *Troubadour* and *Silver Sword*, Gradwell led the procession slowly eastward, picking its way gingerly in poor visibility along the ragged edge of the ice, heading for the west coast of Novaya Zemlya.

Winston-Salem – an emergency war-built EFC Design 1037 from 1920 – was twice attacked by German aircraft on 6 July. It headed north-east as far as the ice permitted until reaching Novaya

HMT *Northern Gem*. Note the painted bow wave to suggest it is underway, despite the fact that it is at anchor, with a black ball in the rigging to indicate this and two men on a staging doing some painting. (Public Domain)

Zemlya, then followed the coast until running aground on a sand bank in Moller Bay in thick weather during the afternoon of 8 July.

Day 11, Tuesday, 7 July

At 0600 hours, *Pan Kraft*, abandoned and on fire since late on 5 July, finally exploded.

At about 0700 hours, *U-355* sank the abandoned and derelict oiler, *Aldersdale*, after a suggestion to salvage it had been summarily dismissed.

As 7 July dawned, the three trawlers *Northern Gem*, *Lord Middleton* and *Lord Austin* entered the Matochkin anchorage. The corvette *Dianella*, assigned to look after the two submarines (*P 614* and *P 615*), and the trawler *Ayrshire* were the only escorts now absent from the group at anchor. *Ocean Freedom*, a coal-burner, topped up the trawlers' bunkers. But, refuelled, where were they expected to go?

Captain Jauncey of *Palomares*, as the senior officer, called a meeting of all the captains at 1600 hours to discuss options, the most obvious of which was to keep heading east through the 100-mile-long twisting strait out into the Kara Sea. *Norfolk*'s Walrus made a reconnaissance of the strait and found the eastern end blocked with ice. Staying put seemed the best alternative, at least until a change in the weather might give a reformed convoy cover from prowling aircraft.

Lotus and *La Malouine* were deployed outside the entrance to Matochkin Strait to detect any U-boats.

Commodore Dowding in the Matochkin anchorage now had a convoy to command. But, where was it to go? On the one hand the anchorage was a haven, on the other a potential death trap. While the small force had quite good protection from the two anti-aircraft auxiliary cruisers, ammunition was limited. The ships could be bottled up in the anchorage and picked off at will by submarines and/or aircraft.

The rescue ship, *Rathlin*, had been unable to keep up with *Palomares*' impromptu convoy on 5 July and fell in with *Bellingham*. At 0740 hours, *Bellingham* was struck by a torpedo from *U-255* which failed to explode. This was not the first instance of torpedoes failing to explode and may have been due to icing-up of the contact fuse mechanism. *Bellingham* claimed to have shot down a FW 200 Condor the next day, but German records have no confirmation of this. It reached Arkhangelsk safely, only to meet its end on 22 September in Convoy QP 14 at the hands of *U-435*.

The busy *U-255* had actually fired two torpedoes at a range of some 6,000 metres, with two merchant ships as its target. Both missed. A single torpedo fired at 0927 hours then struck *Alcoa Ranger* on the starboard side at the number two hold, causing a heavy list. Fifteen minutes later, *Alcoa Ranger* had been abandoned by its 40 crewmen in three lifeboats, two of which reached Novaya Zemlya that day, with the third

SS *Bellingham*. (Public Domain)

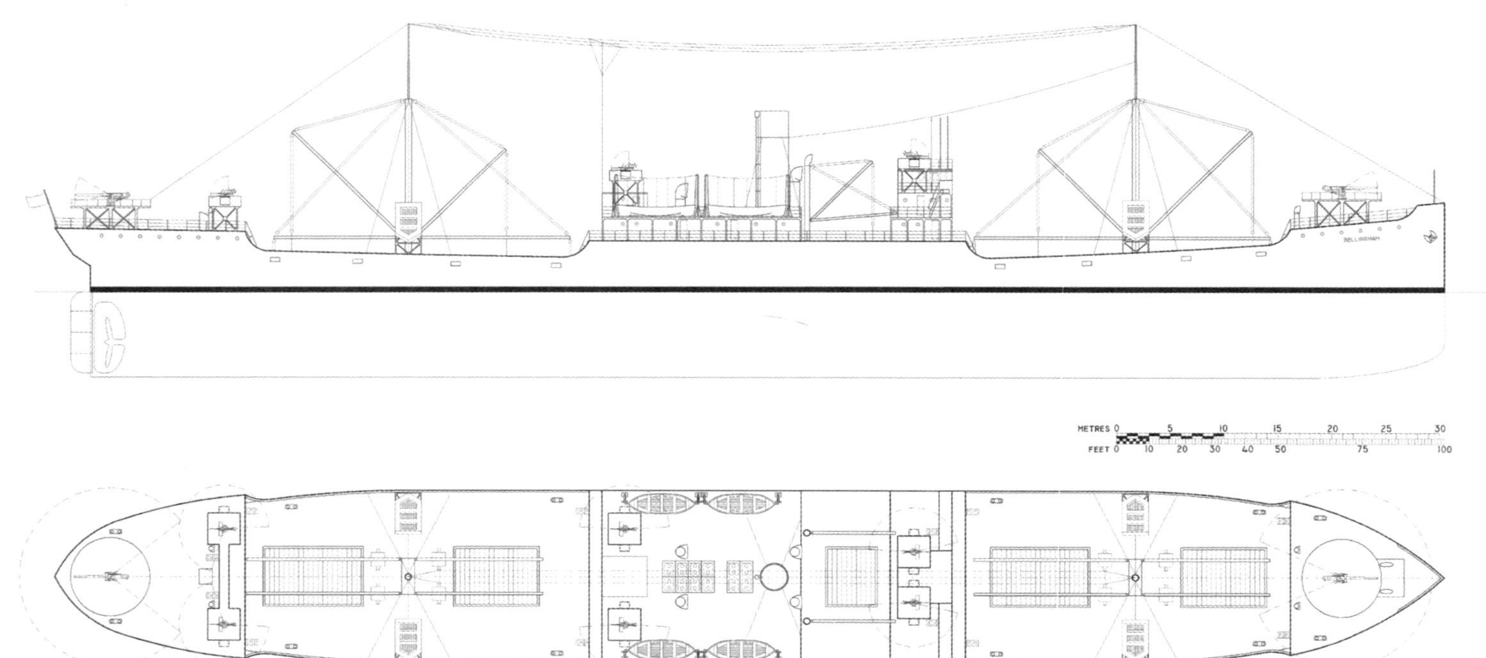

Notes on the drawing: *SS* Bellingham *was a typical example of the 111 of the standardized Design 1013 built for the Emergency Fleet Corporation, in this case one of 30 by Los Angeles Shipbuilding & Drydock Co. They were commonly referred to as the Robert Dollar type.* Bellingham *has been drawn as it was designed to be completed as* West Himrod*, with a 4-inch gun fore and aft but without the tall signalling mast amidships. Six 20 mm Oerlikons have been added in locations typical of Russian convoys.*

SS *Alcoa Ranger* (ex-SS *Sarcoxie*), a typical World War I Emergency Fleet Corporation Design 1022 Hog-Island type. (Public Domain)

SS *Hartlebury* in peace-time livery. (Public Domain)

reaching Cape Kanin a week later. *U-255* surfaced and headed towards the second ship, *Empire Tide*, but turned back to shell *Alcoa Ranger.* It was not until 1200 hours that it sank, having been subjected to at least 60 shells from a range of 100 metres. This was witnessed by *Empire Tide*, some miles to the north and proceeding independently, which turned around and headed for Moller Bay at the southern end of Novaya Zemlya.

At 1835 hours, the *Hartlebury*, proceeding on its own 17 miles south of Novaya Zemlya, was hit by two of three torpedoes that were fired by *U-355*. Without waiting to see if these were fatal, another torpedo was launched and then a fifth, at 1845 hours. *Hartlebury* sank by the bow, taking 36 tanks and seven aircraft with it. Thirty-eight crewmen perished. Seven survivors made it to Novaya Zemlya and were rescued by Russians, being transferred to *Empire Tide* and then to *La Malouine*, finally reaching Arkhangelsk on 25 July. Not so fortunate were the crewmen who were in a swamped lifeboat, of whom only four survived, while nine of the 14 on a raft succumbed to the cold before they made it to shore near the welcoming *Winston-Salem*. One of those lost was the convoy's Vice Commodore, Captain G. W. Stephenson.

At 1900 hours, Commodore Dowding – on *Lotus* – led his rag-tag convoy out of Matochkin Strait and into fog, and they immediately lost formation. *Benjamin Harrison* turned around and headed back. Whatever the reason, this decision saved the ship.

Day 12, Wednesday, 8 July

At 0100 hours, *Olopana* was heading for the White Sea when, about 10 miles west of Moller Bay, it was struck by *U-255*, now running low on torpedoes. *U-255* had manoeuvred ahead of *Olopana* in order to obtain the best short-range firing angle. The torpedo struck on the port side in the engine room; the explosion brought *Olopana* to a halt, blowing in all bulkheads and destroying a lifeboat. However, it did not sink. Forty-one of the 48 crew abandoned ship. At 0116 hours, the submarine surfaced and began firing at *Olopana*, which sank 20 minutes later. Two days later, the survivors made landfall in Moller Bay and were taken by a Soviet Consolidated PBY Catalina flying boat to Matochkin Strait, where they were put aboard *Empire Tide*, which reached Arkhangelsk on 24 July.

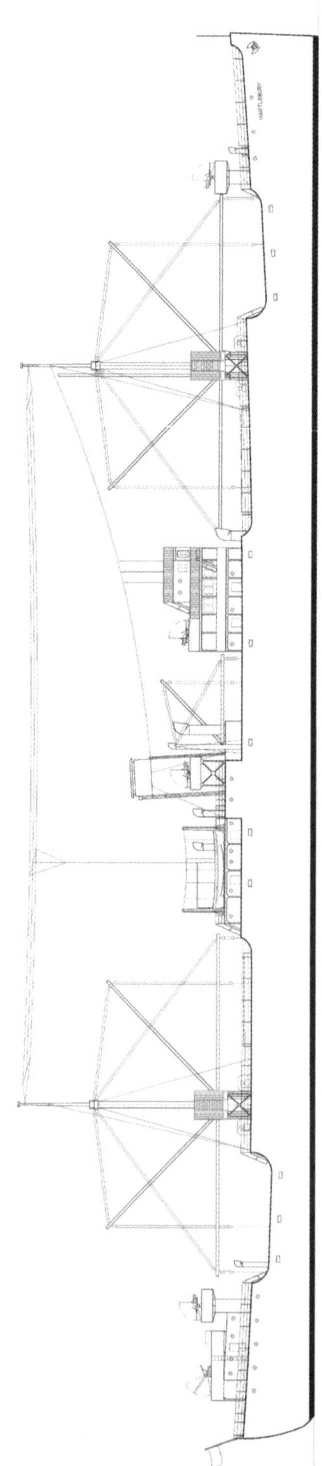

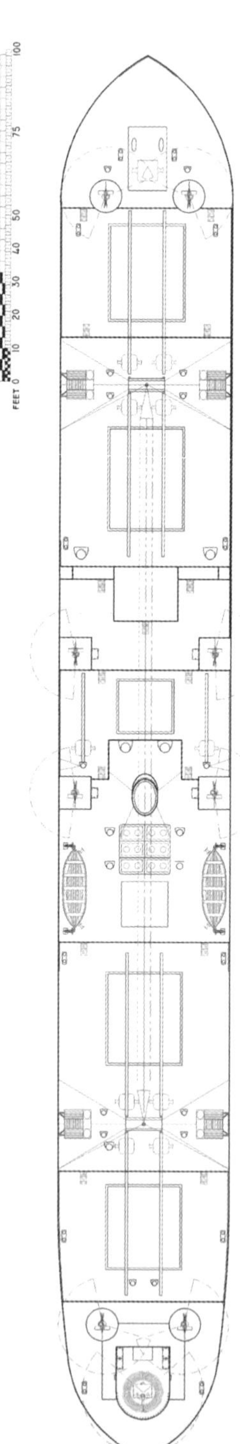

Notes on the drawing: Hartlebury *was drawn from two near-identical photos. It is an unusual configuration, having what could be termed a well deck fore and aft. This may have been to reduce the GRT by having a large shelter deck which was not part of the tonnage calculation. Its unusually large bridge structure was possibly passenger accommodation, although there are only two lifeboats.*

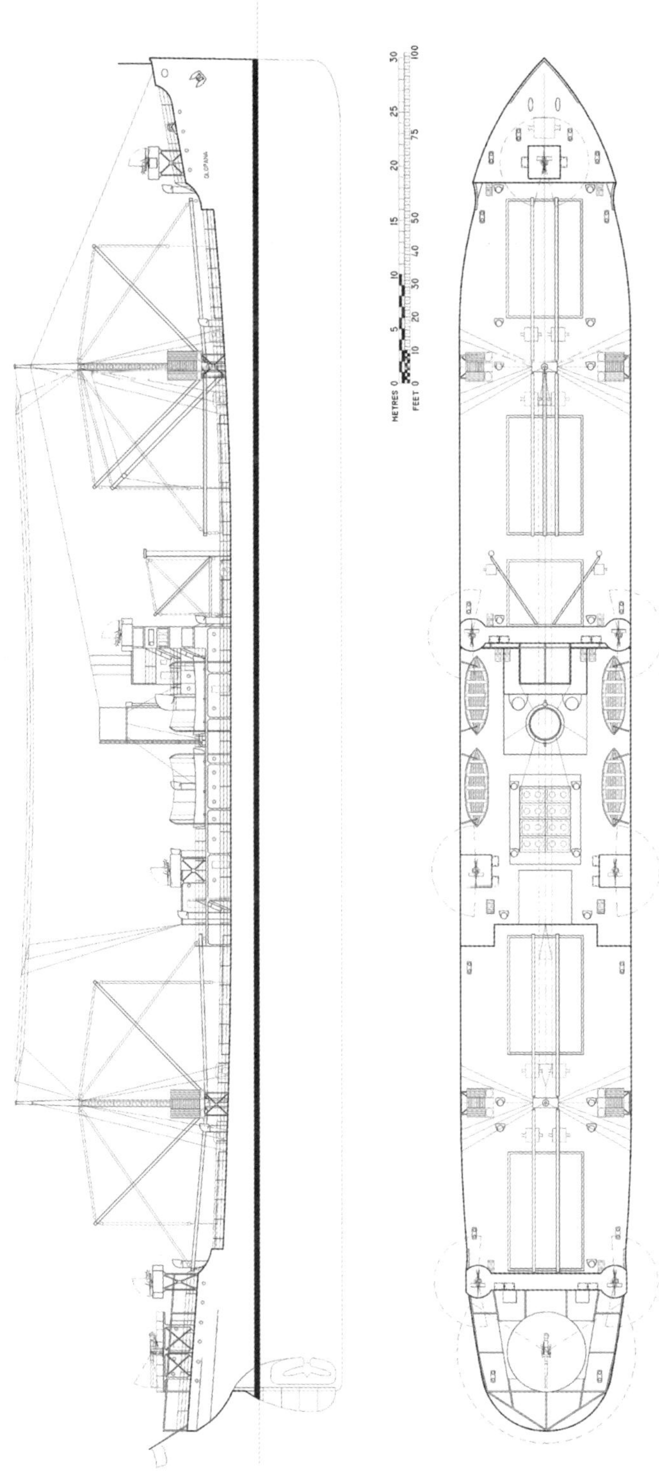

Notes on the drawing: SS Olopana *was yet another of the United States Shipping Board's initiatives implemented through the Emergency Fleet Corporation as Design 1015, more usually referred to as the Moore & Scott type, and is drawn as completed. It was conventional, for the time, except that it was refrigerated (in part) and had goalpost derricks in front of the bridge, probably to serve the refrigerated holds.*

The unmistakable lack of sheer distinguishes SS *Winston-Salem* as an Emergency Fleet Corporation Design 1022 Hog-Islander. (Public Domain)

At 0230 hours, *Bellingham* and *Rathlin* were making their way south, aiming for the entrance to Kola Inlet, ultimately surviving the ordeal. A Focke-Wulf 200 Condor circled and then attacked out of low cloud, only to be met by accurate fire, probably from *Rathlin*'s Bofors and 20 mm Oerlikons, promptly losing two of its four engines, catching fire and crashing into the sea.

The name 'Bellingham' and that part of Russia had something in common. John Bellingham, a Liverpool merchant, was imprisoned in Arkhangelsk for five years (*circa* 1806–11) for debt. After his release, he blamed the British government for lack of assistance and promptly shot and killed Prime Minister Spencer Perceval on 11 May 1812, the only such assassination of a sitting political leader in Britain. He was found guilty and hanged, only a week after the event.

At 1630 hours, Commodore Dowding's little flotilla ran into an ice-field, breaking up what little cohesion had been achieved. *Zamalek* was damaged forward on a submerged ice-ridge and spent some hours stuck before being able to work its way free, leaking forward. *El Capitan* sighted an orange sail and picked up 19 survivors from *John Witherspoon*. The three minesweepers managed to free themselves and, grouped together, joined with *Ocean Freedom* and *Samuel Chase* and two of the trawlers. A separate group formed around *Palomares* and *Pozarica*, comprising *Zamalek*, *El Capitan*, *Hoosier*, corvettes *Poppy* and *La Malouine* and the trawler *Lord Austin*. The balance of *John Witherspoon*'s survivors, 29 in total, were rescued.

Late on 8 July, *Winston-Salem* ran aground on North Gusini Shoal in thick weather while entering Moller Bay. Moller Bay must have appeared in the Sailing Directions as a suitable anchorage, judging by the number of ships which made for it. What the Directions may not have emphasized, or were vague about, was the presence of the North Gusini Shoal. Whatever the case, it was one of three ships from the convoy that ran aground on an island that had little cause to be visited other than by ships with local knowledge. Over the following days, a total of 120 survivors from three other ships sunk from the convoy arrived in their lifeboats. The crew of *Winston-Salem* began to construct a camp ashore in the event the ship was attacked and they had to abandon it.

The corvette *Dianella*, which had discharged its responsibilities with the two submarines it was escorting, was searching for survivors. However, searching for small boats was very much a hit-and-miss affair. *Olopana*'s survivors sighted a searching *Zamalek*, but their flares were unobserved. Similarly, they sighted two corvettes in mist but could not attract attention. On 10 July, they identified the North Gusini lighthouse, presumably located to warn of the shoals, and made it to shore in Moller Bay. A search party discovered the stranded *Winston-Salem*, and *Olopana*'s survivors joined those from other ships there.

Day 13, Thursday, 9 July

After three days hiding in the ice, Lieutenant Gradwell on *Ayrshire* held a conference with the masters in the very early hours and it was decided that they would proceed south to Matochkin Strait. With *Ironclad*, *Troubadour* and *Silver Sword* dutifully following in line astern, they entered a fjord in Northern Novaya Zemlya, where *Ayrshire* was able to transfer much-needed coal from *Troubadour*. Having accomplished this, they proceeded south and entered Matochkin Strait, where *Ironclad* and *Ayrshire* promptly ran aground, *Ayrshire* losing its projecting ASDIC submarine detection dome in the process. Here, they learned of the temporary presence of Dowding's convoy and the presence of survivors further south. *Ayrshire* went off to search and returned with 34 survivors from *Fairfield City*, whom *Ayrshire* took further into the strait to a primitive Russian hospital. *Benjamin Harrison* was duly discovered in the vicinity and was able to make contact with Arkhangelsk, as did *Empire Tide* in Moller Bay to the south.

When about 65 miles north-east of Iokanka on the western shore of the entrance to the large inlet leading to Arkhangelsk, the *Palomares* convoy was attacked by Ju 88s from KG 30 at 2000 hours. The ice had forced it west before it could turn on a welcome south-west heading.

The first stick of three bombs missed *Hoosier*, but the next two were near misses which damaged steam pipes and oil lines, disabled the engine and sprung plates. With *Hoosier* sinking slowly, the 53 crewmen abandoned ship and were picked up by *Poppy* and *La Malouine*. The sighting of *U-255* 4 miles astern put paid to the idea of putting a salvage crew aboard *Hoosier* and attempting a tow. Attempts to sink *Hoosier* by gunfire from the single 4-inch guns of the corvettes proved fruitless, and *U-376* sunk it at 0307 hours on 10 July. Aircraft from KG 30 continued to harry the ships, which were now getting low on ammunition. A call for air cover from the Soviets produced, as was typical in such cases, no result.

A German photograph, believed to be of SS *Hoosier* being sunk by *U-376*. (Public Domain)

Samuel Chase, despite violent changes of direction, was damaged by near misses.[1]

At some-time this day, the Russian tanker *Donbass* arrived at Molotovsk

The Soviet tanker *Donbass*. (Public Domain)

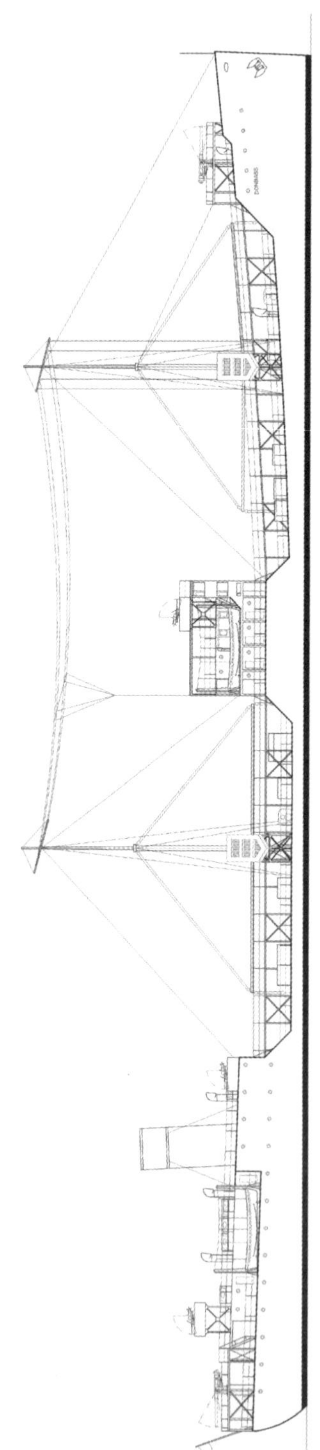

METRES 0 5 10 15 20 25 30
FEET 0 10 20 30 40 50 75 100

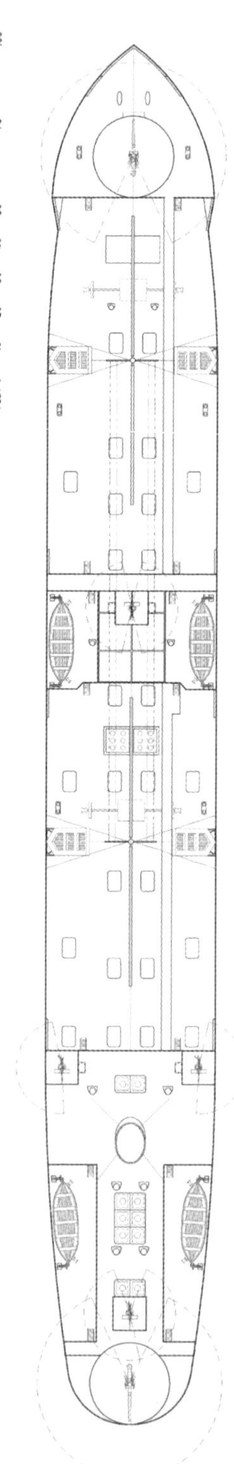

Notes on the drawing: *Unfortunately, but not unexpectedly, finding details about the Soviet ships proved impossible.* Donbass *was an Elba-class tanker, built in 1935. The photograph was the only one I could find and the drawing is an interpretation of how* Donbass *may have looked. Armament may have been a mixture of Soviet and Lend-Lease.*

with survivors from the *Daniel Morgan*, some of whom had manned anti-aircraft guns on *Donbass* and, apparently, damaged an attacking Ju 88.

Day 14, Friday, 10 July

El Capitan met its end at 0200 hours. A three-bomb near miss broke open the after-peak, ruptured the number four hold bulkhead and demolished the starboard side of the engine room. Two hours later, *El Capitan* was attacked again, with another near miss. It was soon obvious that water entering number four and five holds was going to sink the ship, so 67 crew and passengers abandoned ship, to be picked up by the trawler *Lord Austin* and taken to Arkhangelsk. Like *Hoosier*, attempts to sink *El Capitan* by gunfire failed; *U-251* sank it at 0045 hours on 10 July.

At 0400 hours, rescue ship *Zamalek* suffered a near miss which stopped its engines. Among the survivors on *Zamalek* were several engineers, who collectively managed to repair fractured oil pipes, get a generator started and, one hour later, *Zamalek* was doing a creditable 10 knots trying to catch up with the others, believing there was safety in numbers.

At 1230 hours, the *Pozarica* group, which had reached Iokanka, was joined by the Russian destroyers *Grozni* and *Gremyashchi*, which led them past Gourlo into the White Sea and, beyond, the River Dvina and Arkhangelsk, which they reached mid-afternoon on 11 July.

Sometime in the afternoon, a Russian-manned Consolidated PBY Catalina spotted *Winston-Salem*, having earlier landed beside *Empire Tide* some 30 miles further north to evacuate a wounded crewman. The sighting prompted the despatch of a Russian armed trawler, an icebreaker and the battered tanker from PQ 17, *Azerbaijan*, to Moller Bay.

SS *El Capitan* in happier times. (Public Domain)

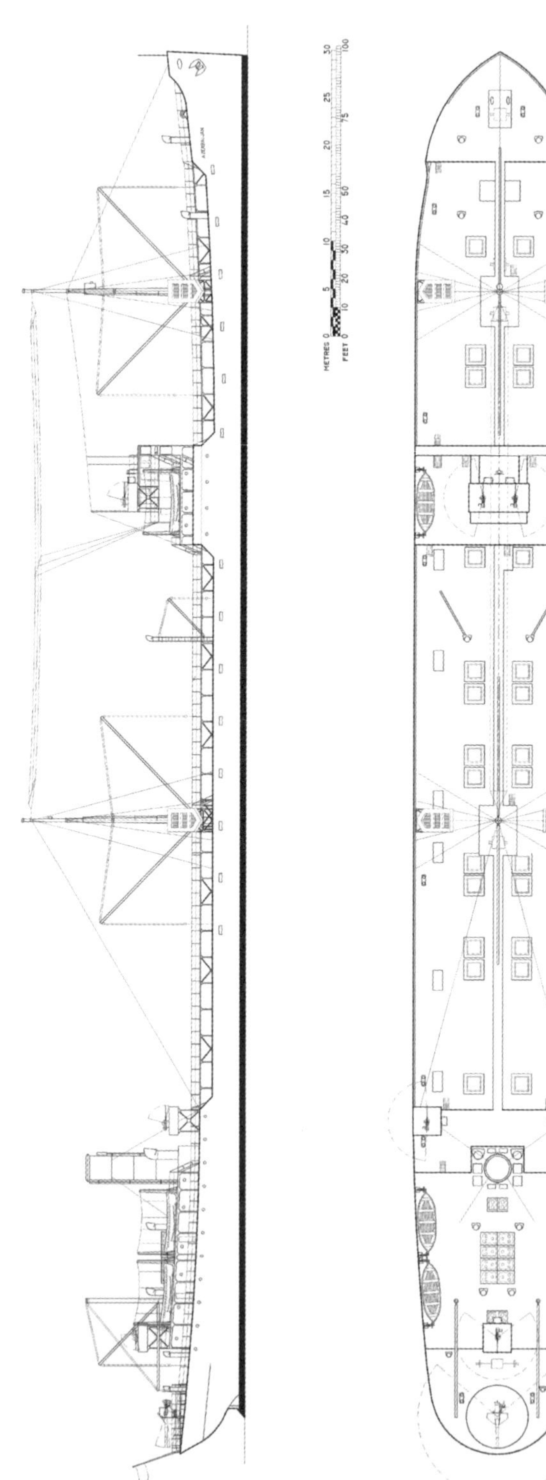

Notes on the drawing: *The only photo I was able to find of* Azerbaijan *was one taken from an unidentified British warship – possibly a WAIR*[1] *conversion of a V & W-class destroyer judging by the twin 4-inch mount and the breakwater – at Hvalfjord, Iceland, prior to the departure of PQ17. It shows* Azerbaijan *in hazy silhouette, some distance away, from which I was able to establish some very basic proportions. Readers should take my drawing only as a basic interpretation.*

At 1100 hours, *Ayrshire*'s 'convoy' reached Matochkin Strait and an armed party was sent ashore to the radio station to determine if it was friendly. Fortunately, it was.

Day 15, Saturday, 11 July

The second group of ships that had formed after the fog lifted was making its own way towards Cape Kanin. It consisted of *Samuel Chase* and *Ocean Freedom*, escorted by *Lotus*, *Halcyon*, *Britomart*, *Lord Middleton* and *Northern Gem*. Inevitably, it came under attack at 1100 hours – 16 Ju 88s from Banak and some from Petsamo. The attack lasted an hour and a half, since the aircraft were close to their bases. Near misses brought *Samuel Chase* to a halt and *Halcyon* took it in tow, with *Lord Middleton* as escort. *Ocean Freedom*, *Britomart* and *Northern Gem* formed up separately. Then it was *Ocean Freedom*'s turn, sustaining damage but not enough to stop its progress.

Late in the afternoon, another attack was forming up when Russian Hurricanes and Petlyakov fighters finally made an appearance. The locally based minesweepers *Hazard* and *Leda*, along with Russian minesweepers, appeared in the White Sea, escorting them to Maimska on the River Dvina.

On 11 July, *Ayrshire* and its charges moved 2 miles deeper into Matochkin Strait and discovered *Benjamin Harrison* at anchor there.

CHAPTER 11

Days 16–32, Sunday, 12 July–Tuesday, 28 July 1942

On 12 July, all ships moved a further 10 miles into the Matochkin Strait to minimize detection, then accompanied by a Russian tanker (probably *Azerbaijan*), a trawler (possibly *Kirov*) and an icebreaker (*Murman*).[1]

On 13 July, the derelict *Paulus Potter* was boarded by men from *U-255*, who took what was deemed useful then gave it the usual *coup de grâce*. Although this is the last we will hear of this submarine in this book, it is of interest that two of the ships of PQ 17 – *Richard Bland* and *Silver Sword* – fell victim to *U-255*, on 20 September 1942 in QP 14 and 10 March 1943 in RA 53, respectively.

On this day too, in London, the British Chiefs of Staff, almost certainly not in possession of all of the bad news concerning PQ 17, recommended that convoys should not be sent to Russia in present circumstances – that is, while the daylight hours persisted.

On 15 July, attempts were made to refloat *Winston-Salem* in Moller Bay. A Russian schooner had arrived, and after this failed it left with the survivors from other ships that had collected there.

On 16 July, the busy corvette *Dianella* returned after an eight-day search which rescued 61 survivors from *Empire Byron*, which finally sank on 5 July after having been attacked and damaged late on 4 July.

The irrepressible Commodore Dowding put to sea in foul weather in *Poppy*, with *Lotus* and *La Malouine* in company, heading for Belushya Bay on Novaya Zemlya, looking to round up the missing ships and look for survivors. They found *Winston-Salem* and nine survivors from *Olopana* in the process, before arriving at Belushya Bay on 19 July and pressing on to Matochkin Strait on 20 July, where they made contact with *Ayrshire*'s flock: *Azerbaijan*, *Murman* and *Kirov*.

On 17 July, *Winston-Salem* was finally spotted by a German aircraft. This was sufficient for the remaining crew to finally abandon their ship, having first made its guns inoperable and flooding the magazine. On 19 July, two Russian armed trawlers and a Russian merchant ship, *Dikson*, arrived and began lightening the stranded ship by removing cargo.

Three corvettes arrived on 20 July, and at 1400 hours all ships raised anchors and headed for the White Sea. Since ammunition was low and gun barrels were worn on the anti-aircraft auxiliaries, three modern M-class destroyers (*Marne*, *Martin* and *Middleton*) and a Hunt-class escort destroyer (*Blankney*) were sent post-haste on 20 July from Scapa Flow to Arkhangelsk, arriving on 24 July without incident. They also carried interpreters, no doubt more necessary

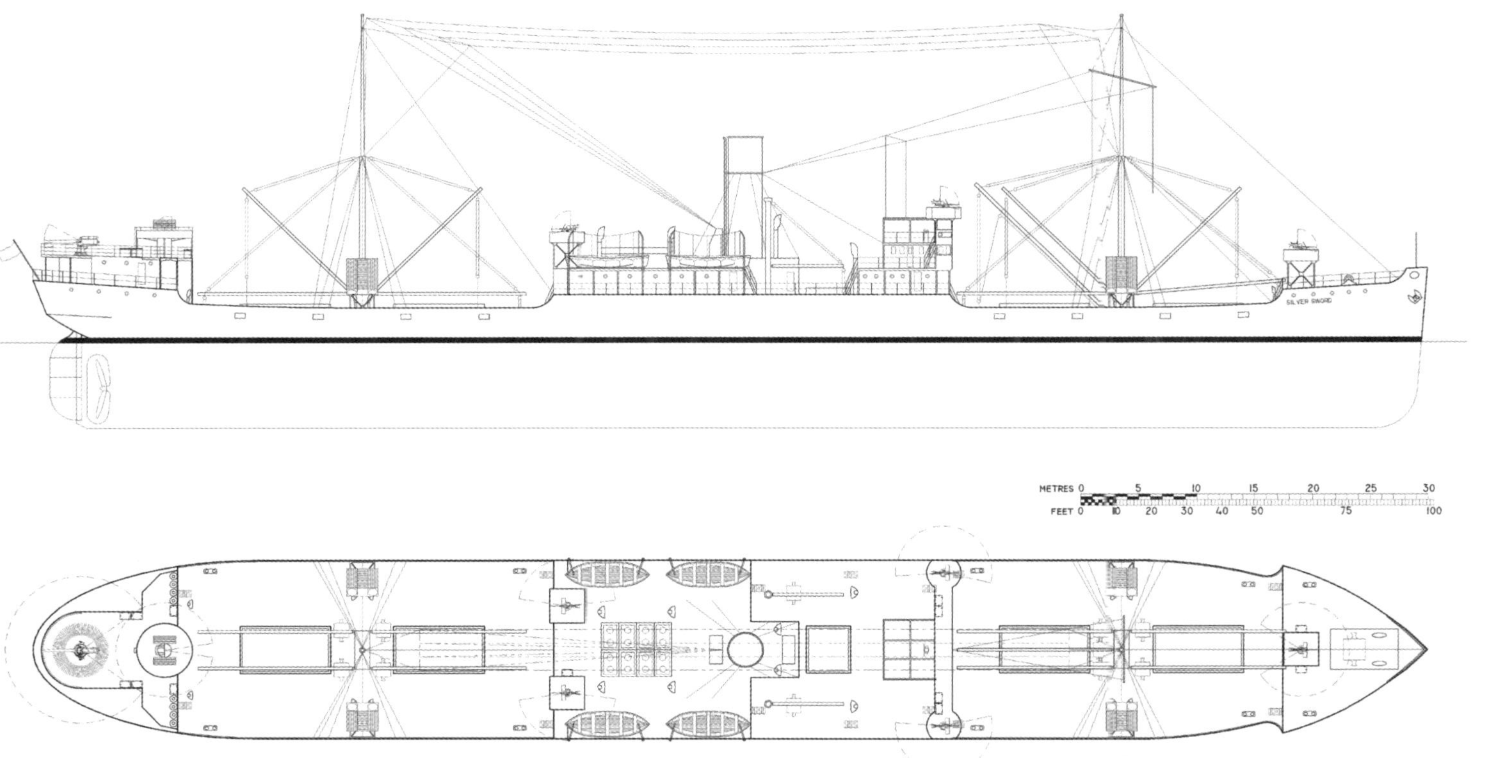

Notes on the drawing: Silver Sword *was one of 11 of the Design 1017 types for the EFC, commonly known as the Downey type after the builder, Downey Shipbuilding Co. of Staten Island, NY. Completed as* New Britain *in July 1919, it appears to have had several changes of ownership and name until 1934, when it joined the Sword Line Inc. While a survivor of PQ 17,* Silver Sword *met its end in March 1943 at the hands of the ubiquitous U-255.*

U-255. (Public Domain)

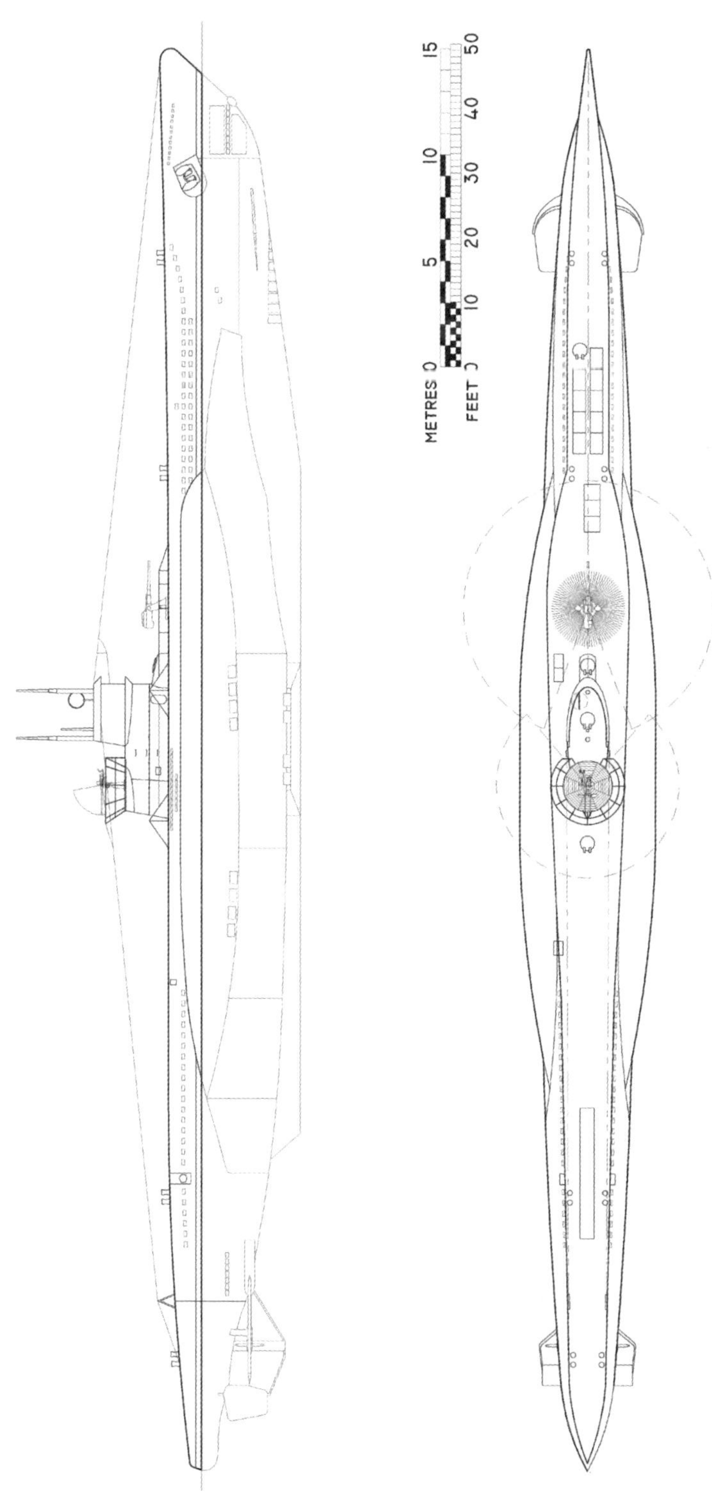

Notes on the drawing: *U-255 was the most-mentioned German U-boat in this book, so it seemed fitting to include a drawing of it. A Type VII C, it was one of 703 Type VIIs built, of which 568 were the C model. The Type IX was a significantly larger submarine, with greater range and heavier armament.*

than ever in order to explain – insofar as they were able – what had happened to PQ 17, although that story would still have been evolving. *Blankney* was damaged in a collision in Murmansk on 30 July and was under repair until mid-September. This was followed up by a larger force comprising the light cruiser USS *Tuscaloosa* and three destroyers (USS *Emmons*, USS *Rodman* and HMS *Onslaught*) carrying 300 tons of ammunition, 20 tons of aircraft parts, radar parts, dehydrated food, 19 tons of mixed cargo and 170 Service passengers, distributed between the four ships at Kola Inlet in late August. These were mainly RAF personnel to service the two Handley Page Hampden bomber squadrons based at Vaenga near Murmansk. A fully equipped mobile hospital was carried to provide a much higher standard of care than offered by the Soviets. In yet another example of Soviet bastardry, they helped themselves to the medical supplies and the hospital was not allowed to be landed.

On 22 July, *Winston-Salem* was finally dragged free and arrived at Arkhangelsk on 28 July. It made the return trip to Britain in QP 14, which left Arkhangelsk on 13 September.

On 24 July, *Pozarica*, with senior officer Commodore J. C. K. Dowding, led *Dianella*, *Hazard*, *Leda* and two Russian destroyers, *Grozni* and *Gremyashchi*, with *Azerbaijan*, *Benjamin Harrison*, *Ironclad*, *Silver Sword* and *Troubadour*, into the relative safety of Arkhangelsk.[2]

And so, 32 days after PQ 17 set out from Iceland, the last merchant ship of that catastrophic convoy made it to harbour, one of the 11 lucky ones.

One man's poor decision, compounded by the pluck and luck of Luftwaffe and Kriegsmarine servicemen, had resulted in what can only be described as the annihilation of PQ 17.

The butcher's bill was 22 of the merchant ships, plus a fleet oiler (RFA *Aldersdale*) and one rescue ship (*Zaafaran*), along with 153 merchant seamen, 430 tanks, 210 aircraft, 3,350 vehicles and 99,316 tons of *matériel*.[3] Eleven merchant ships (71,190 GRT) made it to their destination, albeit two were damaged (*Azerbaijan* and *Winston-Salem*). Three merchant ships (17,888 GRT) turned back, having run aground (*Richard Bland*), developed engine trouble (*West Gotomska*) or had been damaged by ice (*Exford*).

German submarines acting alone accounted for seven merchant ships (41,041 GRT), plus the fleet oiler. Aircraft acting alone claimed eight merchant ships (46,002 GRT) and the rescue ship. A further seven merchant ships (45,691 GRT) were disabled by aircraft and dispatched by submarines, making a grand total of 203,924 GRT of shipping sunk.

On the other side of the ledger, records vary, but what seems to be generally accepted is that five aircraft were lost from the 5th Air Fleet.[4] One must ask: what magnitude of land conflict would it have taken to result in the loss of such a quantity of war *matériel*, and what human losses would have had been sustained in that conflict? So in terms of victors and losers, the actions of the Luftwaffe and Kriegsmarine against PQ 17 resulted in a resounding triumph, way out of proportion to any such action by the Heer (the Germany Army).[5]

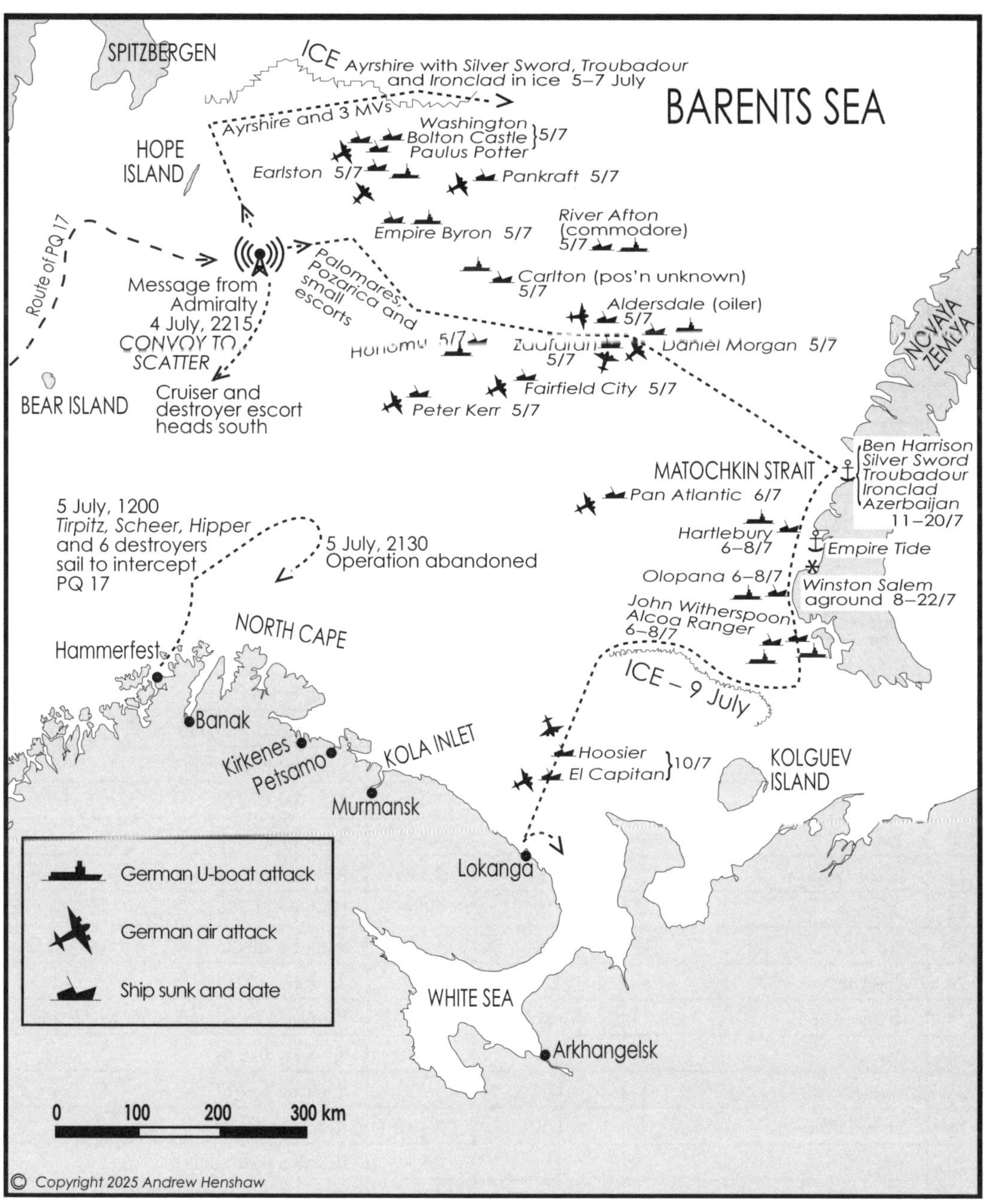

This map shows the approximate movement of PQ 17 ships between 4 and 28 July 1942.

PQ 17 Convoy Ships

	Ship	Flag	GRT	Fate
	Merchant Ships Delivering Aid			
1	*Alcoa Ranger*	US	5,116	Sunk by *U-255*
2	*Azerbaijan*	USSR	6,114	Damaged & reached port safely
3	*Bellingham*	US	5,345	Reached port safely
4	*Benjamin Harrison*	US	7,191	Reached port safely
5	*Bolton Castle*	UK	5,203	Sunk by aircraft
6	*Carlton*	US	5,127	Sunk by *U-88*
7	*Christopher Newport*	US	7,191	Damaged by aircraft, sunk by U-457
8	*Daniel Morgan*	US	7,177	Damaged by aircraft, sunk by *U-88*
9	*Donbass*	Soviet Union	7,925	Reached port safely
10	*Earlston*	UK	7,195	Damaged by aircraft, sunk by *U-334*
11	*El Capitan*	Panama	5,255	Damaged by aircraft, sunk by *U-251*
12	*Empire Byron*	UK	6,645	Damaged by aircraft, sunk by *U-703*
13	*Empire Tide*	UK	6,978	Reached port safely
14	*Fairfield City*	US	5,686	Sunk by aircraft
15	*Hartlebury*	UK	5,082	Sunk by *U-355*
16	*Honomu*	US	6,977	Sunk by *U-456*
17	*Hoosier*	US	5,060	Damaged by aircraft, sunk by *U-251*
18	*Ironclad*	US	5,685	Reached port safely
19	*John Witherspoon*	US	7,191	Sunk by *U-255*
20	*Navarino*	UK	4,841	Sunk by aircraft
21	*Ocean Freedom*	UK	7,173	Reached port safely
22	*Olopana*	US	6,069	Sunk by *U-255*
23	*Pan Atlantic*	US	5,411	Sunk by aircraft
24	*Pan Kraft*	US	5,644	Sunk by aircraft
25	*Paulus Potter*	Dutch	7,168	Damaged by aircraft, sunk by *U- 255*
26	*Peter Kerr*	US	6,476	Sunk by aircraft
27	*River Afton*	UK	5,479	Sunk by *U-703*
28	*Samuel Chase*	UK	7,191	Reached port safely
29	*Silver Sword*	US	4,937	Reached port safely
30	*Troubadour*	Panama	6,428	Reached port safely
31	*Washington*	US	5,564	Sunk by aircraft
32	*William Hooper*	US	7,177	Sunk by aircraft
33	*Winston-Salem*	US	6,223	Bombed, ran aground, reached port
		Sub-total	203,924	

(Continued)

(Continued)

	Ship	Flag	GRT	Fate
	Turned Back			
34	*Exford*	US	4,969	Damaged by ice, turned back
35	*Richard Bland*	US	7,191	Ran aground, towed back to port
36	*West Gotomska*	US	5,728	Developed engine trouble, turned back
		Sub-total	17,888	
		Total GRT	221,812	
	Non-Merchant Ships			
37	RFA *Aldersdale*	RFA	8,402	Damaged by aircraft
38	*RFA Gray Ranger*	RFA	3,313	Damaged by ice, reached port safely
39	*Rathlin*	MFA	1,600	Reached port safely
40	*Zaafaran*	MFA	1,559	Sunk by aircraft
41	*Zamalek*	MFA	1,567	Reached port safely

CHAPTER 12

Aftermath – 'A shameful page in naval history'

United States Navy Captain Daniel V. Gallery described PQ 17, appropriately, as 'a shameful page in naval history'. Gallery, a naval aviator, was stationed at Iceland in charge of the Fleet Air Base in Reykjavík during the time of PQ 17. On the face of it, any comment on the fate of PQ 17 from a man in such an inauspicious posting would seem of little importance. However, Gallery later assumed command of the anti-submarine Task Group (TG) 21.12, then TG 22.3, with the escort carrier *Guadalcanal* as his flagship. He distinguished himself, and his task groups, with pioneering tactics that resulted in the sinking of three U-boats and the capture of another – *U-505* – with its Enigma coding machine on board, earning his group a Presidential Citation. Such was the spirit that Gallery engendered that, while *Guadalcanal* was towing the damaged *U-505*, normal flight operations took place. Having commanded Carrier Division Six during the Korean War, Gallery blotted his copybook by criticizing the then US Secretary of Defense. When he retired in 1960 with the rank of rear admiral, he was second in seniority for advancement. Unfortunately, the long-established principle of an advancement in rank upon retirement without commensurate benefits had been abolished and Gallery missed out on retiring as a vice admiral. His two brothers were also rear admirals.

Commander Jack Broome, commander of PQ 17, wrote the following words as distress calls came in from the scattered convoy:

> That one word; that unforgiveable, tragically misused order, was already busy transforming a perfectly good convoy into one of the most melancholy episodes of the war.[1]

Churchill used a very similar phrase, 'This was one of the most melancholy naval episodes in the whole of the war', in his self-serving memoirs, *The Hinge of Fate: The Second World War, Volume IV*.[2] This was written in 1950. So, did Broome read Churchill or just come up with a very similar phrase? Whatever, I don't think 'most melancholy' cuts it. It is inadequate. What happened to PQ 17 was far more than that. It was an avoidable tragedy. It was more than melancholy. It was, as Gallery stated, a 'shameful page in naval history'.

One hundred and fifty-three merchant seamen of many nationalities – the majority British – serving in PQ 17's ships died on the 22 ships which were sunk, plus one bombed, beached and salvaged. But not one warship was lost; not one person died serving on a naval ship attached to the defence of PQ 17. While this is, of course, a good thing, news of this widened an already-existing gap between the two seafaring services, despite the fact that some 4,000 lives had been lost in the Royal Navy in the preceding months.[3] In PQ 17's case, the 'price of Admiralty'[4] was not paid by the Royal Navy but by the Merchant Navy. Sixteen officers and men of the Merchant Navy received honours: two George Medals, six appointments to the Order of the British Empire at various grades, six British Empire Medals and two King's Commendation for Brave Conduct.

The question posed as to who had won was now unequivocal. The destruction of PQ 17 was very obviously a victory for the Kriegsmarine and the Luftwaffe; more so the latter, because eight ships were sunk directly by aircraft and seven of the ships sunk by U-boats had previously been disabled by the Luftwaffe, to the point where they were abandoned and derelict, becoming simply target practice for the submarines. The victory had greater significance than the statistics. It inflamed an existing schism between the Western Allies and the Soviets. In Soviet eyes, the delay in sending the next convoy, PQ 18, magnified the loss of PQ 17's ships and the aid they contained. The Germans had achieved this result for the loss of only five aircraft and an unknown but small number of Luftwaffe personnel – possibly 10–20.

On 15 July, two weeks before the last ship of PQ 17 limped into harbour, and undoubtedly shamed by the damage done to Britain's reputation by the PQ 17 disaster, Churchill, perhaps just being his belligerent self, pushed Admiral Pound to fight another convoy through without waiting for the conditions of darkness that were now obviously required for any chance of success. However, Pound, presumably chastened by the disaster of his own making, was not to be browbeaten. Nevertheless, there were two extenuating circumstances which made such a repeat convoy impractical: a number of the naval assets involved in PQ 17 were scheduled to be diverted to August's Operation *Pedestal* – an attempt, a last throw of the dice, to relieve Malta – and the ships of the USN's Task Force 39 were reassigned to the Pacific.

Human nature being what it is, a scapegoat was needed for PQ 17's tragedy. It could not – would not – be the man responsible. That was not the British way. Someone else would have to carry the can. Churchill had already gotten rid of generals like Gort, Ironside, Dill, Wavell and Auchinleck, who did not bend to his will.

Eight years after the event, in his *The Hinge of Fate*, Churchill wrote the following opinion of PQ 17's scattering: 'In the light of later knowledge however the decision to scatter was precipitate.'[5] A few sentences earlier, he sets the scene for excusing the 'precipitate' action:

> Admiral Pound would probably not have sent such vehement orders [to scatter] if only our own British warships had been concerned. But the idea that our first large joint Anglo-American operation under British command should involve the destruction of the two United States cruisers as well as our own may well have disturbed the poise with which he was accustomed to deal with these heart-shaking decisions. This is only my surmise from what I knew of my friend, for I never discussed the matter with him. Indeed, so strictly was the secret of these orders being sent on the First Sea Lord's authority guarded by the Admiralty that it was not until after the war that I learned the facts.[6]

On the next page, Churchill states: 'The dismay felt by the merchant ships at witnessing the headlong departure of the cruisers might have been averted if Admiral Hamilton could have remained in the vicinity until the dispersal of the convoy had been accomplished, but from the signals he [Hamilton] had received he could only suppose that the *Tirpitz* was likely to appear over the horizon at any moment.'[7]

Cutting off the proverbial head of the First Sea Lord would have morale ramifications within the over-stressed and under-resourced Royal Navy. It was best to sweep the disaster under the carpet and point the fickle finger of fate at someone less noteworthy than the First Sea Lord. However, this scapegoat should be of significant rank in order that it would appear something serious, some sort of catharsis – a purging – had actually taken place as a result of PQ 17's massacre. That poor individual was the blameless Rear Admiral Louis Hamilton of Cruiser Squadron One. What was worse, it was not done face-to-face; it was done by insidious innuendo, by rumour. Hamilton had followed his orders,[8] indeed had stretched them to advance eastwards further than instructed and stayed longer than was instructed (to try to retrieve *Norfolk*'s Walrus seaplane, which could not be contacted) rather than take the first opportunity to vacate the potential battlefield.[9]

In a minute to the First Lord of the Admiralty, A. V. Alexander, of 15 July, Churchill – either ill-informed or deliberately manipulative, or perhaps an amalgam of both – said:

> I was not aware until this morning that it was the Admiral of the cruisers, Hamilton, who ordered the destroyers to quit the convoy. What did you think of this decision at the time? What do you, think of it now? I awaited the results of the inquiry into the conduct of those concerned. This took a considerable time, and assigned no blame to anyone. How could it do so in view of the signals made on the orders of the First Sea Lord?[10]

Hamilton gave no such orders. Broome offered the services of the destroyer complement of the convoy's escort to Hamilton in the expectation that Cruiser Squadron One was going to engage German forces, including *Tirpitz*. The following message was conveyed by searchlight when the cruisers and Keppel were in visual range:

```
NAVAL MESSAGE
   From: KEPPEL                                          To: CS One
   Propose Close Escort Destroyers join you.
                                                             2230/4
```

Hamilton replied:

```
NAVAL MESSAGE
   From: CS ONE                                          To: KEPPEL
   Approved
```

Later, there was this message from Hamilton:

```
NAVAL MESSAGE
   From: CS ONE                                          To: KEPPEL
Your 2018z/4: Had you any written instructions concerning the conduct
of the escort when the convoy scattered which led you to assume that
the destroyers should concentrate and act under orders of Senior
Officer. Personally I thoroughly approve of your suggestion.
                                                             1439/B5
```

To which Broome responded:

```
NAVAL MESSAGE
   From: KEPPEL                                          To: CS One
Your 1439/5: No instructions. The suggestion to join your force was
my own. My appreciation from slender information at the time was
that action was probable in holding off enemy while convoy scattered
```

> and that destroyers would be most useful under your orders. The decision to leave remaining escorts was most unpleasant and I am always ready to go back and collect them.
>
> 1604B/5

Churchill had a different opinion: 'Nevertheless, while the scattering of the convoy gave little scope for destroyer action against superior surface attack, their withdrawal was certainly a mistake. All risks should have [been] taken in defence of the merchant ships.'[11]

Had the *Tirpitz* threat eventuated, a massed torpedo attack by destroyers would have been a tactical option, albeit a very dangerous one. As fate would have it, Hamilton had to have his appendix removed when in Iceland in August. This event was the perfect excuse for him to be sidelined. He lost command of CS One, never commanded at sea again and saw out the war in a shore command.

The Anglophobic and irascible Fleet Admiral Ernest King[12] (who was said to shave with a blowtorch!), the US Navy's equivalent of the Admiralty's First Sea Lord, condemned Pound's actions and promptly withdrew Task Force 39. While these ships may well have been required in the Pacific, they were also needed in the North Atlantic. But King had lost what little faith he may have had in the Royal Navy. The destruction of PQ 17 provided the perfect justification for his actions.

The Royal Navy's senior representative in Moscow, Rear Admiral Geoffrey Miles, sent a signal to the Admiralty at 1916 hours on 11 July stating that Admiral Kuznetsov, the Soviet Chief of Naval Staff, had met with him. Kuznetsov believed that *K 12* had damaged the *Tirpitz* on 5 July (without any firm evidence to support it), as *Pravda* and *Krasni Flot* (the Soviet Navy newspaper) had prematurely, and typically, lauded the encounter. He expressed his doubts as to the wisdom of dispersing the convoy and believed, correctly, that in doing so the German aims had been achieved. Miles was inclined to agree but diplomatically reserved judgement pending a better appreciation of the facts. He also stated that he did not raise with Kuznetsov the withdrawal of the destroyers in the escort. This issue was obviously a sensitive one even as early as 11 July.

In Russia – indeed in the Russian Embassy in London – there was a warranted disbelief that so many ships could have been lost. The Soviets believed that they were being deliberately lied to. Ambassador Ivan Maisky, never backward in coming forward with criticism or demands, was vocal in both regards. At a meeting in British Foreign Secretary Anthony Eden's office on 28 July with the head of the Soviet military mission, Admiral Harlamov, First Lord Alexander and First Sea Lord Pound, Maisky made it clear in no uncertain terms that he expected another convoy, more or less on the schedule that had been agreed to. He was unmoved by the casualties of PQ 17. In the Russian mindset, disasters of great magnitude with prodigious losses of human life and *matériel* were an everyday occurrence. To their thinking, what happened to PQ 17 – or was likely to happen to any follow-up convoy, for that matter – was not an issue. It was simply the cost of war.

Before the last ships had made it to Russian ports, Stalin was quick off the mark to make his feelings known and to press, once again, for the Western Allies to open a second front and take the pressure off the Red Army, as the following telegram to Churchill demonstrates:

From Stalin to Prime Minister T.1031/2 23.7.42

1. I received your message of 18th July.[13] Two conclusions could be drawn from it. First, the British Government refuses to continue the sending of war materials to the Soviet Union via the Northern Route. Second, in spite of the agreed communique[14] concerning the urgent task of creating a second front in 1942, the British Government postpones this matter until 1943.
2. Our naval experts consider the reasons put forward by the British naval experts to justify the cessation of convoys to the Northern ports of the U.S.S.R. wholly unconvincing. They are of the opinion that with goodwill and readiness to fulfil the contracted obligations these convoys could be regularly undertaken and heavy losses could be inflicted on the enemy. Our experts find it also difficult to understand and to explain the order given by the Admiralty that the escorting vessels of P.Q. 17 should return whereas the cargo boats should disperse and try to reach the Soviet ports without any protection at all. Of course, I do not think that regular convoys to the Soviet Northern ports could be effected without risk or losses. But in war no important undertaking could be effected without risk or losses. In any case, I never expected that the British Government will stop despatch of war materials to us just at the very moment when the Soviet Union, in view of the serious situation on the Soviet-German front, requires these materials more than ever. It is obvious that the transport via Persian Gulf could in no way compensate for the cessation of convoys to the Northern ports.
3. With regard to the second question, i.e., the question of creating a second front in Europe, I am afraid it is not being treated with the seriousness it deserves. Taking fully into account the present position in the Soviet-German front, I must state in the most emphatic manner that the Soviet Government cannot acquiesce in the postponement of a second front in Europe until 1943.

I hope you will not feel offended that I expressed frankly and honestly my opinion as well as the opinion of my colleagues on the question raised in your message.[15]

The paranoid and delusional Stalin questioned Churchill's motives in postponing the convoys, believing that Britain might seek a separate peace with Hitler. Contrast this with Churchill's fear in late 1941 that Stalin might seek a separate peace with Hitler prompting a wary enthusiasm to supply aid to the Soviets.[16]

Victories are easy to celebrate, to emphasize, to be used as stiffeners to boost morale. Defeats have to be played down, glossed over, excused in order not to cause alarm, despondency and to weaken morale.

And so it was with PQ 17: to paraphrase a popular song at the time ('Ac-Cent-Tchu-Ate the Positive' by Bing Crosby and the Andrews Sisters), pandemonium walked upon the scene.

* * * * *

While not directly attributable to PQ 17, three of the destroyers that had brought urgent supplies to Murmansk immediately after the ill-fated convoy – *Marne*, *Martin* and *Onslaught* – were returning to Britain with some survivors from PQ 17 when they came upon the German auxiliary minelayer *Ulm* (a converted 'banana boat') on 25 August off Bear Island. *Ulm* had left Tromsø on 24 August, screened by destroyers initially and then by submarines on its intended route to lay mines, apparently along the edge of the ice barrier between Spitzbergen and Bear Island on 27 August. It had been spotted by RAF reconnaissance aircraft after leaving Tromsø, and the three destroyers had been alerted accordingly. At 2151 hours, they were spread in line abreast, 5 miles apart at 19 knots, course 230°, when *Marne* on the port wing sighted a ship at 7 miles on a reciprocal course. The destroyers closed to engage and opened fire, despite the ruse of *Ulm* flying the American flag. It was a one-sided contest: *Ulm* only had a 105 mm gun forward, a 37 mm gun aft and two 20 mm guns amidships. A torpedo from *Onslaught* at 2231 hours (two fired earlier had missed) caused a huge explosion – possibly the magazine or mines. *Ulm* sank in less than three minutes. Two destroyers began rescuing survivors, while one maintained an A/S patrol. A German aircraft then appeared and it was thought prudent to abandon further rescue attempts, with 30–40 survivors mainly on floats. Of the 181 on board *Ulm*, 114 were lost, making this a far more significant loss than those the Luftwaffe sustained against PQ 17.[17]

KMS *Ulm* was built in 1938 as *Rapide* and designed specifically as a fruit carrier. It was converted to an auxiliary minelayer and entered service in late 1941. The only photograph I could obtain was of poor quality, but there is a schematic drawing from the Naval Intelligence Division's interrogation of survivors: C.B. 4051 (51). Contrast its armament of 105 mm gun forward, a 37 mm gun aft and two 20 mm guns amidships with that of *Marne*.

* * * * *

While the book I considered least likely to cover the post-PQ 17 history was Lund and Ludlam's *I Was There on Convoy PQ 17: The Convoy to Hell*, mainly because it provides no citations and no index, it is based on interviews (with survivors) and its concluding pages set out some observations and details missing from other accounts.

The survivors of PQ 17 – around 1,000 of those who were able and those not previously sent back on *Marne*, *Martin* and *Onslaught* – returned in Convoy QP 14, dispersed among various ships. This dispersal caused problems with overcrowding, particularly in the smaller warships, and also when able survivors who had reached Russia were expected to stand watches. All warships at the time had complements far greater than they were designed for, due to the extra equipment fitted such as ASW, AA, radar etc. The smaller the ship, the worse the overcrowding, usually leading to 'hot bunking', squeezing in extra hammocks on mess decks. Upon arrival at Loch Ewe on 26 September, instead of some sort of rest and recuperation before being made immediately available for reassignment, the survivors were transported by mailboat to Glasgow as a close and closed group. They attended an official reception in St Andrew's Hall and had to face the indignity of being addressed in a patronizing manner by the Under Secretary of State to the Ministry of War Transport, Philip Noel-Baker, and told that the cost had been well worth it. He was, quite rightfully, howled down.[18]

Marne in two-tone camouflage similar to that used in the British Pacific Fleet, probably after repairs following being torpedoed on 12 November 1942 and having its stern blown off. (Public Domain)

The fate of PQ 17 was kept a secret, insofar as it was possible. There was no official communiqué, no press statement. A blanket of secrecy was efficiently spread, smothering news. Reports were censored and, as previously mentioned, the positive was accentuated at the expense of the negative. This was despite the presence of well-informed German reports about PQ 17's fate circulated in the media of neutral countries. Over time, as the survivors returned home or were assigned to new ships, the horror of PQ 17 filtered through. Few, if any, were privy to all the facts – only their own personal experiences and those shared by others.

But the veil of silence could not hold. In 1943, Lord Winster (who had been an officer in the Royal Navy) used Parliamentary Privilege in the House of Lords to try to uncover the facts of PQ 17. While he stated that he (mistakenly) understood that only four of 38 ships survived, the *Daily Express* ran with that information the next day. Still the Admiralty maintained its silence on the subject. That situation was maintained until February 1945, when American seamen who had been prisoners of the Germans were repatriated – 23 of them from PQ 17, who had the same belief as Lord Winster that only four merchant ships had survived. After two days of speculation and resentment – the US Navy Department and the Admiralty declining to comment – the Admiralty finally issued a statement, 'in order to correct erroneous reports recently circulated'. This quantified the losses and referred to an ongoing battle and that an imminent attack by German surface ships resulted in the convoy being ordered to scatter. The statement, accentuating

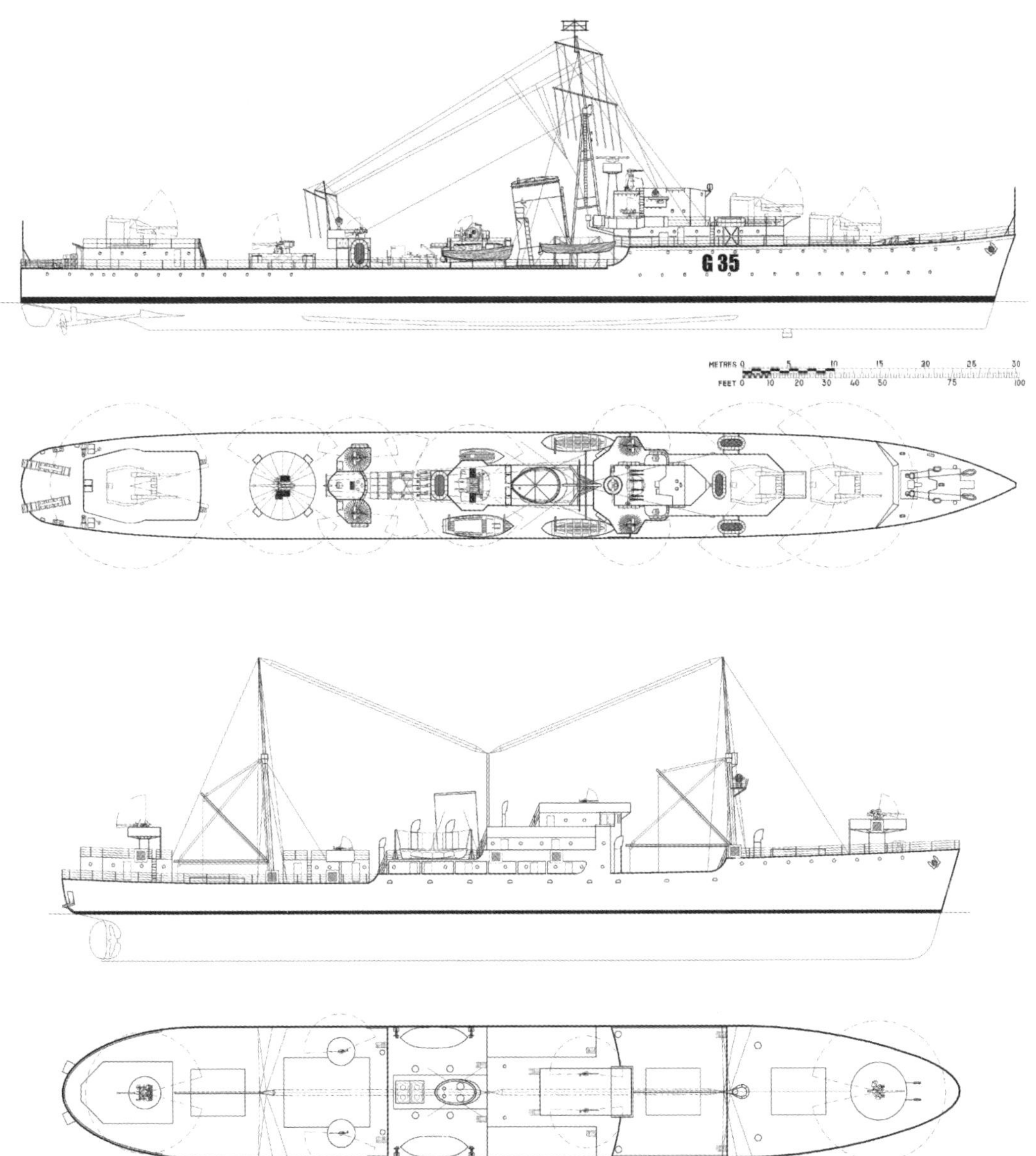

***Notes on the drawings:** The M-class destroyers were basically a follow-on from the L class and the similar J, K and N classes, all of which were conceived as smaller, simpler and less-expensive-to-build replacements for the earlier Tribal class. The Ms and some of the Ls were armed with three twin 4.7-inch Mk XI guns in enclosed mountings – a first for the RN. Although designed to carry eight torpedo tubes in two quad mounts, the aft one was replaced by a single dual-purpose 4-inch Mk V to offer better anti-aircraft protection. While the 4.7-inch guns could elevate to 50°, this was not sufficient to make them an effective anti-aircraft weapon, a problem that dogged the Royal Navy throughout World War II.*

the positive, then pointed out that 91.6 per cent of vital war supplies to the Soviets was getting through, mainly escorted by the Royal Navy.[19]

The issue faded from the public gaze until October 1946, when two articles were published in *Krasni Flot* (the Soviet Navy newspaper) which criticized the Admiralty and the order to scatter, incorrectly blaming the convoy commodore and the commander of the close escort for this. The stories, or the fact that *The New York Times* reported on them, were held by the House of Commons to be outrageous. After two days passed, the Admiralty issued a rebuttal statement 'in order to correct erroneous reports recently circulated'.[20] This re-emphasized the imminence of a surface attack. It added that the convoy was too far to the east to be defended by the Home Fleet (quite possibly true) and that it was inviting disaster for escorts to stand by disabled ships, the latter due to criticism, not entirely unfounded, that merchant ships had been abandoned prematurely.

Milan Vego's opinion of the positioning of the Home Fleet was as follows: 'Positioning of the Home Fleet's Battle Fleet in relation to Convoy PQ 17 on 5 July was clearly unsound: it remained too far away to provide distant cover and support to the convoy, and also too far away to engage the enemy heavy surface group effectively.'[21] More than eight years after the event, on 17 October 1950, extracts from Admiral Tovey's despatches for 1942 were released by the Admiralty in a *Supplement to The London Gazette*. In the Foreword, PQ 17 was finally acknowledged as 'the first and greatest disaster'. The despatches confirmed the loss (incorrectly) of 21 of 34 merchant ships, also presenting data that 62 of 792 (or 7.8 per cent) outward-bound ships to Russia had been lost, along with 28 of 739 (3.8 per cent) homeward-bound vessels. Merchant Navy losses on the convoys were 929 officers and men. The RN, meanwhile, lost two cruisers, six destroyers, three sloops, two frigates, three corvettes and three minesweepers, with the loss of 1,840 officers and men.

Tovey's despatches covered, *inter alia*, recommendations that the Soviets do more to provide protection of the convoys; that fighters provided better cover than AA fire; that convoys should be sailed simultaneously from both ends; that more screening destroyers and escort corvettes were necessary; that convoys should be reduced in those months which favoured German reconnaissance; that if convoys could not be postponed, they should be reduced in size; that the Soviets should bomb German airfields; and that in view of poor Soviet responses, the RAF should station long-range reconnaissance aircraft and fighters in northern Russia.

More telling, and with specific regard to PQ 17, Tovey reported that due to the threat of surface attack, upon reaching 10° east, PQ 17 should turn back for 12–18 hours to tempt German heavy ships to pursue, particularly into the area in which nine RN and three Soviet submarines were stationed. This plan was not approved. The Admiralty instruction stated that the safety of the convoy against surface attack westward of Bear Island must be met by its surface forces and eastward of that meridian by its submarines, and that the cruiser force (Cruiser Squadron One) was not intended to go east of Bear Island unless the convoy was threatened by a surface force which the cruiser force could fight, but in any case not beyond 25° east. Tovey's despatches also revealed Burrough's instruction to Broome to pass further north of Bear Island and laid bare for all to see the hidden truth about PQ 17, in particular the order to scatter and the consequent butcher's bill.[22]

CHAPTER 13

The Balance of 1942 and the 1943–45 Convoys

Although the subject of convoys to Russia after PQ 17 is something of an anti-climax, it is important to have an overview in order to place the significance of PQ 17 in perspective. The campaign to send aid to Russia via this most perilous of routes must be viewed and measured as a whole, not just by one particular failure.

The Remaining 1942 Convoys

The 35-ship Convoy QP 13 (26 June–7 July) ran into heavy fog during its return and 20 ships became lost. QP 13 divided as it approached the north coast of Iceland, following an Admiralty order issued on 2 July. Nineteen ships headed for Scotland's Loch Ewe, arriving without incident on 7 July. The remaining 16, mostly American-flagged, headed for Iceland's Hvalfiordur for assignment to future westbound convoys home. Visibility was poor and navigation had been by DR for three days since the last astronomical fix. The Halcyon-class minesweeper *Niger* spotted what was thought to be land, but this turned out to be an iceberg. Forty minutes later, *Niger* hit a mine in the British-laid minefield (SN 72) off Iceland's North-West Cape at the entrance to the Denmark Strait, and blew up with heavy loss of life. Five merchant ships soon followed, and a sixth was heavily damaged. Sister-ship *Hussar* fortunately obtained an accurate fix and led the remaining merchantmen south out of danger to Reykjavik. A Free French corvette rescued 179 seamen.

Convoy PQ 18 (2–21 September) sailed after an almost 10-week hiatus, this time from Loch Ewe on the north-west coast of Scotland because Iceland was under almost continual aerial observation. In the interim, Operation *Pedestal* – the most heavily defended convoy of all time – struggled through the western Mediterranean to Malta. Only five of fourteen ships survived, all but one damaged by submarines or aircraft. However, the return of Home Fleet warships diverted to *Pedestal* and

A 1940 photograph of *Niger* before the mainmast was removed, before the end of 1941 when the two low-angle 4-inch guns were removed and replaced by a dual-purpose QF 4-inch MK V forward and close-range weapons aft. Type 271 radar replaced the rangefinder on the bridge. (Public Domain)

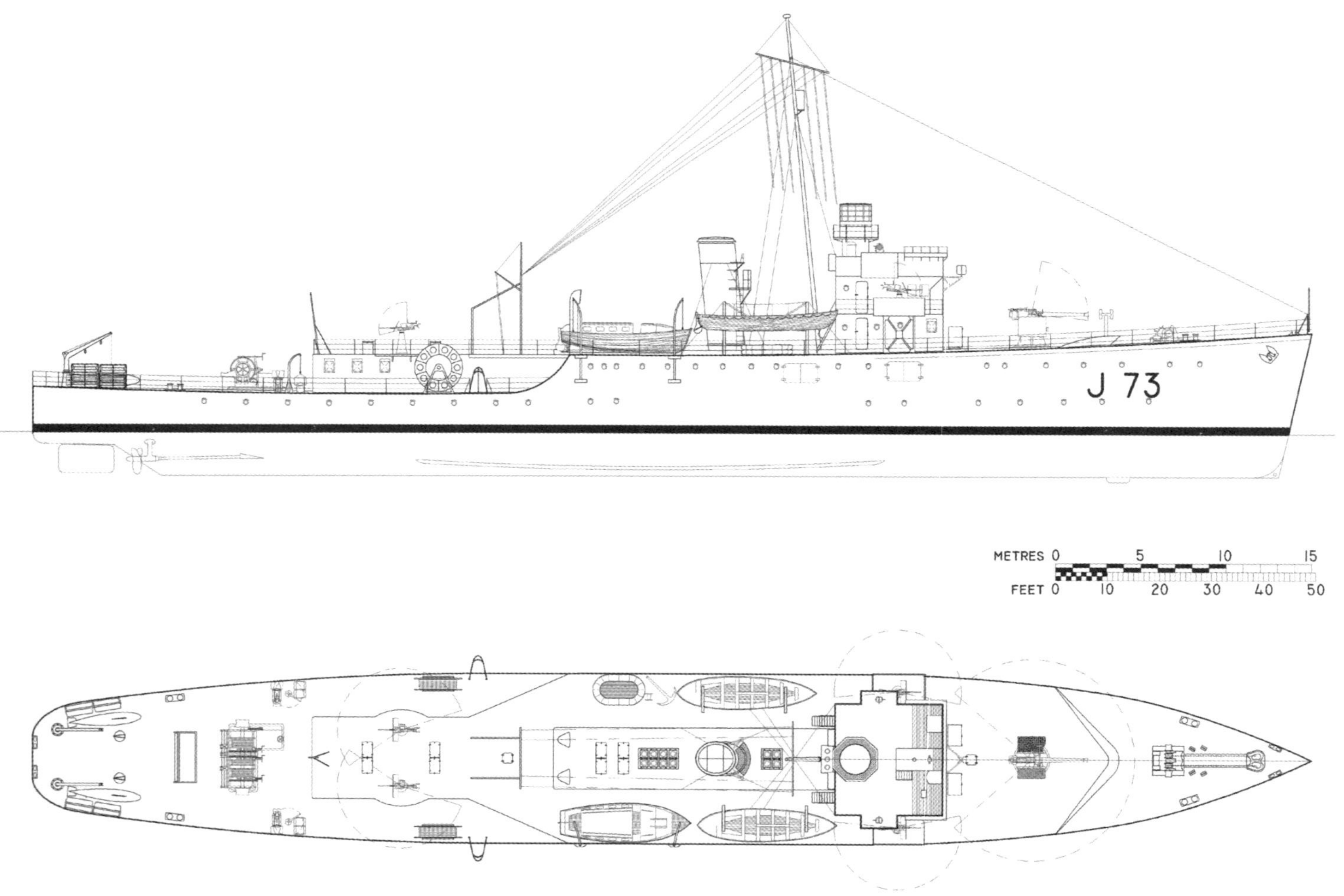

Notes on the drawing: Niger *was one of the 21 minesweepers which made up the Halcyon class but was one of only two which had VTE (Vertical Triple Expansion) steam engines, the others having compound engines or steam turbines. Many of its sister-ships served for long and laborious duty based at Murmansk and Arkhangelsk.*

made available to PQ 18 could not save it, as the convoy lost 13 of its 44 ships: 10 by air attack and three by U-boat. German success came at the cost of four U-boats sunk and as many as 44 aircraft shot down.

A poor-quality yet informative photograph of the stricken Tribal-class destroyer *Somali* with sister-ship *Ashanti* standing by prior to commencing a long but ill-fated towing operation. (Public Domain)

This was the first convoy to have its own air cover in the form of the escort carrier, *Avenger*. The carrier's Fairey Swordfish biplanes conducted anti-submarine sweeps and its Hawker Sea Hurricanes (Hurricanes adapted for carrier use) were able to make intercepts of Luftwaffe reconnaissance aircraft and bomber attacks. Unfortunately, *Avenger*'s aircraft were insufficient in number and, in the case of the Sea Hurricanes, inadequate in performance (speed, endurance and armament) to have been as effective as had been expected.

Another precaution taken was Operation *Orator*: the basing of two squadrons of Handley Page Hampden TB 1 torpedo bombers at Vaenga, along with Consolidated PBY Catalina long-range seaplanes, as an anti-*Tirpitz* measure. However, the Hampden was a pre-war design and obsolete by this time.

A feature of this convoy was the sheer number, intensity and sophistication of Luftwaffe attacks, as evidenced by the results they achieved and the price paid for them.

This was the last of the PQ series of convoys, and thereafter the prefix changed to JW. I have been unable to find any reason for this change, but there was a hiatus of over three months before the JW series commenced. Convoys in almost continual daylight were simply proving too costly.

Convoy QP 14 (13–26 September), with 16 merchant ship plus three escort oilers and a rescue ship, lost four of its number, all to submarines. Yet another valuable Tribal-class destroyer was lost in these waters when *Somali* was torpedoed on 20 September by *U-703*, sinking on 24 September after being towed 420 miles by sister-ship *Ashanti*.

Convoy JW 51 A (15–25 December) and Convoy JW B (22 December 1942–4 January 1943) involved a total of 31 merchant ships, all of which arrived safely, save one which had to turn back.

Operation *FB* was in many ways an experiment to establish the efficacy of having ships proceed independently from 29 October to 9 November, in this case at 12-hour intervals. It could hardly be termed successful: of 13 vessels, five were sunk, three turned back and only five arrived. Twenty-three which sailed from Russia had better luck; 22 survived the journey.

The return convoys, QP 15 (17–30 November) and RA 51 (30 December–11 January 1943) saw 189 merchant ships returned safely to British ports for reassignment.

The tally of valuable ships returned for reuse, often with essential cargoes, was augmented by 22 of 23 or 25 Russian ships (depending on sources) which made independent passages between 29 October 1942 and 23 January 1943.

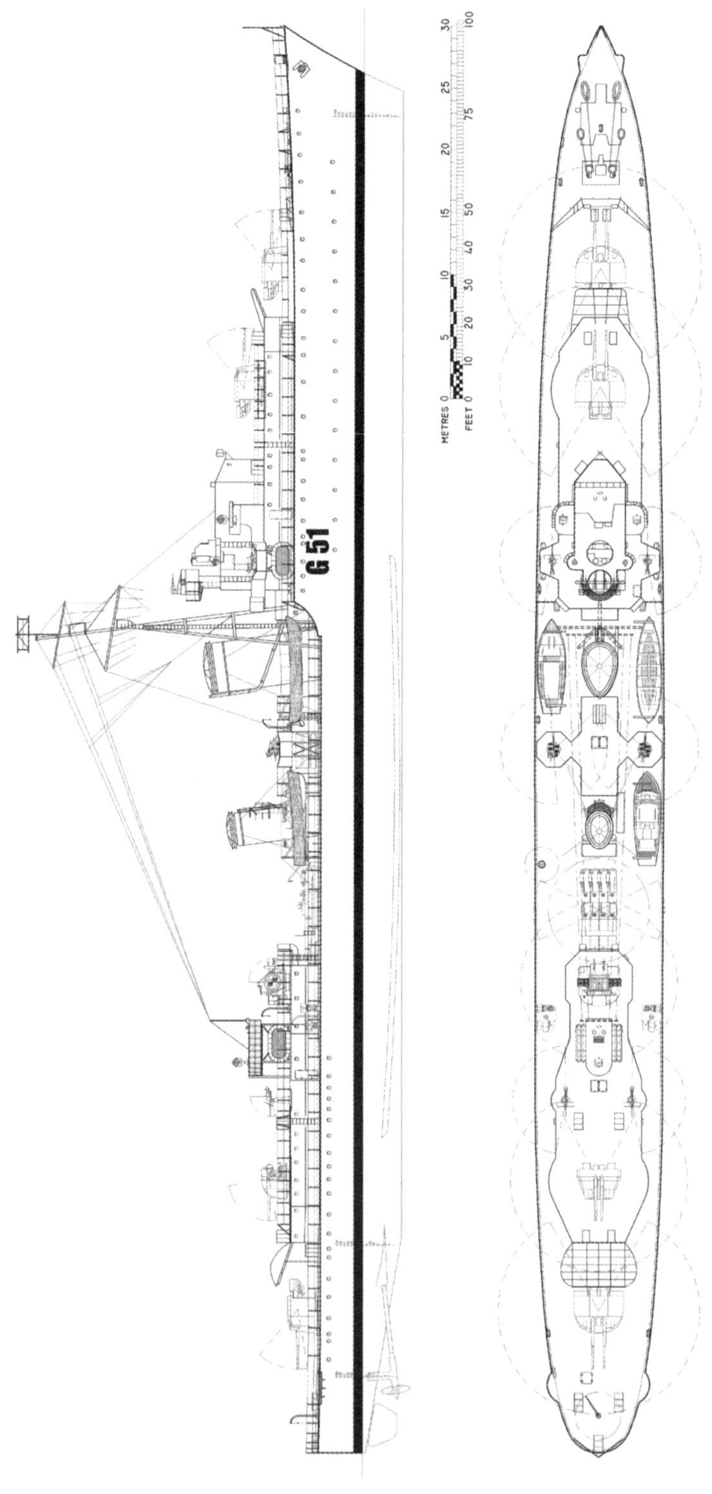

Notes on the drawing: *The 16 destroyers which made up the successful Tribal class of the Royal Navy were large and powerful ships. However, being well-equipped – if a little deficient in torpedo armament, compared particularly with Axis destroyers – they tended to go in harm's way or perhaps attracted commanding officers so inclined. Twelve of them were lost, mainly to aircraft.*

The 1943 Convoys

In contrast with the intensity of convoys in 1942, there were only six convoys to Russia in 1943. After the fall of Stalingrad in February 1943, the initiative was with the Red Army, which pushed the Axis forces forever westward, albeit at great cost of men and *matériel.*

Convoys JW 52 (17–27 January), JW 53 (27 January–15 February), JW 54 A (15–24 November), JW 54 B (22 November–3 December), JW 55 A (12–22 December) and JW 55 B (20–30 December) saw 104 merchant ships make successful voyages without loss, although six ships of JW 53 were forced to turn back.

Convoys RA 52 (29 January–9 February), RA 53 (1–14 March), RA 54 A (1–14 November), RA 54 B (26 November–9 December), RA 55 A (22 December–1 January 1944) and RA 55 B (31 December 1943–8 January 1944) witnessed the return of 82 merchant ships for the loss of five, with three having to turn back.

The 1944 Convoys

The tempo picked up again in 1944, with 10 convoys to Russia.

Convoys JW 56 A (12–28 January), JW 56 B (22 January–1 February), JW 57 (20–28 February), JW 58 (27 March–4 April), JW 59 (15–25 August), JW 60 (15–23 September), JW 61 (20–28 October), JW 61 A (31 October–6 November), JW 62 (29 November–7 December) and JW 63 (30 December 1944–8 January 1945) delivered an incredible 276 ships, with only two ships lost and five forced to turn back.

Convoys RA 56 (3–11 February), RA 57 (2–10 March), RA 58 (7–14 April), RA 59 (28 April–6 May), RA 59 A (28 August–5 September), RA 60 (28 September–5 October), RA 61 (2–9 November), RA 61 A (11–17 November) and RA 62 (10–19 December) delivered 245 ships for the loss of four, with two having to turn back.

The 1945 Convoys

Convoys JW 64 (17–28 February), JW 65 (23 March–1 April), JW 66 (29 April–8 May) and JW 67 (23–30 May) were the last four convoys to Russia. However, with the threat to them substantially reduced, they were larger convoys and for the loss of only two ships delivered an impressive 92 ships—an average of 23 per convoy.

Convoys RA 63 (11–21 January), RA 64 (17–28 February), RA 65 (23 March–1 April), RA 66 (29 April–8 May) and RA 67 (23–30 May) rounded up ships left in Russia, such as specialized heavy-lift ships retained there to assist in the unloading process: a total of 134 for the loss of two ships.

CHAPTER 14

Analysis and Conclusions

Hindsight is a wonderful thing. We can look into the past and, from the comfort of the present, state with authority what happened, when, how and why. But only the 'when' is chiselled in stone; providing we are only looking far enough back for accurate records to have been kept. The 'how' and 'why' questions – where hindsight fails or is subject to criticism – all depend on the prism through which hindsight is directed, since hindsight is individual, peculiar to the viewer and their depth of knowledge and understanding of all the circumstances which pertained. It depends, too, on the bias of the viewer and the context in which the hindsight observations are made, and in which the circumstances are examined.

And so it is with PQ 17. We can deplore what happened. We must do so. It was a debacle of the first magnitude. How could it be otherwise, with 22 of the final 33 ships lost – a two-thirds loss rate. We can hypothesize what should have happened, that Admiral Pound should not have ordered PQ 17 to scatter, but to what end? 'What-ifs' are pointless. The facts cannot change, but the interpretation of the facts can, and did.

If one was to read Soviet versions of World War II, or watch the plethora of Russian film and television depictions of what they know as the Great Patriotic War, then the *matériel* assistance from the United States and United Kingdom, and the trials and tribulations to deliver it to the Soviets, barely receive a mention. Take the television series *Soviet Storm: World War II in the East*, also known as *The Great Patriotic War*, created by Anna Grazhdan. 15,000 aircraft, 7,000 tanks and self-propelled artillery, 350,000 tons of explosives, 51,000 jeeps, 375,000 trucks, 2,000 locomotives, 11,000 rail wagons, 3 million tons of gasoline and 15 million pairs of boots provided by the USA, and the 5,000 tanks and 7,000 aircraft provided by Britain, seem an irrelevance in the Russian interpretation of the Great Patriotic War. To this must be added coal (Soviet production fell during the conflict), aluminium, radios, radar and medical supplies, plus the 2,600 tons of food, 90 cargo vessels, 107 million yards of cotton cloth and 62.5 million yards of woollen cloth. Ten per cent of the Soviet Union's Gross National Product (GNP) was made up of Allied aid when at its peak.[1]

However, there are many variations and interpretations of the data relating to what was supplied to the USSR via Lend-Lease. The US Department of State's 'Report on War Aid Furnished by the United States to the USSR' of 28 November 1945 provides the following data:

Shipments to USSR, 22 June* 1941 to 20 September 1945 (tons)

Year	All Routes	Persian Gulf	Soviet Far East	Northern Russia	Black Sea	Soviet Arctic
1941	360,000	13,000	193,000	154,000	0	0
1942	2,453,000	705,000	734,000	950,000	0	64,000
1943	4,795,000	1,607,000	2,389,000	681,000	0	118,000
1944	6,218,000	1,789,000	2,848,000	1,453,000	0	128,000
1945	3,675,000	45,000	2,079,000	727,000	681,000	143,000
	17,501,000**	4,159,000	8,243,000	3,965,000	681,000	453,000
	100.00%	23.76%	47.10%	22.66%	3.89%	2.59%

Notes:

* 22 June – the commencement of Operation *Barbarossa* – is irrelevant as a starting date since the first deliveries did not commence until Operation *Dervish*, 21–31 August 1941.

** In the absence of information to the contrary, it is assumed that these figures relate to all Allied aid and not just that from the United States.

The overall shipment loss rate was 3.05 per cent, comprising 4 per cent for the Persian Gulf, 1 per cent for the Soviet Far East, 7 per cent for northern Russia (Murmansk/Arkhangelsk convoys) and 1 per cent for the Mediterranean/Black Sea.

Shipments to Northern Russia, 22 June 1941 to 20 September 1945 (tons)

Year	All Routes	Northern Russia Only		All Routes Accumulative		Northern Russia Accumulative	
1941	360,000	154,000	42.78%	360,000	2.06%	154,000	0.88%
1942	2,453,000	950,000	38.73%	2,813,000	16.07%	1,104,000	6.31%
1943	4,795,000	681,000	14.20%	7,608,000	43.47%	1,785,000	10.20%
1944	6,218,000	1,453,000	23.37%	13,826,000	79.00%	3,238,000	18.50%
1945	3,675,000	727,000	19.78%	17,501,000	100.00%	3,965,000	22.66%
Total	17,501,000	3,965,000					

In order to foster the politically correct message to the Soviet people at the time, Lend-Lease vehicles were 'sanitized' on arrival, with slogans of support for Stalin and the Soviet people painted out upon being unloaded. One of the advantages of the internet is the ability now to source documentary film that was not previously available to the public, particularly Soviet-originated. The absence of British or American Lend-Lease military equipment in these 'documentaries' is quite obvious. Occasionally, a recognizable Studebaker 2½-ton truck might be seen briefly. But despite watching many of these over time, thanks to YouTube particularly, I am yet to see a Matilda, Valentine, Churchill, M3 Lee/Grant or M4 Sherman tank, and certainly the commentaries make no reference to them. Any contribution by the Western Allies is simply airbrushed from the Soviet visual version of the Great Patriotic War.

Mk 2 Valentine tanks bound for Russia, Birmingham Railway Carriage and Wagon Company, 22 September 1941. (Public Domain)

Admiral Nikolai Kuznetsov, the Soviet Chief of Naval Staff, wrote a begrudging acknowledgement in his memoirs:

> Summing up, I would like to point out that the Allied aid in armaments, means of transportation and foodstuffs was, of course, of definite importance to us. However, it should be mentioned that Allied deliveries accounted only for a small share of the USSR's needs in war. The volume of these deliveries was incomparable with the war effort of the Soviet people who shouldered the main burden of the struggle against Nazi Germany and its satellites. I shall not quote any figures, because they have appeared in many publications. But it is necessary to bring this point to light, because bourgeois falsifiers of the history of the Second World War have continued to exaggerate the importance of Allied wartime deliveries to our country.[2]

As historian David Wragg comments in his book, appropriately titled *Sacrifice For Stalin*:

> Stalin worked hard to convey the impression that while Russia suffered, her new Allies were doing nothing. Insult was added to injury as later Russian records failed to note the achievements made possible by Western aid. One can scan official Russian accounts in vain for the mention of British and American equipment.[3]

Noted historians on the war on the Eastern Front, David M. Glantz and Jonathan M. House, stated:

> Although Soviet accounts have routinely belittled the significance of Lend-Lease in the sustainment of the Soviet war effort, the overall importance of the assistance cannot be understated. Lend-Lease aid did not arrive in sufficient quantities to make the difference between defeat and victory in 1941–1942; that achievement must be attributed solely to the Soviet people and to the iron nerve of Stalin, Zhukov, Shaposhnikov, Vasilevsky, and their subordinates.[4]

The Soviet Union was not a country to admit that assistance from capitalist countries ever happened, let alone provided the Soviets with any advantage. Basically, Russians still have the belief that they won the Great Patriotic War *despite* the Western Allies, not in any way *because* of them or in any way due to their assistance. During the Cold War, the Western Allies' contribution was written out, expunged from Russian history.

So effective has this misinformation been that British historian Sir Antony Beevor stated in a 2017 address to the Hillsdale College, titled 'The Soviet Role in World War II', that a June 2017 survey by the Russian Levada Centre showed that 63 per cent of Russians believed that the USSR would have been victorious in the Great Patriotic War without the assistance of the Allies. Curiously, in that same poll, only 12 per cent of Russians believed that Joseph Stalin was most to blame for the Red Army's high casualty rate in that war. Beevor also stated that 'the rehabilitation of Stalin has been gathering speed'. He went on to say: 'Putin, like Stalin, refuses to acknowledge the Western Allies' contribution to Russia's survival and, ultimately, to the Allied victory.'

In some respects, one can begin to sympathize with this view, particularly if one compares the magnitude and ferocity of the Eastern Front to that of the Western Front. Compare, just for one moment, the numbers of combatants, and particularly the number of military deaths, on both sides. Of the approximately 5.3 million German military deaths during World War II, around 80 per cent were incurred fighting the Soviets on the Eastern Front; that is, some 4.2–4.25 million deaths. These numbers were inflicted at a cost of some 8.7 million Soviet military deaths.[5] On the other hand, data as to the Western Allied military deaths in the whole European theatre total less than 1.0 million (possibly 868,000, according to some sources).

I realize that this comparison of military deaths may appear as though I am belittling the Allied effort. I am not. I simply wish to put the two fronts into perspective, to achieve some sort of balance as to where the majority of fighting took place which ultimately defeated Nazi Germany.

We have grown up believing a view, presented by politicians, the media, even some historians and certainly the many 'documentaries' now common on YouTube, that overemphasized the Western Allies' contribution to winning World War II in Europe, overemphasized the importance and success of campaigns such as D-Day, the Battle of the Bulge and the round-the-clock strategic bombing and underemphasized the Red Army's contribution. The post-war Cold War did nothing to reverse this attitude.

Much has been written about the losses suffered and the trials and tribulations of the Russian convoys. The facts need some examination. As Arnold Hague points out, 'the overall loss was not significantly higher than North Atlantic convoys. The true nature of the operations has been somewhat obscured by the scale of losses in two convoys.' Hague goes on to say that 'it is questionable whether there would have been a significant, strategic effect on the outcome of the war if the summer convoys of 1942 had been suspended'.[6]

Building on Hague's proposition: did the Russian convoys and the aid provided by them make any difference to the war's outcome?

Referring to Tables A and B above, of the 17,501,000 tons of aid shipped in total via five different routes to the USSR, the 3,965,000 tons that were dispatched via the Russian convoys to either Murmansk or Arkhangelsk represented 22.66 per cent of the total tonnage. However, the loss rate was 7 per cent overall, reducing the total to some 3,687,500 tons and 21.07 per cent. I could not find any data to separate the loss rate into yearly totals, of which 1942 must surely have represented the lion's share. Nevertheless, it is worth examining the data as to the yearly shipment data and accumulated total from Table B. Ignoring losses, the total dispatched to northern Russia in 1941 and 1942 was 1,104,000 tons, or only 6.31 per cent of the final total. From early 1943, after the battle for Stalingrad marked the turning point on the Eastern Front, only 681,000 tons (3.89 per cent) were despatched for the remainder of the year, by the end of which only 1,785,000 tons, or 10.20 per cent of the total, had been despatched. The vast majority of the aid, a further 1,453,000 tons (12.46 per cent), was delivered in 1944. Therefore, did the 22.66 per cent of aid despatched via the Russian convoys, most of it after Stalingrad, make a difference?

To answer this, one needs to ask what difference the whole of Lend-Lease aid made to the Great Patriotic War. It is my opinion that even if Lend-Lease aid or similar had not been provided, the defeat of Nazi Germany was inevitable. But the big question is: when? One must consider just what type of Lend-Lease aid was delivered, when and by what means. The Red Army learnt from the mistakes made early in the war that allowed large encirclements to take place. Tactics generally improved, becoming more flexible and less doctrinal. Control and communication improved. But the predominant tactic was to use overwhelming force, to hurl seemingly endless quantities of personnel and armoured vehicles on broad fronts, supported by massive artillery barrages. Most of this took effect, forcing the Axis ever westward, after the tide had turned – commonly accepted to be the failure of *Fall Blau* and the surrender at Stalingrad in February 1943. However, without Lend-Lease, victory would have been substantially delayed and would have resulted in more deaths for the Western Allies and Soviets, particularly the latter. Hitler's reliance on 'wonder weapons', on technology, on quality overcoming quantity, would not have made the difference. Ultimately, of course, the atomic bomb might have been the determinant.

However, in a substantially delayed victory, it might well have been the case that some of the countries that came under the Soviet yoke would have been liberated by the Western Allies. On the other hand, there is ample evidence to indicate that the Western Allies were more than happy to see Russian blood shed rather than their own—the so-called 'race to Berlin', the US Ninth Army's enforced halt at the River Elbe and the lack of will to occupy Prague being examples. The Western Allies simply wanted the war to be over, as soon as practicable and with the minimum of Western bloodshed. Stalin wanted the war to finish too, but with Soviet hegemony paramount. Both got their wishes.

David Wragg argues, effectively, in his last chapter 'Stalin Prepares to Dominate Europe', that 'the Soviet Union had been rigging the shape of post-war Europe as its influence spread westwards with the German retreat',[7] and that the Yalta Conference of February 1945 – and Churchill's earlier meeting with Stalin in October 1944, known as the Tolstoy Conference – gave Stalin Eastern Europe.[8] It is hard not to come to the same conclusion.

Having looked at the bigger picture, it is now time to focus on PQ 17 itself and post-war reactions to it. The question of Broome's destroyers leaving the now-scattering PQ 17 was the subject of a comment by Winston Churchill: 'Unfortunately, the destroyers of the convoy escort also withdrew [with the cruisers].'[9] In a letter to the *Daily Telegraph* on 30 October 1950, Commander Broome, leader of the 1st Escort Group and by then a captain on the retired list with a Distinguished Service Cross to his name, responded to Churchill's statement:

> This statement may reasonably create the impression that the destroyer force was free to remain with the convoy or withdraw. It was no misfortune that the destroyers under my command withdrew. It resulted from a direct order from the Admiralty to scatter the convoy. This order could only have been justified by the proximity of the enemy, and it demanded therefore that I should concentrate my destroyer force with the nearby cruisers. The responsibility for the tragic events which followed must rest with those who, in contradiction to normal naval practice, elected to direct an Arctic convoy from London, instead of passing information and leaving decisions to the commander on the spot.[10]

In his 1972 autobiography *Convoy is to Scatter*, Broome has this to say on the same subject: 'This basic fact which no improvement in communication can alter: the situation confronting the man on the spot will never be exactly the same as that visualized anywhere else.'[11] That Broome felt that he needed to attack the Admiralty's decision (that is, Pound's decision), five years after the war's end, is significant in itself.

David Irving's *The Destruction of Convoy PQ 17* was first published in 1968 by Cassell. A pre-release batch of 60 copies resulted in Broome suing Irving for libel as the publication (later a full release in paper-back form in 1970) maintained that Broome, with the destroyers that formed part of 1st Escort Group under his command, disobeyed Admiral Hamilton's instructions, misunderstood Admiralty signals and abandoned the convoy when they joined Cruiser Squadron One, and that this was a primary cause of the convoy's destruction. In March 1968, Broome issued a writ for libel against both Irving and Cassell, the publishing firm having been warned that the material was contentious, as it had been rejected previously by publishers William Kimber for that reason. Cassell published Irving's book on the condition that Irving provided them with an indemnity in the event that the publication was libellous. That indemnity was to backfire on Irving, as he lost the case and the subsequent appeal, having to pay Broome £15,000 compensation and £25,000 punitive damages.[12]

The copy I obtained of Irving's book was published in 1987 and would appear to have been toned down. I could find no particular criticism of Broome by Irving, although Broome was, perhaps, damned by faint praise. Irving's criticism was his point of view – wrong, as it turned out – and is only of passing interest to the story of PQ 17, although it created a furore at the time.

What was of more interest was an impromptu meeting Broome apparently had with the First Lord of the Admiralty, A. V. Alexander, when *Keppel* (Broome's command) was in a London commercial dockyard on one of two occasions – in either late 1942 or late 1943 – for an annual refit. Alexander addressed the ship's company and Broome says that the words Alexander used were 'treacle' and 'too thick, overspilt'. Broome said that they 'were a ship's company, not a constituency'. Later, in his cabin, Broome asked Alexander outright, 'Why was PQ 17 scattered?' Broome did not enlighten us with Alexander's words. All he remembered was that 'it was no answer, or moment of truth. My question was precisely what he had come, armed with evasive politics, to decry … the Right Honourable A.V. Alexander left my cabin in no doubt whether I was both disappointed and disgusted. My conclusion: had the Admiralty's conscience about PQ 17 been clear, I would never have had the doubtful pleasure of that meeting'.[13]

Just as the Soviets put their particular spin on the war, so did the Admiralty view PQ 17 – not its finest moment, but somewhat camouflaged to hide the obvious: the failure of the First Sea Lord to avoid micro-managing long-distance action and without a proper appreciation of intelligence.

No matter what spectacles we use, what magnifying glass we use, what microscope we bring to the forensic examination of PQ 17's fate, that failure is obvious.

I trust this work has shed a little more light on the matter, some 80-plus years hence.

Glossary

AA	Anti-aircraft.
'A' Position, etc.	In British ships, main armament positions – almost invariably on the centreline of the ship – were given alphabetical designations, starting with 'A' and 'B' at the bow and finishing with 'X' and 'Y' at the stern. Midships turrets usually had something like a 'Q' designation. The reason the designations did not follow the alphabet was to ensure that when giving orders, the names sounded sufficiently distinct so they would not be confused.
A/S	Anti-submarine.
ASDIC	The primary device for detecting submarines via echolocation. Called sonar by the USN.
ASV	Air-to-Surface-Vessel radar carried by, in this instance, Fairey Swordfish, Fairey Albacore and Catalina aircraft.
AW or A/W	Air Warning – as in Air Warning radar. Air-Search was another term used.
BHP	Brake Horsepower – the power measured at the crankshaft just outside the engine, before the losses of power caused by the gearbox and drive train.
BL	Breech loading – that is, where the projectile and propellant charge are loaded separately, as distinct from QF (Quick-firing), where the projectile and propellant are in one self-contained round.
Bofors	The Swedish armaments manufacturer whose name was simply used to describe its famous 40 mm anti-aircraft gun that was made under licence. The first models were simple single-barrelled air-cooled models, but were developed by the licensees into two- and four-barrelled water-cooled versions.
Carley Float	A life raft made from a steel or copper inner tube, divided into watertight sections and covered in a buoyancy material such as cork, in turn covered in painted canvas with a floor of webbing or slatted wood. They came in various sizes and shapes from 8 ft × 5 ft to 14 ft × 9 ft.
DC	Depth Charge, a drum-shaped canister filled with high explosive detonated via a hydrostatic valve set at predetermined depths.
DCT	Depth Charge Thrower, hydraulic or explosively detonated projector to launch a depth charge clear of a ship. Called a Depth Charge Projector in USN ships.
Displacement	By the Archimedes Principle: the weight of the water displaced by the vessel when floating.

DR	Dead Reckoning: the process of calculating the current position of a moving object by using a previously determined position, or fix, and incorporating estimates of speed, heading (or direction or course) and elapsed time, all of which are subject to significant errors of approximation.
F	Flag – an indication that a ship is the senior ship of a detachment/squadron, etc.
Full Load	That is, Full Load Displacement, the weight of the water displaced by the vessel when floating at its greatest allowable draft.
GRT	A ship's total internal volume expressed in register tons, each of which is equal to 100 cubic feet (2.83 m^3). GRT tonnage uses the total permanently enclosed capacity of the vessel below the uppermost continuous deck plus all enclosed spaces above this deck, less exempted spaces (such as accommodation), as its basis for volume.
HA	High Angle, in effect anti-aircraft capable only.
HA/LA	High Angle/Low Angle, in effect both capable of surface and anti-aircraft action.
HACS	High Angle Control System: an obsolescent RN anti-aircraft fire control system based on the premise that a target moved at a constant course, speed and height throughout the engagement. Its shortcomings were particularly evident as target speeds increased and attack methods changed. It expended huge amounts of ammunition to little effect, as evidenced by the number ships lost during the intense AA engagements in the Mediterranean.
IHP	Indicated Horsepower – the total power produced by the engine measured at the crankshaft, such as a reciprocating engine.
LA	Low Angle, in effect surface action capable only.
Laid Down	The term applied to the keel being laid down, which was traditionally the first and major structural item on which the rest of the framework of the ship was constructed.
Launched	Ships are seldom launched in a completed state – that is, fully fitted out. The slipways are needed for the next ship, so ships are launched when they are substantially complete and moved to fitting-out berths.
LBP	Length Between Perpendiculars – sometimes expressed as bp or pp, especially prior to World War II. It is measured from the forward surface of the stem, or main bow perpendicular member, to the after surface of the sternpost, or main stern perpendicular member.
LOA	Length Overall – measured from the extreme forward end of the bow to the extreme aft end of the stern. Watercraft operators must be familiar with this and similar dimensions to safely maneuver the ship. The dimension is commonly found in lists of data for each vessel.
LWL	Length Load Waterline – an important dimension because length at the waterline is a key factor in the complex problem of speed, resistance, and friction. In simple terms, the maximum speed of a displacement hull is $1.34 \times \sqrt{LWL}$.

MG	Machine gun.
mm	Millimetre, in this case the calibre, the bore, of the weapon.
NHP	Nominal Horsepower – an antiquated and complicated method of estimating the power of steam engines, particularly because it assumed a very low steam pressure of 7 psi (pounds per square inch).
Oerlikon	A Swiss armament manufacturer, but the name more commonly used to describe their high-velocity 20 mm cannon made under licence in large numbers in Britain and the USA, primarily as a light, short-range, anti-aircraft weapon.
Pendant Number	Pronounced 'Pennant Number', the numbers or letters, or combination of numbers and letters, used to identify individual ships.
Pom-pom	The name is derived from the sound the Vickers 40 mm QF 2 pdr Mk II made when fired. It was, in effect, an oversized Maxim machine gun. The later Mk VIII model was made in single, quad and eight-barrel mountings and capable of a high rate of fire.
QF	Quick-Firing, using fixed ammunition where the projectile and propellant are in one piece, offering a higher rate of fire, as distinct from Breech-Loading (BL), where the projectile and propellant are separate and slower to load.
QF 12 pdr 12 cwt	This weapon dated back to 1894. Twelve pounds (12 pdr) was the weight of the projectile and 12 hundredweight (12 cwt) the weight of the barrel and breech. It was not a Quick-Firing gun in the true sense of the word in that the projectile and propellant were separate but were loaded together on a special tray, although it did achieve 15 rounds per minute. The gun stayed in production throughout World War II, with improvements, such was demand.
QF 2 pdr Mk VIII	A single-barreled, manually operated and updated version of the QF 2-pdr Mk II, commonly referred to as a pom-pom from the noise it made when firing. Usually replaced by 20 mm Oerlikon or, later, 40 mm Bofors.
Radar	Originally called RDF – Range and Direction Finding – the acronym came from Radio Detection and Ranging. An object-detection system that uses radio waves to determine the range, angle or velocity of objects via a transmitter producing electromagnetic waves through an emitting antenna and a receiving antenna to capture any returns from objects in the path of the emitted signal, plus a receiver and processor to determine the properties of the object.
RAF	Royal Air Force.
RN	Royal Navy.
RNR	Royal Naval Reserve; at the time of World War II it was a volunteer reserve force, formed mainly from professional merchant seaman officers.
RNVR	Royal Naval Volunteer Reserve. a 'hostilities only' volunteer force of officers formed mainly from volunteers with some form of seagoing experience, however slight.

R/T	Radio Telephony.
Shp	Shaft Horsepower: the power delivered to the propeller shafts of a steamship. This measure is not commonly used in the automobile industry, because in that context drive train losses can become significant.
Standard	That is, Standard Displacement, the weight of the water displaced by the vessel complete, fully manned, engined and equipped ready for sea, including all armament and ammunition, equipment, outfit, provisions and fresh water for crew, miscellaneous stores and implements of every description that are intended to be carried in war, but without fuel or reserve boiler feed water on board.
SW	Surface Warning, as in Surface Warning radar.
USN	United States Navy.
VTE	Vertical Triple Expansion – a compound engine that expands the steam in three stages. That is, an engine which has cylinders operating at three different pressures. Exhaust steam from the small, high-pressure cylinder goes to the medium-pressure, middle-sized cylinder and thence to the lowest-pressure and biggest-sized sized cylinder before going to a condenser to be turned back into water, and then to the boiler to be turned back into steam.
W/T	Wireless Telegraphy.
Work Up	The British equivalent of the USN Shakedown: the process of bringing a ship and its crew up to operational capability.

Appendix A: Orders of Battle

Allied

PQ 17 Convoy Merchant Ships

Ship Name & Nationality	Built	Type/Design
Alcoa Ranger (US)	1919	Emergency Fleet Corporation Type 1022
Azerbaijan (Soviet)	1935	No details available
Bellingham (US)	1918	Emergency Fleet Corporation Type 1013
Benjamin Harrison (US)	1942	Liberty Ship EC2-S-C1
Bolton Castle (UK)	1939	British-built – no details
Carlton (US)	1920	Emergency Fleet Corporation Type 1022
Christopher Newport (US)	1942	Liberty Ship EC2-S-C1
Daniel Morgan (US)	1942	Liberty Ship EC2-S-C1
Donbass (Soviet)	1935	Emba-class tanker
Earlston (UK)	1941	British World War II emergency design
El Capitan (Pan)	1917	Emergency Fleet Corporation, type unknown
Empire Byron (UK)	1941	British World War II emergency Ba Type
Empire Tide (UK)	1941	British World War II emergency X Type
Exford (US)	1919	Emergency Fleet Corporation Type 1022
Fairfield City (US)	1921	Built for US Steel
Hartlebury (UK)	1934	British-built – no details
Honomu (US)	1919	Emergency Fleet Corporation Type 1079
Hoosier (US)	1920	Emergency Fleet Corporation Type 1022
Ironclad (US)	1919	No details available
John Witherspoon (US)	1942	Liberty Ship EC2-S-C1
Navarino (UK)	1937	No details available
Ocean Freedom (UK)	1942	US-built, Ocean class
Olopana (US)	1920	Emergency Fleet Corporation Type 1015

Ship Name & Nationality	Built	Type/Design
Pan Atlantic (US)	1920	Emergency Fleet Corporation Type 1019
Pan Kraft (US)	1919	Emergency Fleet Corporation Type 1019
Paulus Potter (Dutch)	1942	British standard World War II emergency design
Peter Kerr (US)	1920	Emergency Fleet Corporation Type 1127, Japanese-built
Richard Bland (US)	1942	Liberty Ship EC2-S-C1
River Afton (UK) (Commodore)	1935	No details available
Samuel Chase (US)	1942	Liberty Ship EC2-S-C1
Silver Sword (US)	1919	Emergency Fleet Corporation Type 1017
Troubadour (Pan)	1920	British World War I emergency-build N-type
Washington (US)	1919	Emergency Fleet Corporation Type 1019
West Gotomska (US)	1918	Emergency Fleet Corporation Type 1013
William Hooper (US)	1942	Liberty Ship EC2-S-C1
Winston-Salem (US)	1920	Emergency Fleet Corporation Type 1037

For ship details, refer to Appendix B.

Rescue Ships *(all British)*

Rathlin

Zaafaran

Zamalek

For ship details, refer to Appendix B.

Close Escort/Ocean Escort

(All RN unless specified otherwise.)

Destroyers: *Fury*, *Keppel* (F), *Leamington*, *Ledbury*, *Offa*, *Wilton*

Corvettes: *Dianella*, *Lotus*, *Poppy*, *La Malouine* (Free French)

A/S (anti-submarine) Trawlers: *Ayrshire*, *Lord Austin*, *Lord Middleton*, *Northern Gem*

Minesweepers: *Bramble*, *Britomart*, *Leda*, *Salamander*

Auxiliary AA ships: *Palomares*, *Pozarica*

For ship details, refer to Appendix C.

Supply Group (Force Q)

Fleet Oilers: RFA *Gray Ranger*, RFA *Aldersdale*

Destroyer: *Douglas*

For ship details, refer to Appendix C.

Covering Force

Cruiser Squadron 1 (CS One) (all RN unless specified otherwise)

Heavy Cruisers: *London* (F), *Norfolk*, *Tuscaloosa* (USN), *Wichita* (USN)

Destroyers: *Somali*, *Rowan* (USN), *Wainwright* (USN)

For ship details, refer to Appendix C.

Battle Fleet/Distant Cover Force

(All RN unless specified otherwise.)

Battleships: *Duke of York* (F), *Washington* (USN)

Aircraft carrier: *Victorious*

Heavy cruiser: *Cumberland*

Light cruiser: *Nigeria*

Destroyers: *Ashanti*, *Blankney*, *Escapade*, *Faulknor*, *Marne*, *Martin*, *Middleton*, *Onslaught*, *Onslow*, *Wheatland*, *Mayrant* (USN), *Rhind* (USN)

For ship details, refer to Appendix C.

Submarines

Sahib, *Sea Wolf*, *Sturgeon*, *Tribune*, *Trident*, *Unrivalled*, *Unshaken*, *Ursula*, *Minerve* (Free French) + 5 Soviet

For ship details, refer to Appendix C.

Axis

Kriegsmarine

1st Combat Group (Trondheim)

Tirpitz (Battleship) Flagship

Admiral Hipper (Heavy Cruiser)

5th Destroyer Flotilla: *Z-4 Richard Beitzen, Z-14 Friedrich Inh*

Torpedo boats: *T-7, T-15*

2nd Combat Group (Narvik)

Lützow (Pocket Battleship/Heavy Cruiser)

Admiral Scheer (Pocket Battleship/Heavy Cruiser)

8th Destroyer Flotilla: *Z-24, Z-27, Z-28, Z-29, Z-30*

Submarines: *U-88, U-251, U-255, U-334, U-355, U-376, U-456, U-457, U-703*

For ship details, refer to Appendix D.

Luftwaffe

5th Air Fleet

108 Ju 88 bombers

42 He 111 bombers

15 He 115 floatplane bombers

30 Ju 87 dive-bombers

74 reconnaissance aircraft including FW 200 Condors and BV 138 seaplanes

For ship aircraft details, refer to Appendix E.

Appendix B: Merchant Ships of PQ 17

Typical EC2-S-C1 Liberty Ship (*Benjamin Harrison, Christopher Newport, Daniel Morgan, John Witherspoon, Richard Bland, Samuel Chase, William Hooper*)

Displacement:	7,176 GRT
Dimensions:	441 ft 6 in LOA, 57 ft 0 in beam, 26 ft 10 in draught
Propulsion:	3-cylinder VTE, 2,500 ihp to 1 shaft
Maximum speed:	11–11.5 kn

SS *Ocean Freedom* (Ocean-class war emergency tramp ship)

Displacement:	7,157 GRT
Dimensions:	441 ft 6 in LOA, 57 ft 0 in beam, 26 ft 11 in draught
Propulsion:	3-cylinder VTE, 2,500 ihp to 1 shaft
Maximum speed:	11–11.5 kn

EFC Type 1022, Hog Island (*Alcoa Ranger, Carlton, Exford, Hoosier*)

Displacement:	5,116 GRT
Dimensions:	390 ft 0 in LOA, 54 ft 1½ in beam, 26 ft 6–27 ft 6 in draught
Propulsion:	2 geared turbines, 2,500 shp to 1 shaft
Maximum speed:	15 kn

EFC Type 1013, Robert Dollar (*Bellingham, West Gotomska*)

Displacement:	5,345 GRT
Dimensions:	423 ft 9 in LOA, 54 ft 0 in beam, 24 ft 2 in draught
Propulsion:	3-cylinder VTE, 422 nhp or Curtis turbine, 2,500 shp to 1 shaft
Maximum speed:	10.5 kn

EFC Type 1019, Ferris (*Pan Atlantic, Pan Kraft, Washington*)

Displacement:	5,411 GRT
Dimensions:	410 ft 5 in LOA, 54 ft 0 in beam, 27 ft 0 in draught
Propulsion:	3-cylinder VTE, 2,800 ihp to 1 shaft
Maximum speed:	10.5 kn

EFC Type 1127, Osaka (*Peter Kerr*)

Displacement:	7,192 GRT
Dimensions:	429 ft 0 in LOA, 55 ft 5 in beam, 27 ft 7 in draught
Propulsion:	3-cylinder VTE, 553 nhp to 1 shaft
Maximum speed:	10.5 kn

EFC Type 1037, Federal (*Winston-Salem*)

Displacement:	6,501 GRT
Dimensions:	410 ft 3 in LOA, 55 ft 0 in beam, 35 ft 0 in draught
Propulsion:	2 × Scotch boilers, VTE, 590 nhp to 1 shaft
Maximum speed:	11.0 kn

British Standard N Type (*Troubador/Troubadour*)

Displacement:	6,590 GRT
Dimensions:	428 ft 0 in LOA, 55 ft 5½ in beam, 28 ft 0 in draught
Propulsion:	Geared turbine, 2,300 hp to 1 shaft
Maximum speed:	11 kn

MV *Empire Tide* (MoWT Type X, CAM ship)

Displacement:	6,978 GRT
Dimensions:	433 ft 0 in LOA, 56 ft 0 in beam, 32 ft 2 in depth (not draught)
Propulsion:	6-cylinder diesel, details unknown, to 1 shaft
Maximum speed:	11 kn (assumed)

SS *Rathlin* (Rescue Ship)

(Laid down – date unknown, launched 3 September 1936, completed November 1936)

Displacement:	1,599 GRT
Dimensions:	272 ft 6 in LOA, 38 ft 6 in beam, draught unknown
Armament:	2 × 40 mm Bofors (2 × 1)
	4 × 20 mm (4 × 1)
Propulsion:	3-cylinder VTE, 196 nhp to 1 shaft
Maximum speed:	12 kn
Range:	Unknown
Crew:	Unknown

Appendix C: Home Fleet – Battle Fleet or Distant Cover Force

HMS *Duke of York*

King George V-class Battleship

Ordered:	16 November 1937
Builder:	John Brown & Company, Clydebank
Laid down:	5 May 1937
Launched:	28 February 1940
Commissioned:	2 November 1941
Pennant number:	17
Displacement:	42,000 tn standard
Length:	745 ft 1 in LOA
Beam:	103 ft 2 in
Draught:	34 ft 4 in
Propulsion:	8 Admiralty 3-drum boilers driving 4 geared turbines delivering 110,000 shp to 4 shafts
Speed:	28.3 kn
Range/endurance:	15,000 nm at 10 kn
Complement:	1,550
Armament:	As in July 1942:
	10 × 14 in (2 × 4, 1 × 2)
	16 × 5.25 in
	48 × 40 mm/2 pdr AA (6 × 8)
	6 × 20 mm AA
Aircraft:	4 × Supermarine Walrus seaplanes (sometimes only 1–2 carried), 1 catapult
Armour:	Belt: 5.4–14.7 in
	Deck: 5–6 in
	Bulkheads: 10–12 in
	Turrets: 12¾ in
	Conning tower: 3–4 in

Sensors:	Type 279 air warning radar
	Type 271 surface warning
	Type 282 ranging radar for 2 pdr pom-poms
	Type 284 ranging radar for main armament

USS *Washington*

North Carolina-class Battleship

Builder:	Philadelphia Navy Yard
Laid down:	14 June 1938
Launched:	1 June 1940
Commissioned:	15 May 1941
Pennant number:	BB-56
Displacement:	36,000 tn standard, 44,800 tn full load
Length:	728 ft 9 in LOA
Beam:	108 ft 4 in
Draught:	33 ft 0 in
Propulsion:	8 × Babcock & Wilcox Admiralty boilers delivering 121,000 shp to General Electric geared turbines to 4 shafts
Speed:	28 kn
Range/endurance:	17,450 nm at 15 k
Complement:	1,800
Armament:	As in July 1942:
	9 × 16 in (3 × 3)
	20 × 5 in (10 × 2)
	16 × 1.1 in AA (4 × 4)
	Numerous 0.5 in HMG (heavy machine guns), possibly some 20 mm Oerlikons
Aircraft:	3 × Curtiss SOC Seagull seaplanes, 2 catapults
Armour:	Belt: 12 in
	Deck: 5½ in
	Bulkheads: 10–12 in
	Turrets: 16 in
	Conning tower: 16 in
Sensors:	CXAM-1 air search radar
	May have had Mk 3 and Mk 4 radars for main and secondary armament

HMS *Victorious*

Illustrious-class Aircraft Carrier

Ordered:	13 January 1937
Builder:	Vickers-Armstrong Ltd, Newcastle upon Tyne, England
Laid down:	4 May 1937
Launched:	14 September 1939
Commissioned:	14 May 1941
Pennant number:	38, R38
Displacement:	23,000 tn standard
Length:	753 ft 6 in LOA, 673 ft 0 in LBP
Beam:	95 ft 9 in
Draught:	24 ft 0 in
Propulsion:	6 Admiralty 3-drum boilers with superheaters at 400 psi driving 3 Parsons geared turbines delivering 111,000 shp to 3 shafts
Speed:	31 kn
Range/endurance:	11,000 nm at 14 kn
Complement:	1,392, including air group
Armament:	As at July 1942:
	16 × 4.5 in/45 DP (8 × 2)
	48 × 40 mm/2 pdr AA (6 × 8)
	3 × 20 mm AA
Aircraft:	As designed – 72
	In June 1942 – 34 (6 Hawker Sea Hurricanes, 885 Sqd; 20 Fairey Fulmars, 809 & 884 Sqd; 14 Fairey Albacores, 832 & 817 Sqd)[1]
Armour:	Belt: 4½ in
	Hangar side: 4½ in
	Deck: 2½–3 in
Sensors:	Type 72DM aircraft homing beacon
	Type 79 air warning radar
	Type 282 ranging radar for 2 pdr pom-poms
	Type 285 ranging radar for main armament

HMS *Nigeria*

Crown Colony-class Light Cruiser

Ordered:	Under the 1937 estimates
Builder:	Vickers-Armstrong Ltd, Newcastle upon Tyne, England
Laid down:	8 February 1938
Launched:	18 July 1939
Commissioned:	23 September 1940
Pennant number:	60
Displacement:	8,253 tn standard (10,534 tn full load)
Length:	555 ft 6 in LOA, 538 ft 0 in LBP
Beam:	62 ft 0 in
Draught:	15 ft 6 in forward, 17 ft 6 in aft
Propulsion:	4 Admiralty 3-drum boilers driving Parsons single reduction geared turbines of 72,500 shp to 4 shafts
Speed:	32¼ kn (31¼ full load)
Range/endurance:	8,000 nm at 16 kn
Complement:	738
Armament:	As in July 1942:
	12 × BL 6 in/50 cal. Mk XXIII (4 × 3)
	8 × QF 4 in Mk. XVI/45 cal. (4 × 2)
	8 × QF 2 pdr Mk VII
	8 × 0.5 in Vickers MG Mk III (2 × 4)
	6 × 21 in torpedo tubes (2 × 3)
Aircraft:	3 × Supermarine Walrus Mk I (1 catapult)
	Capacity was 3 but, in this instance, there may have only been 1 on board
Armour:	Belt: 3¼ in
	Deck: 2 in
	Turrets: 2 in
	DCT: 4 in
Sensors:	Unknown

HMS *Ashanti*

Tribal-class Destroyer

Ordered:	19 June 1936
Builder:	William Denny and Brothers Limited, Dunbarton, Scotland

Laid down:	23 November 1936
Launched:	5 November 1937
Commissioned:	21 December 1938
Pennant number:	L 51/F 51/G 51
Displacement:	1,960 tn standard (2,520 tn full load)
Length:	377 ft 0 in LOA, 355 ft 6 in LBP
Beam:	36 ft 6 in
Draught:	9 ft 0 in (13 ft 0 in full load)
Propulsion:	3 Admiralty 3-drum boilers at 300 psi driving Parsons single reduction geared turbines delivering 44,000 shp at 350 rpm to 2 shafts
Speed:	36 kn (32½ kn full load)
Range/endurance:	5,700 nm at 15 kn, 3,200 nm at 20 kn
Complement:	190
Armament:	As in July 1942:
	6 × QF 4.7 in/45 cal. Mk XII (3 × 2)
	2 × QF 4 in/45 cal. Mk XVI (1 × 2)
	4 × QF 2 pdr 40 mm/40 cal. Mk VIII AA (1 × 4)
	6 × 20 mm Oerlikons (6 × 1)*
	4 × 21 in torpedo tubes (1 × 4)
	2 × DCT
	2 DC rails
Sensors:	Type 290 air warning radar
	Type 285 gunnery ranging radar
	ASDIC

* The replacement of the 0.5 in MGs by 20 mm Oerlikons was on an 'as available' basis.

HMS *Marne*

M-class Destroyer

Ordered:	1939 Programme
Builder:	Vickers-Armstrong Ltd, Newcastle upon Tyne, England
Laid down:	23 October 1939
Launched:	30 October 1940
Commissioned:	2 December 1941
Pennant number:	G 35
Displacement:	1,920 tn standard (2,725 tn full load)

Length:	362 ft 6 in LOA, 345 ft 6 in LBP
Beam:	37 ft 0 in (14 ft 6 in full load)
Draught:	10 ft 0 in
Propulsion:	2 Admiralty 3-drum boilers at 300 psi driving Parsons single reduction geared turbines delivering 48,000 shp at 340 rpm to 2 shafts
Speed:	36 kn
Range/endurance:	5,500 nm at 12 kn, 4,000 nm at 20 kn
Complement:	190
Armament:	As completed and probably as at July 1942:
	6 × QF 4.7 in/50 cal. Mk XI (3 × 2)
	1 × QF 4 in/45 cal. Mk V HA Mk III
	4 × QF 2 pdr 40 mm/40 cal. Mk VIII AA (1 × 4)
	4 × 20 mm Oerlikons (4 × 1)
	4 × 0.5 in Vickers MG Mk III (2 × 2)
	4 × 21 in QR Mk VIII torpedo tubes (1 × 4)
	2 DCT
	2 DC rails, 42 DCs
Sensors:	Type 290 air warning radar
	Type 285 gunnery ranging radar
	ASDIC

HMS *Onslow*

O-class Destroyer

Ordered:	2 October 1939 (2nd Emergency Flotilla)
Builder:	John Browne & Company, Clydebank
Laid down:	1 July 1940
Launched:	31 March 1941
Commissioned:	8 October 1941
Pennant number:	G 17
Displacement:	1,550 tn standard (2,250 tn full load)
Length:	345 ft 0 in LOA, 328 ft 9 in LBP
Beam:	35 ft 0 in
Draught:	9 ft 0 in (12 ft 3 in full load)
Propulsion:	2 Admiralty 3-drum boilers with Melesco superheaters at 300 psi driving Parsons single reduction turbines delivering 40,000 shp at 350 rpm to 2 shafts

Speed:	36¾ kn (33 kn full load)
Range/endurance:	3,850 nm at 20 kn
Complement:	176
Armament:	As completed and as in July 1942:
	5 × QF 4 in/45 cal. Mk V on HA MK III** mounting (5 × 1)*
	4 × QF 2 pdr/40 cal. Mk VIII (1 × 4)
	4 × 20 mm Oerlikons (4 × 1)**
	4 × 21 in QR Mk VIII torpedo tubes***
	4 DCT
	2 DC rails, 70 depth charges
Sensors:	Type unknown air warning radar
	Type 285 gunnery ranging radar
	HF/DF
	ASDIC type unknown

* March states 4; ** March states 2 and 2 Mk twin 0.5 in MG; *** March states 8 (page 386); the aft bank of torpedo tubes replaced the 4 in gun at some stage but this is unlikely to have happened before August 1942.

Covering Force – Cruiser Squadron 1

HMS *London*

County-class Heavy Cruiser (London Group)

Ordered:	Details unknown
Builder:	Portsmouth Dockyard
Laid down:	23 February 1926
Launched:	14 September 1927
Commissioned:	31 January 1929
Pennant number:	69
Displacement:	9,750 tn standard (13,315 tn full load)
Length:	633 ft 0 in LOA
Beam:	66 ft 0 in
Draught:	21 ft 0 in
Propulsion:	8 Admiralty 3-drum boilers driving Parsons single reduction geared turbines of 80,000 shp to 4 shafts
Speed:	32 kn

Range/endurance:	9,120 nm at 12 kn
Complement:	784
Armament:	In July 1942
	8 × BL 8 in/50 cal. Mk VIII (4 × 2)
	8 × QF 4 in Mk XVI/45 cal. (4 × 2)
	8 × QF 2 pdr Mk VII (2 × 4)
	7 × 20 mm Oerlikons (7 × 1)
	8 × 21 in torpedo tubes (2 × 4)
Aircraft:	1–2 × Supermarine Walrus Mk I (1 catapult)
Armour:	Belt: 4½ in
	Deck: 1¼–1 ½in
	Turrets: 1 in
	DCT: 1–4 in
Sensors:	Type 279 air warning radar
	Type 273 surface warning radar
	Type 282 ranging radar for 2 pdr pom-poms
	Type 284 main armament gunnery ranging radar
	Type 285 secondary armament gunnery ranging radar

HMS *Norfolk*

County-class Heavy Cruiser (3rd Group)

Ordered:	1924
Builder:	Fairfield Shipbuilding & Engineering Co Ltd, Govan
Laid down:	8 July 1927
Launched:	12 December 1928
Commissioned:	30 April 1930
Pennant number:	78
Displacement:	9,975 tn standard
Length:	630 ft 0 in LOA
Beam:	66 ft 0 in
Draught:	17 ft 0 in
Propulsion:	8 Admiralty 3-drum boilers driving Parsons single reduction geared turbines of 80,000 shp to 4 shafts
Speed:	32¼ kn
Range/endurance:	9,120 nm at 12 kn

Complement:	650
Armament:	In July 1942:
	8 × BL 8 in/50 cal. Mk VIII (4 × 2)
	8 × QF 4 in Mk XVI/45 cal. (4 × 2)
	8 × QF 2 pdr Mk VII (2 × 4)
	4 × 20 mm Oerlikons (4 × 1)
	8 × 0.5 in HMG (2 × 4)
Aircraft:	1 Supermarine Walrus (1 catapult)
Armour:	Belt: 4½ in
	Deck: 1¼–1½ in
	Turrets: 1 in
	DCT: 1–4 in
Sensors:	Type 279 air warning radar
	Type 282 ranging radar for 2 pdr pom-poms
	Type 284 main armament gunnery ranging radar
	Type 285 secondary armament gunnery ranging radar

USS *Tuscaloosa*

New Orleans-class Heavy Cruiser

Ordered:	13 February 1929
Builder:	New York Shipbuilding
Laid down:	3 September 1931
Launched:	15 November 1933
Commissioned:	17 August 1934
Pennant number:	CA-37
Displacement:	9,975 tn standard
Length:	588 ft 0 in LOA
Beam:	61 ft 9 in
Draught:	19 ft 5 in
Propulsion:	8 × Babcock & Wilcock boilers delivering 107,000 shp to Parsons single reduction geared turbines to 4 shafts
Speed:	32¾ kn
Range/endurance:	Unknown
Complement:	708

Armament:	In July 1942:
	9 × 8 in/55 cal. (3 × 3)
	8 × 5 in/28 cal. (8 × 1)
	8 × 1.1 in (2 × 4)
	10 × 20 mm (10 × 1)
Aircraft:	3–4 Curtiss SOC Seagull seaplanes (2 catapults)
Armour:	Belt: 3–5 in
Deck:	1¼–2¼ in
Barbettes:	5 in
Turrets:	1½–8 in
DCT:	5 in
Sensors:	CXAM -1 search radar
	Mk 3 or Mk 4 fire control

USS *Wainwright*

Sims-class Destroyer

Builder:	Norfolk Navy Yard
Laid down:	7 June 1938
Launched:	21 June 1939
Commissioned:	15 April 1940
Pennant number:	DD-419
Displacement:	1,570 tn standard, 2,211 tn full load
Length:	348 ft 3¼ in LOA
Beam:	36 ft 1 in
Draught:	13 ft 4½ in
Propulsion:	3 Babcock & Wilcock boilers delivering 50,000 shp to Westinghouse single reduction geared turbines to 2 shafts
Speed:	35 kn
Range/endurance:	3,660 nm at 20 kn
Complement:	192–251
Armament:	In July 1942:
	4 × 5 in/38 cal. (4 × 1)
	4 × 20 mm (4 × 1)
	8 × TT (2 × 4)
	2 × DC rails

Sensors:	SC 1 search radar (photographs indicate that this may not have been fitted at the time)
	Sonar

Close Escort

HMS *Keppell*

Shakespeare-class – Thornycroft Destroyer Leader

Ordered:	Mid-March 1918
Builder:	John I. Thornycroft & Company, Woolston, England
Laid down:	7 October 1918
Launched:	23 April 1920
Commissioned:	15 April 1925
Pennant number:	D 84/I 84
Displacement:	1,554 tn standard (2,080 tn full load)
Length:	329 ft 0 in LOA, 318 ft 3 in LBP
Beam:	31 ft 6 in
Draught:	9 ft 0 in (13 ft 6 in full load)
Propulsion:	4 Yarrow boilers at 250 psi driving Brown-Curtis single reduction geared turbines delivering 40,000 shp at 360 rpm to 2 shafts
Speed:	36 kn (32½ kn full load)
Range/endurance:	5,000 nm at 15 kn
Complement:	164–83
Armament	As at July 1942:
	2 × BL 4.7 in/45 cal. Mk I on CP Mk VI mounting (2 × 1)
	1 × QF 3 in 20 cwt HA on Mk III mounting
	4 × 20 mm Oerlikons (4 × 1)
	6 × 21 in torpedo tubes
	1 Hedgehog ATW
	4 × DCT
	2 × DC rails
Sensors:	HF/DF
	Type 271 surface warning radar
	Type 291 air warning radar
	ASDIC

HMS *Fury*

F-class Destroyer

Ordered:	17 March 1933, 1932 Programme
Builder:	J. Samuel White and Company, Cowes, Isle of Wight, England
Yard number:	Unknown
Laid down:	19 May 1933
Launched:	10 September 1934
Commissioned:	18 May 1935
Pennant number:	H 76
Displacement:	1,405 tn standard (1,940 tn full load)
Length:	329 ft 0 in LOA, 318 ft 3 in LBP
Beam:	33 ft 3 in
Draught:	8 ft 6 in (12½ ft deep load)
Propulsion:	3 Admiralty 3-drum boilers at 300 psi driving Parson single reduction geared turbines delivering 36,000 shp at 350 rpm to 2 shafts
Speed:	35½ kn (31½ kn full load)
Range/endurance:	6,350 nm at 15 kn, 1,275 nm at 35½ kn
Complement:	145
Armament:	As in July 1942:
	4 × BL 4.7 in Mk IX/45 cal. on CP Mk XVIII mounting (3 × 1)
	1 × QF 12 pdr/40 cal. 12 cwt HA Mk VIII mounting
	4 × 20 mm Oerlikons (4 × 1)
	4 × 21 in QR Mk VI torpedo tubes (1 × 4)
	2 × DCT
	1 × DC rail, 20 DCs
Sensors:	Type 286 target indication radar
	ASDIC

HMS *Leamington*

Town-class Destroyer

Builder:	New York Shipbuilding Corporation
Laid down:	23 January 1918
Launched:	28 September 1918

Commissioned:	28 July 1919 (as USS *Twiggs*, DD-127)
Pennant number:	G 19
Displacement:	1,306 tn standard
Length:	314 ft 4 in LOA
Beam:	30 ft 11 in
Draught:	9 ft 9 in
Propulsion:	4 Normand return flame boilers at 260 psi delivering 24,200 shp Parsons geared turbines to 2 shafts
Speed:	35 kn
Range/endurance:	3,400 nm at 20 kn
Complement:	145
Armament:	As in July 1942:
	3 × BL 4 in 50 cal. Mk 12 (3 × 1)
	1 × QF 12 pdr/40 cal. 12 cwt HA Mk VIII mounting
	2 × 0.5 in HMG (2 × 1)
	3 × 21 in torpedo tubes (1 × 3)
	2 × DCT
	2 × DC rail
Sensors:	Type 286 target indication radar
	ASDIC

HMS *Ledbury*

Hunt-class (Type II) Destroyer

Ordered:	20 December 1939
Builder:	John I. Thornycroft & Company Limited, Woolston, England
Laid down:	24 January 1940
Launched:	27 September 1941
Commissioned:	11 February 1942
Pennant number:	L 90
Displacement:	1,050 tn standard (1,490 tn full load)
Length:	280 ft 0 in LOA, 264 ft 6 in LBP
Beam:	31 ft 6 in
Draught:	7 ft 9 in (12 ft 9 in full load)
Propulsion:	Two Admiralty 3-drum boilers at 300 psi driving two Parsons single reduction geared turbines of 19,000 shp at 380 rpm to 2 shafts

Speed:	27 kn (25½ kn full load)
Range/endurance:	2,100 nm at 20 kn, 1,100 nm at 25½ kn
Complement:	168
Armament:	As completed and probably as in June 1942:
	6 × 2 × QF 4 in/45 cal. Mk XVI (3 × 2)
	4 × QF 2 pdr 40 mm/40 cal. Mk VIII AA (1 × 4)
	2 × 20 mm Oerlikons (2 × 1)
	4 × DCT
	1 × DC rail initially, increased to 2 and possibly 3 rails, and 110 DCs
Sensors:	Type 286 target indication or Type 290 air warning radar
	Type 285 gunnery ranging radar
	ASDIC type unknown

HMS *Dianella*

Flower-class Corvette

Ordered:	25 July 1939
Builder:	John Lewis & Sons, Aberdeen
Laid down:	8 December 1939
Launched:	3 December 1940
Commissioned:	6 January 1941
Pennant number:	K 07
Displacement:	925 tn standard
Length:	205 ft 0 in LOA, 190 ft 0 in LBP
Beam:	33 ft 0 in
Draught:	11 ft 6 in
Propulsion:	2 Scotch cylindrical boilers driving a 4-cylinder Vertical Triple Expansion Reciprocating Engine of 2,750 ihp to 1 shaft
Speed:	16 kn
Range/endurance:	3,500 nm at 12 kn
Complement:	85
Armament:	As in July 1942:
	1 × BL 4 in/45 cal. Mk IX
	1 × QF 2 pdr/40 cal. Mk VIII
	4 × 20 mm (4 × 1)

	2 × .303 in Lewis MG (2 × 1)
	4 × DCT
	2 × DC rails, depth charges increased in number
Sensors:	Type 271 surface warning radar
	ASDIC Type 123A or Type 127

HMS *Palomares*

Auxiliary Anti-aircraft Ship/Vessel

Builder:	William Doxford & Sons, Sunderland
Laid down:	Unknown
Launched:	Unknown
Completed:	20 October 1937
Pennant number:	F 98
Displacement:	1,896 tn standard
Length:	306 ft 6 in LOA, 295 ft 6 in LBP
Beam:	57 ft 0 in
Draught:	17 ft 6 in
Propulsion:	Doxford diesel engine, 2,640 bhp to 1 shaft
Speed:	16¼ kn
Range/endurance:	Unknown
Complement:	Unknown
Armament:	6 × 4 in Mk XVI (3 × 2)
	8 × 2 pdr/40 mm (4 × 2)
	8 × 0.5 in HMG (2 × 4)
Sensors:	Type 79 or 279 air-warning radar
	Type 285 gunnery ranging radar

HMT *Ayrshire*

Anti-submarine Trawler

Note: Very little is known about HMT *Ayrshire* or indeed any of the many hundreds of trawlers and drifters taken up from trade. A typical armament was either a QF 12 pdr 12 cwt or an antique 4 in low-angle mount forward on the forecastle – perhaps a QF 4 in Mk IV or a BL 4 in Mk VIII. Close-range anti-aircraft weapons varied considerably depending on the size and basic design of the trawler and what was available at the time. A common fit-out was a single 20 mm aft and machine guns in what amounted to extended bridge wings. Anti-submarine trawlers had at least one depth-charge rack and two depth-charge throwers and ASDIC.

Supply Group (Force Q)

HMS *Douglas*

Scott-class Destroyer Leader

Ordered:	April 1917
Builder:	Cammell-Laird, Birkenhead, Merseyside, England
Laid down:	27 March 1918
Launched:	29 May 1919
Commissioned:	14 December 1919
Pennant number:	D 19/I 19
Displacement:	1,530 tn standard (2,130 tn full load) Lenton
Length:	332 ft 6 in LOA, 320 ft 0 in LBP
Beam:	31 ft 9 in
Draught:	9 ft 3 in (13 ft 6 in full load)
Propulsion:	4 Yarrow boilers at 250 psi driving Parsons single reduction geared turbines delivering 40,000 shp at 360 rpm to 2 shafts
Speed:	36½ kn (32 kn full load)
Range/endurance:	5,000 nm at 15 kn
Complement:	164/183
Armament:	As in July 1942*
	3 × BL 4.7 in/45 cal. Mk I on CP Mk VI mounting (3 × 1)
	1 × QF 12 pdr/40 cal. 12 cwt HA Mk VIII mounting
	2 × QF 2 pdr/40 cal. Mk 2 (2 × 1)
	2 × 20 mm Oerlikons (2 × 1)
	3 × 21 in torpedo tubes (1 × 3)
	4 × DCT
	2 × DC rails
Sensors:	Type 271 surface warning radar
	Type 286M target indication radar
	ASDIC

Note: * Estimated only. The full conversion to a Short-Range Escort did not take place until January–February 1943 refit when Hedgehog, Type 271 radar and HF/DF were fitted. (https://www.naval-history.net/xGM-Chrono-10DD-03Scott-Douglas.htm)

RFA *Gray Ranger*

Ranger-class Fleet Attendant Oiler

Builder:	Caledon Shipbuilding & Engineering Company, Dundee
Laid down:	24 June 1940
Launched:	27 May 1941
Completed:	25 September 1941
Official number:	Unknown
Displacement:	6,700 tn standard
Length:	365 ft 4 in LOA
Beam:	47 ft 0 in
Draught:	22 ft 0 in
Propulsion:	1 × 4-cylinder Doxford diesel delivering 2,800 shp to 1 shaft
Speed:	13 kn
Crew:	40
Range:	6,000 nm at 13 kn
Armament:	1 × 4 in LA (type unknown)
	1 × QF 12 pdr/40 cal. 12 cwt HA Mk VIII mounting
	1 × 40 mm Bofors Mk III
	4 × 20 mm Oerlikons

RFA *Aldersdale*

Dale-class Tanker (1st Group)

Ordered:	Unknown
Builder:	Cammell Laird & Co. Ltd, Birkenhead
Laid down:	September 1935
Launched:	7 July 1936
Completed:	17 September 1937
Official number:	X 34
Displacement:	8,192 tn standard (16,836–17,000 tn full load, depending on sources)
Length:	479 ft 5 in LOA (some sources state 482 ft 6 in, others 483 ft 0 in)
Beam:	61 ft 10 in (some sources state 58 ft 6 in)
Draught:	27 ft 6 in
Propulsion:	4-cylinder Doxford diesel delivering 6,800 hp to 1 shaft
Speed:	11½ kn

Crew:	44
Armament:	1 × 4 in LA (type unknown)
	1 × QF 12 pdr/40 cal. 12 cwt HA Mk VIII mounting
	6 × 20 mm Oerlikons

Submarines

HMS *Sturgeon*

S-class Submarine (1st Group)

Ordered:	1929 Programme, 2 July 1930
Builder:	Chatham Dockyard, England
Laid down:	3 January 1931
Launched:	8 January 1932
Commissioned:	27 February 1933
Pennant number:	73 S
Displacement:	640 tn surfaced, 935 tn submerged
Length:	202 ft 6 in LOA
Beam:	24 ft 0 in
Draught:	10 ft 6 in
Propulsion:	2 × 8-cylinder Admiralty Diesel engines delivering 1,900 bhp at 460 rpm or 2 electric motors delivering 1,300 hp to 2 shafts
Speed:	13¾–14¾ kn surfaced, 9–10 kn submerged
Range/endurance:	6,000 nm at 10 kn surfaced, 120 nm at 3 kn submerged
Complement:	36–44
Armament:	6 × 21 in torpedo tubes (6 bow)
	1 × 3 in/45 cal. 20 cwt QF HA Mk I on CPV mounting
	1 × 20 mm Oerlikon
	3 machine guns
Sensors:	ASDIC Type 129AR and Type 138
	Type 291 air warning radar

HMS *Unshaken*

U-class Submarine (3rd Group)

Ordered:	23 August 1940
Builder:	Vickers-Armstrong Ltd, Barrow-in-Furness, England
Laid down:	12 June 1941

Launched:	17 February 1942
Commissioned:	21 May 1942
Pennant number:	P 54
Displacement:	545 tn surfaced, 630–740 tn submerged
Length:	191 ft 0 in LOA
Beam:	16 ft 1 in
Draught:	15 ft 2 in
Propulsion:	2 × 6-cylinder Paxman-Ricardo 6RXS types each developing 800 bhp at 425 rpm coupled to a 550 kW generator by Wellman-Bibby flexible couplings to 2 shafts
Speed:	11¾ kn surfaced, 9 kn submerged
Range/endurance:	4,500 nm at 11 knots surfaced
Complement:	27–31
Armament:	6 × 21 in torpedo tubes
	1 × 3 in/45 cal. 20 cwt QF HA Mk I on CPV mounting
	3 × .303 in MG
Sensors:	ASDIC Type 129AR and Type 138
	Type 291 air warning radar

Kola Inlet-Based

HMS *Niger*

Halcyon-class Minesweeper (Second Group)

Ordered:	Unknown
Builder:	J. S. White & Co., Cowes, Isle of Wight, England
Laid down:	1 April 1935
Launched:	29 January 1936
Commissioned:	4 June 1936
Pennant number:	J 73
Displacement:	815 tn standard (1,330 tn full load)
Length:	241 ft 6 in LOA
Beam:	33 ft 6 in
Draught:	9 ft 0 in
Propulsion:	2 × Admiralty 3-drum boilers delivering 2,000 ihp driving 2 VTE to 2 shafts
Speed:	17 kn

Range/endurance:	7,000 nm at 10 kn, 4,200 nm at 15 kn
Complement:	80 peacetime (157 wartime)
Armament:	1 × QF 4 in/45 cal. Mk V HA Mk III (2 × 1)
	4 × 20 mm Oerlikons (4 × 1)
	2 × .303 in MG (2 × 1)
	4 × DCT*
	2 × DC rails*
Sensors:	Type 271
	ASDIC

* May have been deleted when used for minesweeping.

Appendix D: German Warships

KMS *Admiral Von Tirpitz*

Bismarck-class Battleship

Laid down:	2 November 1936
Launched:	1 April 1939
Commissioned:	25 February 1941
Displacement:	42,900 tn standard
Length:	823 ft 6 in LOA
Beam:	118 ft 1 in
Draught:	30 ft 6 in
Aircraft:	1 catapult, 4 × Arado 196 floatplanes
Complement:	2,608 (potential)
Armament:	8 × 15 in (4 × 2)
	12 × 5.9 in (6 × 2)
	16 × 4.1 in (8 × 2)
	16 × 37 mm AA (8 × 2)
	18 × 20 mm AA guns (2 × 4, 10 × 1)
Armour:	Main deck: 3.9–4.7 in
	Upper deck: 2 in
	Main turrets: 14 in
	Bulkheads: 7–8.7 in
Propulsion:	12 Wagner boilers (Blohm & Voss type) delivering 160,800 shp to Wagner single reduction-geared turbines to 3 shafts
Speed:	30 kn
Range:	8,870 nm at 19 kn

KMS *Admiral Scheer*

Deutschland-class Pocket Battleship – *Lützow* similar

Laid down:	25 June 1931
Launched:	1 April 1932
Commissioned:	12 November 1934
Displacement:	13,660 tn standard
Length:	610 ft 3 in LOA
Beam:	70 ft 0 in
Draught:	23 ft 9 in
Aircraft:	1 catapult, 2 × Arado 196 floatplanes
Complement:	1,070
Armament:	6 × 11 in (2 × 3)
	8 × 5.9 in (8 × 1)
	8 × 21 in TT (2 × 4)
Armour:	Main belt: 3.1 in
	Main deck: 1.8 in
	Main turrets: 3.5 in
Propulsion:	8 M.A.N. diesels delivering 53,260 shp to 2 shafts
Speed:	28.3 kn
Range:	9,100 nm at 20 kn

KMS *Admiral Hipper*

Admiral Hipper-class Heavy Cruiser

Laid down:	6 July 1935
Launched:	6 February 1937
Commissioned:	29 April 1939
Displacement:	16,170 tn standard
Length:	665 ft 4 in LOA
Beam:	69 ft 11 in
Draught:	24 ft 0 in (full load)
Aircraft:	1 catapult, 3 × Arado 196 floatplanes
Complement:	1,600
Armament:	8 × 8 in (4 × 2)
	12 × 5.9 in (6 × 2)

12 × 4.1 in (6 × 2)
12 × 37 mm AA (8 × 2)
10 × 20 mm AA guns (10 × 1)
12 × 21 in TT (4 × 3)

Armour: Main belt: 2.8–3.1 in
Main deck: 0.8–2 in
Main turrets: 4.1 in
DCT: 2–6 in

Propulsion: 12 La Mont-type boilers delivering 133,631 shp to Blohm & Voss single-reduction geared turbines to 3 shafts

Speed: 32.5 kn

Range: 6,500 nm at 17 kn

Type 34 – Maas Class

Destroyer – *Richard Beitzen*

Laid down: 7 January 1935

Launched: 30 November 1935

Commissioned: 13 May 1937

Displacement: 2,259 tn standard

Length: 390 ft 5 in LOA

Beam: 37 ft 1 in

Draught: 13 ft 11 in (full load)

Complement: 325

Armament: 5 × 5 in (5 × 1)
4 × 37 mm AA (2 × 2)
5–10 20 mm AA guns (singles)
8 × 21 in TT (2 × 4)
4 × DCT
60 mines could be carried

Propulsion: 6 boilers delivering 60,000 shp to single-reduction geared turbines to 2 shafts

Speed: 36 kn

Range: 1,530 nm at 19 kn

Type 1936A

Z 23-class Destroyer

Laid down, launched and commissioned: 1938–43

Displacement:	2,584 tn standard
Length:	416 ft 8 in LOA
Beam:	39 ft 4 in
Draught:	14.4 ft
Complement:	325–35
Armament:	4 × 5 in (4 × 1) or 5 × 5 in (1 × 2, 3 × 1)
	4 × 37 mm AA (2 × 2)
	5–10 × 20 mm AA guns
	8 × 21 in TT (2 × 4)
	4 × DCT
	60 mines could be carried
Propulsion:	6 boilers delivering 60,000 shp to single-reduction geared turbines to 2 shafts
Speed:	36 kn
Range:	2,600 nm at 19 kn

Type 35

Torpedo Boat

Laid down, launched and commissioned: 1938–40

Displacement:	873 tn standard
Length:	276 ft 7 in LOA
Beam:	28 ft 3 in
Draught:	9 ft 3 in
Complement:	120
Armament:	1 × 4.1 in
	1 × 37 mm AA
	2 × 20 mm AA guns (2 × 1)
	6 × 21 in TT (2 × 3)
	30–60 mines could be carried
Propulsion:	4 boilers delivering 31,000 shp to single-reduction geared turbines to 2 shafts
Speed:	35 kn
Range:	1,200 nm at 19 kn

Type VIIC

Submarine

Laid down, launched and commissioned: 1940–45

Displacement:	757 tn standard surfaced, 857 tn submerged
Length:	220 ft 2 in LOA
Beam:	20 ft 4 in
Draught:	15 ft 7 in
Complement:	44–55
Armament	1 × 88 mm
	5 × 21 in TT (4 bow, 1 stern)
Propulsion:	2 × 6-cylinder diesels, 2,800–3,200 shp to 2 shafts. Electric motors of 750 hp
Speed:	17.7 kn surfaced, 7.6 kn submerged
Range:	8,500 nm at 10 kn surfaced, 80 nm at 4 kn submerged

Appendix E: German Aircraft

Junkers Ju 87 D (Stuka)

Crew:	2 (pilot, radio operator/rear gunner)
Length:	36 ft 6 in
Wingspan:	45 ft 4 in
Height:	12 ft 9 in
Weight:	12,600 lb normal flying weight, 14,500 lb maximum take-off weight
Engine:	Junkers Jumo 2221 J 12-cylinder inverted V, liquid-cooled engine, 1,300 hp
Speed:	255 mph at 13,500 ft
Range:	1,200 miles with maximum fuel, 620 miles with maximum bomb load
Service ceiling:	24,000 ft
Rate of climb:	15,000 ft in 19 min (1,267 ft/min)
Armament:	2 × 7.92 mm MG 17 and 1 × 7.92 mm MG 15, bombs up to 3,960 lb

Junkers Ju 88 A-17

Crew:	3–4 (pilot, bomb aimer/front gunner, radio operator/rear gunner)
Length:	47 ft 1 in
Wingspan:	65 ft 10 in
Height:	15 ft 11 in
Weight:	26,700 lb normal loaded weight, maximum take-off weight 31,000 lb
Engines:	2 Junkers Jumo 211 F-1 or J-2, 12-cylinder inverted V, liquid-cooled engines, each 1,060 hp at 17,000 ft, 1,340 hp for take-off
Speed:	295 mph at 17,500 ft
Range:	1,900 miles with maximum fuel load, 650 miles with maximum bomb load of 6,600 lb

Service ceiling:	27,000 ft
Rate of climb:	17,500 ft in 23 min (761 ft/min)
Armament:	4–5 × 7.92 mm MG 812s, 2 torpedoes

Heinkel He 111 H-6

Crew:	5 (pilot, navigator/bombardier/nose gunner, ventral gunner, dorsal gunner/radio operator, side gunner)
Length:	54 ft 6 in
Wingspan:	74 ft 3 in
Height:	13 ft 9 in
Weight:	17,000 lb empty, normal loaded weight 26,500 lb
Engines:	2 Junkers Jumo 211F-1, 12-cylinder inverted V, liquid-cooled engines, each 1,300 hp
Speed:	250 mph at 17,000 ft
Range:	1,750 miles with maximum fuel load
Service ceiling:	27,500 ft
Rate of climb:	17,000 ft in 20 min (1,176 ft/min)
Armament:	6–7 MGs, 2 torpedoes

Heinkel He 115 C-4

Crew:	3 (pilot, navigator, rear gunner)
Length:	56 ft 9 in
Wingspan:	73 ft 1 in
Height:	21 ft 8 in
Weight:	11,662 lb empty, 22,928 lb maximum load
Engines:	2 × BMW 132 K, 9-cylinder air-cooled radial engines of 950 hp
Speed:	203 mph
Range:	1,300 miles
Service ceiling:	17,100 ft
Rate of climb:	N/A
Armament:	1 × 7.92 mm MG 17, 2 × 7.92 mm MG 15, 1 torpedo

Focke-Wulf Fw 200C (Condor)

Crew:	8 (2 pilots, flight engineer, radio operator, 4 gunners)
Length:	78 ft 3 in
Wingspan:	108 ft 3 in
Height:	23 ft 4 in

Weight:	50,000 lb maximum take-off weight
Engines:	4 BMW 323 R-2 9-cylinder, air-cooled radial engines each of 940 hp at 12,000 ft
Speed:	240 mph at 13,120 ft
Range:	2,200 mi, 9¾ hr
Service ceiling:	20,000 ft
Rate of climb:	N/A
Armament:	2 × MG 151 20 mm cannon, 4–6 × MG 131, 3,200 lb bombs

Blohm & Voss Bv 138 C-1

Crew:	6 (pilot, navigator, radio operator, 3 gunners)
Length:	72 ft 3 in
Wingspan:	88 ft 7 in
Height:	19 ft 4 in
Weight:	34,100 lb normal flying weight, 36,300 lb maximum normal take-off weight, 39,600 lb with rocket assistance
Engines:	3 × Junkers Jumo 205 C or D, 6-cylinder opposed piston diesel engines each of 880 hp
Speed:	170 mph at sea level
Range:	2,000 mi with maximum fuel load
Service ceiling:	16,000 ft
Rate of climb:	10,000 ft in 24 min (417 ft/min)
Armament:	2 × 20 mm MG 151, 1 × 13 mm MG 131, 660 lb bombs

Arado Ar 196

Crew:	2 (pilot and radio operator/gunner)
Length:	36 ft 1 in
Wingspan:	40 ft 10½ in (15 ft 9 in when folded)
Height:	14 ft 6 in
Weight:	6,580 lb empty, 8,200 lb fully loaded
Engine:	BMW 132K, 9-cylinder air-cooled radial engine
Speed:	193 mph at 13,120 ft
Range:	1,070 mi
Service ceiling:	23,000 ft
Rate of climb:	980 ft/min
Armament:	2 × 20 mm MG FF in wings, 1 × 7.92 mm MG 17 in fuselage, 2 × MG 17 in rear cockpit

Endnotes

Preface

1 The Soviets built a monument in Khimki on 6 December 1966 in the form of a giant tank trap. Some sources hold that the furthest effectively reached and held for a time by German forces was Krasnoya Polyana, 29 kilometres north-west of Moscow.
2 The sanctions basically involved an embargo on Japan importing scrap steel and oil – considered strategic materials – plus Japanese assets in the United States were frozen. America required Japan to withdraw from the Tripartite Pact (with Germany and Italy), withdraw from China and southern Indochina and terminate its concept of a Greater East Asia Co-Prosperity Sphere. Japan was never going to agree on these, so some sort of conflict was inevitable.
3 Alfred Thayer Mahan, *The Influence of Sea Power Upon History, 1660–1783* (1890).
4 Winston Churchill, 'Alliance with Russia', The Churchill Centre, https://churchillcentre.com.au/?s=alliance+with+russia.
5 The Geographic North Pole is where all the 360 meridians of longitude meet, each meridian representing one arc degree. The Magnetic North Pole is that point on Earth where a compass needle will point directly downwards. Therefore, the closer one gets to the Magnetic North Pole, the more inaccurate a magnetic compass will become.

Chapter 1: Background

1 The First Reich was the Holy Roman Empire (800–1806) and the second was the German Empire (1871–1918).
2 www.admiral.centro.ru, 'Admiral Kuznetsov, Memoirs of Wartime Minister of the Navy, The Northern Sea Routes'.
3 A. J. P. Taylor, *Origins of World War II*, p. 112.
4 Admiralty War Diaries, Home Fleet 1942, www.naval-history.net.
5 John Terraine, *Business in Great Waters: The U-Boat Wars 1916–1945,* pp. 767–68.
6 John Henshaw, *Liberty's Provenance; The Evolution of the Liberty Ship from its Sunderland Origins.*
7 Arnold Hague, *The Allied Convoy System, 1939–1945: Its Organization Defence and Operation*, p. 187.

Chapter 2: Arctic Convoys Begin

1 The 'Daylight Sun' extends over some 76 days between May and June in northern Norway. Above the Arctic Circle (approximately 66° 30'N), the sun does not set until around 21 June or rise until around 21 December. Even when the sun dips 10 to 12 degrees below the horizon, twilight prevails. For four months, the sun does not rise at all and noon is a twilight at best.
2 Richard Woodman, *Arctic Convoys 1941–1945*, p. 54.

Chapter 3: Aid Now Comes at a Price

1 John Henshaw, *Malta's Savior: Operation Pedestal August 1942.*
2 ULTRA was the term used to designate the most secret of the signals intelligence derived from the Government Code and Cypher School (GC&CS) at Bletchley Park breaking encrypted German radio and teleprinter communications, such as the Enigma machines.

3 Www.admiral.centro.ru, 'Admiral Kuznetsov, Memoirs of Wartime Minister of the Navy, The Northern Sea Routes'. Emphasis added by author.
4 National Archives PREM 3/403/4.
5 National Archives PREM 3/403/4.

Chapter 4: Prelude to Disaster

1 Richard Woodman, *Arctic Convoys 1941–1945*, p. 115.
2 Milan Vego, 'The Destruction of Convoy PQ 17: 27 June–10 July 1942', *Naval War College Review*, Vol. 69, No. 3, Article 7.92016, p. 10.
3 Ibid., pp. 11–12.
4 A detailed gruesome account of medical matters ashore in Russia can be found at http://www.halcyon-class.co.uk/ashore_in_russia.htm for those with a strong stomach.
5 Patrick Beesly, *Very Special Intelligence: The Story of the Admiralty's Operational Intelligence Centre 1939–1945*, p. 131.
6 Hugh Sebag-Montefiore, *Enigma: The Battle of the Code*, quoting Tovey's papers held at the Churchill Archives Centre.
7 The priority of signals was as follows: '[nothing mentioned as to priority] IMPORTANT, IMMEDIATE, MOST IMMEDIATE, EMERGENCY'. The security scale of signals was as follows: 'UNCLASSIFIED, CLASSIFIED, CONFIDENTIAL, SECRET, MOST SECRET, HUSH, AIDAC'.
8 Captain Jack Broome, *Convoy is to Scatter: The Story of PQ 17*, pp. 110–12. Regrettably, none of the signals before this relate to the HUSH message. Please note that the list omits the letter 'i' to avoid the possibility of it being confused with the Roman numeral 'i', as per the original source.

Chapter 5: Days 1–7, Saturday, 27 June–Friday, 3 July 1942

1 Richard Woodman, *Arctic Convoys 1941–1945*, p. 195.
2 Arnold Hague, *The Allied Convoy System, 1939–1945: Its Organization Defence and Operation*, p. 188.
3 Woodman, p. 199.
4 Rescue ships were introduced to convoys in early 1941. Previously, the escorts had been responsible for rescuing survivors of sunken or sinking ships and dedicated rescue ships proved a better option, having dedicated facilities to pick up and treat survivors. They were converted from small, manoeuvrable coastal vessels, but late in the war converted Castle-class corvettes were used. Rescue ships flew the Blue Ensign with a mixed crew of RN and Merchant Navy sailors. They were not protected by the Geneva Convention and were armed for self-defence, often having HF/DF fitted to assist escorts with locating U-boats.
5 These submarines were two of an order of four for the Turkish Navy from Vickers Armstrong, based on the S-class in service.
6 Milan Vego, 'The Destruction of Convoy PQ 17: 27 June–10 July 1942', pp. 116–17.
7 Ibid., pp. 114–15.
8 Ibid., p. 117.
9 Ibid., p. 117.
10 Ibid., p. 117.
11 Captain Jack Broome, *Convoy is to Scatter: The Story of PQ 17*, p. 128.

Chapter 6: Day 8, Saturday, 4 July (Part 1)

1 Milan Vego, 'The Destruction of Convoy PQ 17: 27 June–10 July 1942', p. 118.
2 It is an unpleasant fact that eight of the nine merchant ships that had been damaged, but were still afloat and seaworthy to various degrees and were abandoned, were American. The same thing happened with the two American ships in Operation *Pedestal* (*Almeria Lykes* and *Santa Elisa*). Contrast this propensity to abandon ship with the Russian tanker *Azerbaijan*, where the crew – including a large number of women – fought fires, made good damage and caught up with the convoy.

3 Patrick Beesly, *Very Special Intelligence: The Story of the Admiralty's Operational Intelligence Centre 1939–1945*, p. 133.
4 Vego, p. 120.
5 Www.u-boat.net.
6 Beesly, p. 133.

Chapter 7: Admiral Pound and the Operational Intelligence Centre

1 High Angle Control System: an obsolescent RN anti-aircraft fire control system based on the premise that a target obligingly moved at a constant course, speed and height throughout the engagement. Its shortcomings were particularly evident as target speeds increased and attack methods changed. It expended huge amounts of ammunition to little effect, as evidenced by the number of ships lost during the intense AA engagements in the Mediterranean.
2 Admiral Sir Dudley North was dismissed for his failure to challenge a Vichy French naval squadron in September 1940. Admiral Sir Charles Forbes was dismissed after the Denmark Strait and *Bismarck* episode, and Vice Admiral Tovey took command of the Home Fleet.
3 Video transcript available at available at https://www.iwm.org.uk/history/why-convoy-pq-17-was-doomed-to-destruction.
4 Operation *Catherine* was a 1940 plan for a substantial naval force – three battleships specially modified, an aircraft carrier, five cruisers and 16 destroyers – to enter the Baltic Sea and disrupt German sea traffic to and from Russia, Sweden (iron ore in particular) Finland, Estonia and Latvia.
5 Quoted in Captain Jack Broome, *Convoy is to Scatter: The Story of PQ 17*, p. 320.
6 Denning had four brothers. Two were killed in World War I. One became Lord Denning, a prominent and influential judge, the other became Lieutenant General Sir Reginald in the British Army. In a strange twist, the author of *The Destruction of Convoy PQ 17*, David Irving, was sued by then-Captain J. E. Broome for libel. Irving lost the case but went to appeal, involving Lord Denning also upholding the guilty verdict.
7 Patrick Beesly, *Very Special Intelligence: The Story of the Admiralty's Operational Intelligence Centre 1939–1945*, p. 135.
8 Ibid., p. 135.
9 Ibid., p. 135.
10 Correlli Barnett, *Engage the Enemy More Closely, The Royal Navy in the Second World War*, p. 722.
11 Ibid., pp. 136–37.
12 Milan Vego, 'The Destruction of Convoy PQ17: 27 June–10 July 1942', p. 121.
13 Ibid., p. 135.
14 David Irving, *The Destruction of Convoy PQ 17*, p. 128.
15 'Admiral Kuznetsov, Memoirs of Wartime Minister of the Navy, The Northern Sea Routes', translated on www.admiral.centro.ru/memor08.htm#Northern. Emphasis added by author.
16 Comparisons can be made with the significant battle of Midway (only a month earlier on 4 June 1942). Admiral Yamamoto, Commander in Chief of the Japanese Combined Fleet, sought to run the conflict from the battleship *Yamato* that was the flagship of the Main Body, a battleship-centric covering force similar to the Distant Cover Force of PQ 17. Yamamoto was some 500–600 miles distant from where the First Air Fleet's four aircraft carriers were engaged with three USN aircraft carriers in Yamamoto's plan to invade Midway Island and bring the US Pacific Fleet into a decisive battle. Not only was the Main Body too far away to be effective when action was joined, and the battle was being lost, but Yamamoto, like Pound, was not aware of the tactical situation. He was not content to leave decisions to the commander on the spot, Admiral Nagumo (whom he relieved of command) or the commanders of the other forces involved. Instead, he tried to run the battle from afar by remote control. Also, like Pound, he was not a delegator.

Chapter 8: Day 8, Saturday, 4 July (Part 2)

1 *Brown's Signalling*, 8th Edition.
2 At 0115 hours, 5 June, Hamilton signalled Dowding: 'I know you will all be feeling as distressed as I am at having to leave that fine collection of ships to find their own way to harbor. The enemy under the cover of his shore-based aircraft has succeeded in concentrating a far superior force in this area. We were therefore ordered to withdraw. We are all sorry that the good work of the close escort could not be completed. I hope we shall all have a chance of settling this score with them soon.' Irving, pp. 135–36.

Chapter 9: Day 9, Bloody Sunday, 5 July 1942

1 Captain Jack Broome, *Convoy is to Scatter: The Story of PQ 17*, p. 219.
2 Ibid., p. 220.
3 A special pawn capture that can only occur immediately after a pawn makes a move of two squares from its starting square, and it could have been captured by an enemy pawn had it advanced only one square.
4 In a strange coincidence, the assassin of British Prime Minister Spencer Perceval on 11 May 1812 was John Bellingham, a Liverpool merchant who had spent five years incarcerated at Arkhangelsk on charges related to debt and blamed the British government for lack of assistance.
5 Michael G. Walling, *Forgotten Sacrifice: The Arctic Convoys of World War II*, p. 165.
6 Ibid., p. 165.
7 Www.uboat.net.

Chapter 10: Days 10–15, Monday, 6 July–Saturday, 11 July 1942

1 Michael G. Walling, *Forgotten Sacrifice: The Arctic Convoys of World War II*, p. 166.

Chapter 11: Days 16–32, Sunday, 12 July–Tuesday, 28 July

1 WAIR refers to anti-aircraft conversions of W-class destroyers.
1 Michael G. Walling, *Forgotten Sacrifice: The Arctic Convoys of World War II*, p. 166.
2 Ibid., p. 253.
3 Ibid., p. 170.
4 One BV 138, two He 111s, one He 115 and one Fw 200.
5 The German Army is frequently and incorrectly referred to as the Wehrmacht and not the Heer. The Wehrmacht (lit. 'defence power') is the term applied to the three branches of the German armed forces as a whole: Heer, Luftwaffe and Kriegsmarine. The SS was separate again.

Chapter 12: Aftermath – 'A Shameful Page in Naval History'

1 Captain Jack Broome, *Convoy is to Scatter: The Story of PQ 17*, p. 229.
2 Winston Churchill, *The Second World War, Volume 4, The Hinge of Fate*, p. 240.
3 Richard Woodman, *Arctic Convoys 1941–1945*, p. 256.
4 Attributed to Rudyard Kipling's 'Song of the English' (1893): 'If blood be the price of admiralty Good God, we ha' paid in full'.
5 Churchill, *The Hinge of Fate*, p. 236.
6 Ibid., pp. 235–36.

7 Ibid., pp. 236–37.
8 It is important to distinguish between 'instructions' and 'orders'. The former are guideline and not necessarily binding, as they cannot be tailor-made to cover all circumstances and eventualities. Orders, on the other hand, are sacrosanct and must be obeyed.
9 On 4 July, at 1520 hours, Hamilton signalled that CS One would stay with PQ 17 until the location of the enemy force was known or until 1200 hours on 5 July – whichever was the earlier.
10 Churchill, *The Hinge of Fate*, pp. 237–38.
11 Ibid., p. 238.
12 King served on secondment with the RN's Home Fleet during World War I and is said to have developed his dislike for the British by being admonished by a senior officer in the presence of crew members. However, there is plenty of evidence that King was always angry, at everyone!
13 This refers to Churchill's telegram to Stalin advising that further convoys to northern Russia would be postponed.
14 The reference to a communiqué relates to the American Communiqué to the effect that there could be a second front in Europe as early as 1942.
15 National Archives, PREM 3/403/4.
16 Milan Vego, 'The Destruction of Convoy PQ17: 27 June–10 July 1942', p. 131.
17 Www.uboatarchive.net/Int/ULMINT.htm.
18 Woodman, pp. 255–56.
19 Lund and Ludlam, *I Was There on Convoy PQ 17: The Convoy to Hell*, pp. 223–28.
20 Lund and Ludlam, *I Was There*, p. 224.
21 Vego, 'The Destruction of Convoy PQ17: 27 June–10 July 1942', p. 134.
22 Supplement to *The London Gazette*, 17 October 1950, pp. 5139–54.

Chapter 14: Analysis and Conclusions

1 David Wragg, *Sacrifice for Stalin: The Cost and Value of the Arctic Convoys Re-assessed*, pp. 50–51; by comparison, in 2021, prior to the invasion of Ukraine, Russia's defensive spending was estimated by the International Institute for Strategic Studies as being 4.3 per cent of GDP.
2 'Admiral Kuznetsov, Memoirs of Wartime Minister of the Navy, The Northern Sea Routes', translated on www.admiral.centro.ru/memor08.htm#Northern.
3 Wragg, pp. 48–49.
4 David M. Glantz and Jonathan M. House, *When Titans Clashed: How the Red Army Stopped Hitler* (Lawrence University Press of Kansas, 1995), 285.
5 G. I. Krivosheev, *Soviet Casualties and Combat Losses*, pp. 85–97.
6 Arnold Hague, *The Allied Convoy System, 1939–1945: Its Organization Defence and Operation*, p. 187.
7 Wragg, p. 198.
8 Ibid., p. 197.
9 Michael G. Walling, *Forgotten Sacrifice: the Arctic Convoys of World War II*, p. 170.
10 Ibid., p. 197.
11 Captain Jack Broome, *Convoy is to Scatter: The Story of PQ 17*, p. 52.
12 In a strange twist of fate, one of Commander Denning's two brothers, Lord Denning, Master of the Rolls, was one of the three judges who heard, and rejected, Irving's appeal.
13 Broome, pp. 231–32.

Appendix C: Home Fleet – Battle Fleet or Distant Cover Force

1 https://www.armouredcarriers.com/hms-illustrious-armoured-aircraft-carrier-design.

Bibliography

Published Sources

Beesly, Patrick, *Very Special Intelligence: The Story of the Admiralty's Operational Intelligence Centre 1939–1945* (London: Greenhill Books, 2000).

Broome, Captain Jack, *Convoy is to Scatter: The Story of PQ 17* (London: Futura Publications, 1974).

Hague, Arnold, *The Allied Convoy System, 1939–1945: Its Organization, Defence and Operation* (Ontario: Vanwell Publishing Limited, 2000).

Henshaw, John, *Liberty's Provenance; The Evolution of the Liberty Ship from its Sunderland Origins* (Barnsley: Pen & Sword, 2020).

Henshaw, John, *Malta's Savior: Operation Pedestal August 1942* (Jefferson, North Carolina: McFarland, 2024).

Irving, David, *The Destruction of Convoy PQ 17* (New York: St Martin's Press, 1987).

Koop, Gerard, and Klaus Peter Schmolke, *German destroyers of World War II* (Annapolis: Naval Institute Press, 2014).

Krivosheev, Colonel-General G. I., ed., *Soviet Casualties and Combat Losses* (London: Greenhill Books, 1997).

Lund, Paul, and Harry Ludlam, *I Was There on Convoy PQ 17: The Convoy to Hell* (Berkshire: W. Foulsham & Co. Ltd, 1968).

Mitchell, W. H., and L. A. Sawyer, *British Standard Ships of World War I* (London: The Journal of Commerce and Shipping Telegraph, 1968).

Mitchell, W. H., and L. A. Sawyer, *Empire Ships of World War II* (London: The Journal of Commerce and Shipping Telegraph, 1965).

Roskill, S. W., *The War At Sea 1939–1945, Vol. I, The Defensive* (London: HMO, 1954).

Roskill, S. W., *The War At Sea 1939–1945, Vol. II, The Period of Balance* (London: HMO, 1956).

Roskill, S. W., *The War At Sea 1939–1945, Vol. III, The Offensive* (London: HMO, 1960).

Ruegg, Bob, and Arnold Hague, *Convoys to Russia: Allied Convoys and Naval Surface Operations in Arctic Waters 1941–1945* (Kendal: World Ship Society, 1992).

Taylor, A. J. P., *Origins of the Second World War* (New York: Simon & Schuster Paperbacks, 2005).

Taylor, Theodore, *Battle in the Arctic Seas: The Story of Convoy PQ 17* (New York: Thomas Y. Crowell & Co., 1976).

Terraine, John, *Business in Great Waters: The U-Boat Wars 1916–1945* (London: Mandarin Paperbacks, 1990).

Vego, Milan, 'The Destruction of Convoy PQ 17: 27 June–10 July 1942', *Naval War College*, Vol. 69, No. 3 (summer 2016).

Walling, Michael G., *Forgotten Sacrifice: The Arctic Convoys of World War II* (Oxford: Osprey Publishing, 2012).

Woodman, Richard, *Arctic Convoys 1941–1945* (London: John Murray [Publishers] Ltd, 1995).

Wragg, David, *Sacrifice for Stalin: The Cost and Value of the Arctic Convoys Re-assessed* (Barnsley: Pen & Sword, 2005).

Other Sources

'Arctic Convoys 1941–1945: Battle Summary No. 22, Naval Staff History Second World War', issued as a Confidential Book (CB 3305[4]) in December 1954 by the Historical Section of the British Admiralty.

Grazhdan, Anna, *Soviet Storm: World War II in the East* (also known as *The Great Patriotic War*), MMX Star Media Pro, 2011.

'Home Fleet and Home Fleet Destroyer Command War Diaries', from the British National Archives (TNA ADM 199/427).

McKellar, N. L., 'Steel Shipbuilding Under the U.S. Shipping Board 1917–1921', *The Belgian Shiplover*, No. 87 (May–June 1962).

Supplement to the London Gazette, Friday, 13 October 1950, 'Convoys to North Russia, 1942', pp. 5139–54.

Electronic Sources

Note: the hyperlinks referenced below were accessed between 2019 and 2022.

http://admiral.centro.ru/start_e.htm.

https://www.clydeships.co.uk.

https://www.halcyon-class.co.uk/.

https://www.history.navy.mil/.

https://www.naval-history.net./.

https://www.shipbuildinghistory.net./.

https://www.shipbuildinghistory.net./.

http://www.unithistories.com./.

https://www.wrecksite.eu/.

Index